Praise for
Art Critiques: A Guide

"Elkins introduces refreshing commonsense in the tired and tiresome activity of the critique of art works by students. A dissection geared to avoid or delay a future autopsy of the field, the book uses case studies that teach as much about "how to" as they do about "how not to" A nice and often funny exercise in debunking, *Art Critiques: A Guide* is also a fascinating analysis of the successes and failures in communication among people."

—Luis Camnitzer, Professor Emeritus, State University of New York, and Pedagogical Advisor to the Cisneros Foundation.

"James Elkins is one of the world's leading educators in the visual arts. In *Art Critiques: A Guide*, Elkins shines his bright light across the long overlooked shadowland of studio education. Beautifully written and easy to use, this book is an absolute must for art students and faculty alike."

—George Smith, Founder & President, Institute for Doctoral Studies in the Visual Arts.

Art Critiques

A Guide

By the same author

ARTISTS WITH PhDs: On the New Doctoral Degree in Studio Art
Second Definitive Edition (New Academia Publishing, 2014)

Read an excerpt at www.newacademia.com

Art Critiques

A Guide

James Elkins

Third Definitive Edition
Revised and Expanded

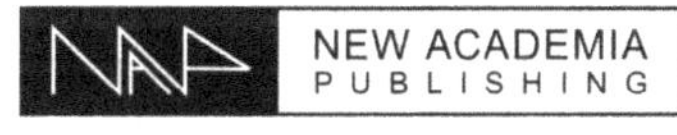

Washington, DC

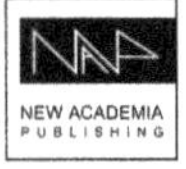

New Academia Publishing
P.O. Box 24720, Washington, DC 20038-7420
info@newacademia.com - www.newacademia.com

Contents

Part Three: MFA Issues

Part Four: Theories

Part Five: Projects

Part Six: PhD Issues

Preface

The first year I was hired at the School of the Art Institute in Chicago, I was on a panel with four other instructors. We sat down on five chairs in an empty ballet practice room. An MFA student from the Performance Art Department walked out in front of us. The lights went down, and the spotlight went on her. She was wearing a 1950s-style calico dress. She spoke for ten minutes about her childhood, staring into the darkness over our heads. When the performance was over, we all went into a backstage room and sat on filthy couches for the critique. One instructor said the lighting was overly dramatic. The student had a little note pad, and she wrote that down. Another said the student's story was interesting but too disjointed. And then a third instructor said something that changed the way I thought about critiques forever. He said:

"You know, you have very hairy legs."

I expected the student to be outraged. She hadn't mentioned her legs at all, so the instructor's remark seemed way off topic, way out of bounds. There was a pause, and then the student said:

"Yes, I know, all the women in my family have hairy legs. My mother never shaves."

The instructor—his name was Tom Jaremba, the wonderful founder of the Performance Art department at the School of the Art Institute of Chicago, where I teach—grinned. "Wow," he said, "I think that's fabulous. Hairy legs on a woman have such an *amazing* effect. It's so strong."

"I haven't thought about that," the student said, taking notes.

The conversation got very animated after that, and everyone started talking about shaving. I don't remember if I said much: I was probably just taking it all in. I didn't mind the subject, as long as the student didn't mind. It was obviously more fun to talk about than lighting or narrative. What amazed me, and continues to amaze me, is that there was no sense that the conversation had strayed off topic. This is an art critique, I thought: a place where all possible subjects are permitted, all at once. There are no rules. Anything at all might be pertinent. It was one of the strangest conversations I had ever been part of. Not because it is strange to talk about who shaves themselves, when, or where, or why, but because it is weird to mix that kind of talk with talk about art, theater, lighting, and narrative, and then to try to understand it all together as a way of teaching art.

It might have been shortly after that day that I decided to make a special study of critiques. Ever since then I have participated in as many critiques as I can. I have made audiotapes and transcripts; I've taken reams of notes and photographs; I've talked to students and instructors; and I've read what little there is to read on the subject. For me, critiques are the most interesting, infuriating, and challenging part of art teaching. Of all the things that happen when art is taught, critiques the hardest to understand, the trickiest to make use of, the least understood, and potentially the most helpful and rewarding.

Terminology

A quick word about terminology. I call studio art teachers "instructors," "professors," and "teachers" indiscriminately. Sometimes I call the teachers in a critique "panelists." In most of the world, "professor" is a special category, higher than an ordinary university teacher. In North America, every department is full of professors. I am not observing those distinctions here. This book is about visual art instruction wherever it happens: in a two-year liberal arts college, a community college, a research university, an art department, an art academy, an art school, or a technical or design school. I take examples from all of those, without stressing the differences, which often hardly exist anyway.

The same goes for the expressions "art school," "art department," "art academy," and "art university." Different parts of the world use different names. There are over twenty "art universities" in Japan, which sounds odd to someone from North America. On the other hand the "art schools" in North America sound strange to people from Europe and South America, where art is usually taught in art academies.

I also don't distinguish between BA and BFA, or MA and MPhil and MFA, or PhD and DCA. Degree-granting differences can be significant, but not often, I think, at the level of the critique itself.

Acknowledgments

This book wouldn't have been possible without all the colleagues I've shared critiques with over the years. I'd like to especially remember six colleagues who have died since I started work in 1988: Tom Jaremba; Shellie Fleming, a thoughtful presence in film critiques; Paul Hinchcliffe, an adventurous painter and teacher; George Roeder, an Americanist political historian who managed, somehow, to bridge the gap between his field and art; Kathryn Hixson, whom most people remember as the editor of the *New Art Examiner*; and Robert Loescher, one of the art world's real originals. You won't find much trace of Bob on the internet, because he gave his life to teaching his three specialties: Hispanic art, the history of sexuality, and the history of food. He was outrageously good at all three subjects.

There's no way I can name all the colleagues who have been part of critique culture at the School, but I especially want to thank Joan Livingstone, John Manning, Claire Pentecost, Frank Piatek, Chris Sullivan, Lisa Wainwright, Faith Wilding, Michiko Itatani, Anders Nereim, Helen Maria Nugent, Anne Wilson, Gaylen Gerber, Jim Nutt, Simon Anderson, Lin Hixson, Alan Labb, Michael Miller, Stephanie Brooks, Beth Nugent, Werner Herterich, Tiffany Holmes, Michael Newman, Susanne Doremus, Carol Becker, Candida Alvarez, Gregg Bordowitz, Jesse Ball, Mary Jane Jacob, Sharon Cousin, Frances Whitehead, and Barbara DeGenevieve, for their many insights over many years.

Thanks, too, to the student artists who gave me permission to tape and transcribe their critiques and reproduce their work: Sean Lamoureux, Alexandra Helene Copan, Chris Fennell, Diego Gutierrez, Rebecca Gordon, Chris Campe, Catherine Arnold (now Schaffner), elin o'Hara slavick, and Andrea Schumacher. And special thanks to Joanne Easton, who shared her MA thesis on critiques with me; to the gang on my Facebook page for lots of ideas (you're all thanked in footnotes); to Jerry Saltz (who posted my project on his Facebook page on June 23, 2011, resulting in 900 responses) and all his friends (they're all thanked too); to Buzz Spector; and to Tom Mapp, who was once my teacher when I was in the MFA program at the University of Chicago.

And finally, to all the students in my critique classes over the years. Sadly, I don't have a list of all those classes, so the spring 2014 class will have to stand in for all of them: thanks to Catalina Acosta-Carrizosa, Kyle Riley, David Albert, Ke Wang, Amy Stoker, Keith Tolch, Aubrey Manson, Fabienne Zuijdwijk, Annelies Kamen, Leonard Suryajaya (not in the photo), Ilan Gutin, and Laís Pontes, for putting up with all the experiments and proposals in this book. There we are in the photo.

How This Book is Organized

Learning about critiques is like walking into a swamp. Ever walked into a swamp? At first you squish along in the mud, and it seems like everything will be fine. But then the mud gets sticky, and it grabs your shoes, and there are sticks underwater that you can't see, and they snag your legs, and soon you can hardly move. (Why did you walk into a swamp to begin with?)

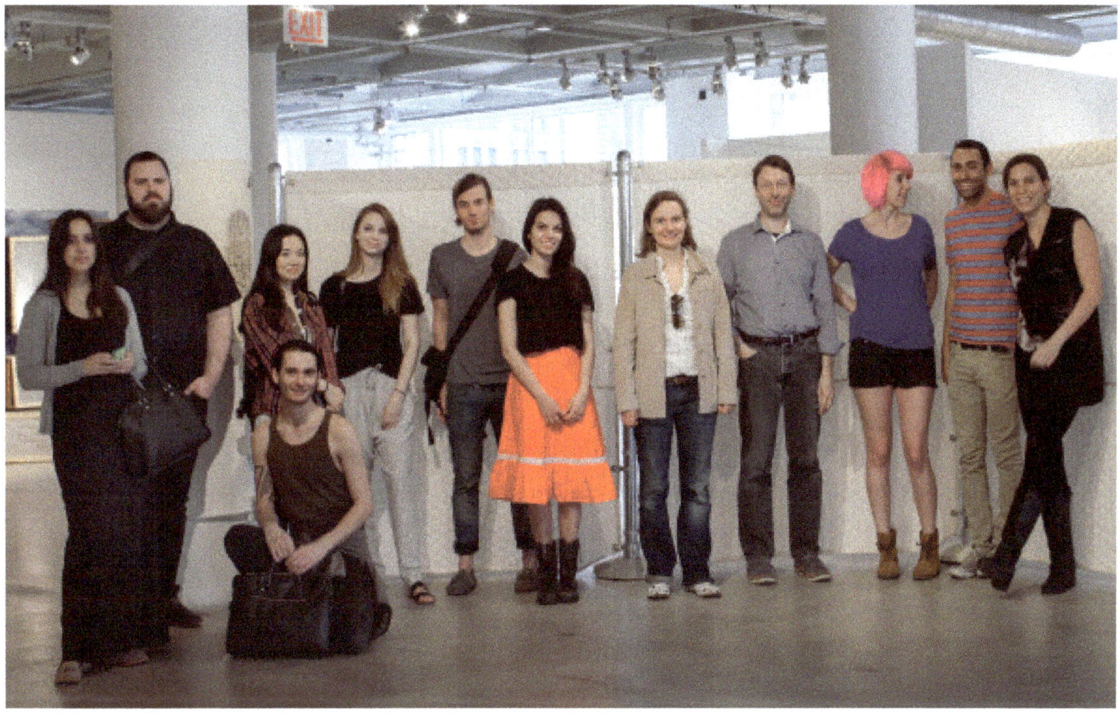

There is no yellow brick road to understanding critiques, no simple solution, no standard advice. And so there really is no way to organize a book on critiques so that it builds from one thing to the next.

On the other hand, there is often a difference between what happens in the first year (Freshman year, Foundation year) and what happens later in the undergraduate (college, BA, BFA) curriculum. And there is often, but by no means always, a distinction between what happens at the BA level and what happens at the MA (or MFA, or MPhil) level. And there is very definitely always a difference between what happens at all those levels and in the PhD.

The first two editions of this book scrambled all those levels together, because that's how I feel about critiques. Teachers pointed out that some sections are over the head of beginners and introductory classes. One reviewer, on Amazon, even said this book was only for MFA students. So for this third edition I have reluctantly separated the "Basics" from the BFA, MFA, and PhD. I have also reluctantly gathered some chapters on the theory of the critique, and on practical experiments you can make with critiques (they're called "Projects").

I am full of misgivings about this organization, and I strongly recommend you read at random anywhere you'd like in the book. Critiques are disorderly things: that is why they are interesting. It's easy to think that there are good ways to distinguish between the first year, the BFA, and the MFA, and for administrators there have to be ways to do that. But in real life everything is tangled together.

Why There Are So Few Books on This Subject

I think it is weird that something as universal as art critiques—practiced all around the world, at all levels of education—has so little written about it. Part of the explanation is that the people who write books about teaching are mainly administrators and educators, and not art teachers. There is a large literature on how to assess and grade art students, for people who run art departments and art schools, and that counts as writing on art critiques. That literature is full of ideas like "the student should be able to articulate her influences," or "the student should show that she can connect and synthesize different ideas," or "the student should provide evidence that she can work innovatively and develop new content." Administrators, deans, and chairs of departments need writing like that to assess students: but it just doesn't get near what is actually said in studio critiques. If you're interested in that literature, you might look up writing in the field of art education; or you might look at the websites of organizations that help monitor education standards, like the commissions on higher learning in the US and Europe. This book isn't about that.

There may be up to five thousand institutions in the world that grant the equivalent of BFA, MFA, and PhD degrees in the visual arts,[2] and if each one of those holds just five critiques a semester (and surely the number is much higher) then there are at least fifty thousand art critiques each year. And yet there is no standard literature on critiques: nothing about how to run them, what they're supposed to accomplish, what standards they might employ.

There is a book called *The Critique Handbook*, but two-thirds of it is about the basic terms and ideas that are used in art instruction, like "form" and "space." If you're new to the art world and you're looking for a book that will introduce you to critiques but also to form, space, scale, format, line, color, realism, and abstraction, then *The Critique Handbook* may be a good choice.[3] There is a fun chapter called "The Crit" in Sarah Thornton's *Seven Days in the Art World*; and some passages in the edited volumes *Rethinking the Contemporary Art School*, *The Routledge Companion to Research in the Arts*, and *Agonistic Academies*.[4]

There's a good book by Timothy Van Laar and Leonard Diepeveen, *Active Sights: Art as Social Interaction*, but it's more about artists in the world than students.[5] And there's a book by Deborah Rockman called *The Art of Teaching Art*, geared to introductory-level drawing classes.[6] All of these books spend a lot of time on things other than critiques.

The only book I know, other than this one, which is exclusively on art critiques is the very entertaining *Q-Art Presents / Art Crits: 20 Questions, A Pocket Guide*, edited by Sarah Rowles (2013). It's about open critiques, including self-trained artists, so it's especially good on ways critiques can be supportive, and how to gain confidence with them. I have incorporated references to that book in this one.

What's New in This Edition

This is the third, final, and definitive edition of this book: I will not be expanding it further, so it's a safe book to buy. Previous editions have been available in less expensive black and white versions, but this time I decided color really does make a difference, so there is no black and white option. The cover was painted especially for this book by Mark Staff Brandl.

About 10 chapters are expanded from chapter 4 in my book *Why Art Cannot be Taught: A Handbook for Art Students.*[7] It is the only time I have ever repeated anything from one book to another. I re-used that material because *Why Art Cannot be Taught* should really have been a book about art critiques, but it grew into something bigger. The chapters on art critiques were buried, and students didn't see them. I wanted to bring that material out and write something focused on art critiques. *Why Art Cannot be Taught* also has a history of art schools, discussions of common problems in teaching art, and a section about whether or not art can be taught.[8] If you're interested in the history of art teaching, or in the philosophic problem about whether or not art can be taught (in studios, or even in classrooms), then that book might be better than this one.

This book is not just an extract from that one. I have worked hard on this book: everything's been reorganized, and lots has been rewritten; lots of material is crowd sourced from Facebook; and this edition also adds five new chapters that weren't in the second edition—2, 5, 7, 10, and 43. It's as good as I can make it.

How To Contact the Author

You can write at jameselkins@fastmail.fm or through the contact form on the website www.jameselkins.com. I am always glad to hear from people with new critique experiences, questions, or problems.

I have traveled widely as a guest speaker, and participated in art critiques in most states of the US (I seem to be missing Maine, Idaho, Missouri, Oklahoma, Vermont, Alaska, and Hawaii), and in about 15 foreign countries. (I have been to art departments and academies in 60 countries, but I have only been in critiques in about 15 of those.) My traveling—on average once a week during the academic year—has given me a wide, nebulous, and unquantifiable sense of the flavor and style of critiques in many places. I've tried to incorporate as much of that into this book as I could.

Even though there's hardly anything more annoying than an advertisement, I'd like to say that if your institution would like a workshop on critiques, just let me know.

Your Future Outside Art School

One last word before we get started. This book is all about individual and group critiques in institutions like schools, universities, colleges, and academies. Critiques happen in many places: among friends, in bars, in artist's residencies, in community centers, in commercial galleries, in project spaces. Those critiques can often be less formal, because there's less of a power relation, and—most important!—because there is no money involved. I hope that some of what I say can be helpful in those real-life situations.[9]

I have one piece of advice about critiques out there in the real world. After you graduate, the chances are you'll have a circle of friends, and you'll all critique each other's work. The danger is that as the years go on, you'll get to know each other very well, and your friends won't be giving you the serious, fundamental critiques you may need. I've seen this happen many times: good friends after ten or twenty years support one another, but that is not always what is needed.

So here's my advice, which no one ever takes:

1. When you graduate, gather a group of friends, and try to find a space you can all share.

2. Then after four or five years, dump them and find another group.

Critiques depend on honesty.

James Elkins
School of the Art Institute, Chicago

Art Critiques

A Guide

Part One

The Basics

1

Time for Critique!

A critique is an opportunity to see how your work looks to other people. The ingredients are you, your work, and people. Some of those people have authority, and some don't. Some make sense, and some don't. Some are helpful, and others have their own agendas.

Critiques take place in space (often a cinder block room with a concrete slab floor, or a classroom repurposed), in time (from five minutes to six hours), in language (sometimes very abstruse and philosophic, sometimes technical), and in gestures (people walk, and point, and mimic art making). Critiques can be:

Confusing	Frightening
Inspiring	Traumatic
Brilliant	Personal
Challenging	Aggressive
Too challenging	Predictable
Over your head	Worthless
Beneath you	Irrelevant
Annoying	Useless
Misguided	Expensive and useless
Repetitive	Intellectual
Boring	Too intellectual
Exhausting	Anti-intellectual
Unbelievably boring	Too anti-intellectual
Mind numbing	Eloquent
Too short	Too verbal
Incomprehensible	Intuitive
Strict	Supportive
Like an examination	Touchy-feely
Like boot camp	Inappropriate
Like therapy	Fabulous
Chaotic	

Your goal is to take it all in, and use it to understand your work more fully.

Critiques Aren't Tests

Art critiques are very different from the exams, quizzes, and tests in most other subjects. Critiques are more free form, more conversational. Critiques are sometimes one-on-one, but more often they involve a number of people. Sometimes there's an audience. Sometimes the audience participates. In the end, critiques don't always result in a grade: usually they're pass / fail, and sometimes they are just intended to encourage the student, and there's no way to fail. An exam is on one subject, which everyone agrees on in advance. A critique can be about anything from the politics of the day to the student's hairy legs.

How boring tests are by comparison! I have taken, and graded, enough tests to appreciate how they measure very limited properties. An IQ test, an Iowa Test, a GRE, an SAT, a Leaving Cert in Ireland, an A-level or an O-level in England, the

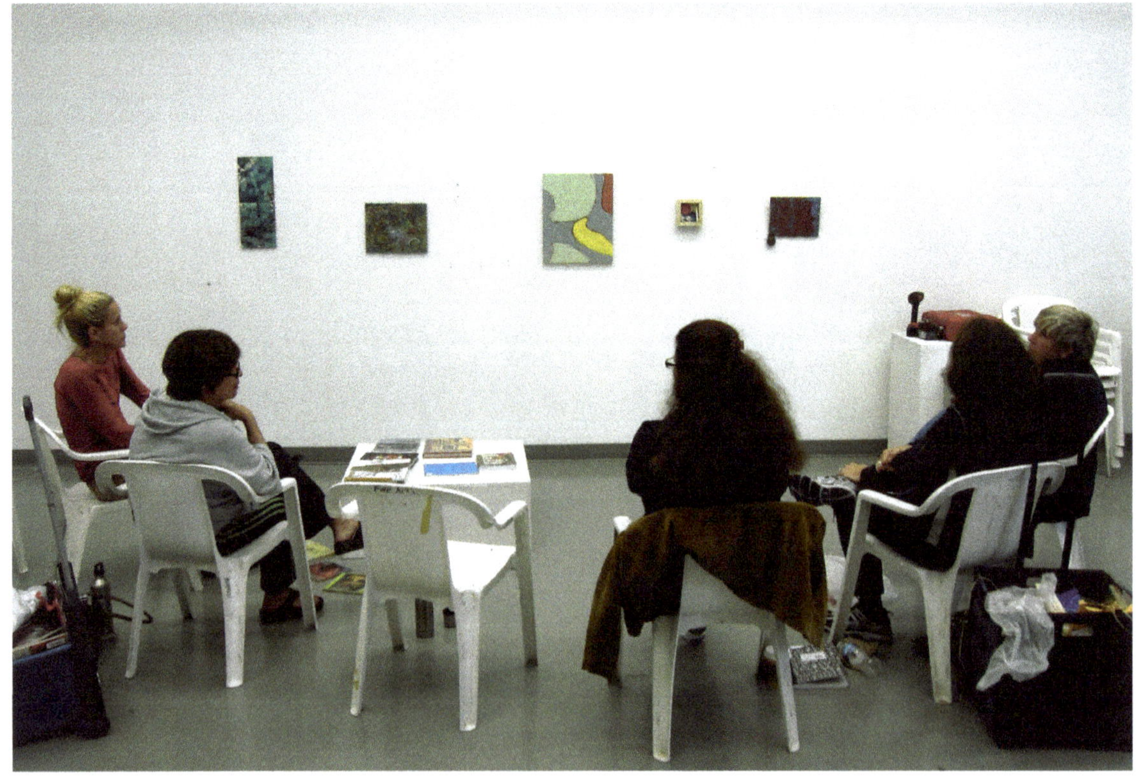

Abitur or Matura in the European Union, or any multiple-choice test in college, is usually a dreary affair. It tells me next to nothing about myself, if I'm taking it—and if I'm administering it, it tells me only a few things about the student.

A typical test is just a set of little puzzles, like a wheel for a hamster or a maze for a mouse. Tests have the virtue of ensuring that everyone in the class is on the same page. They promote the accumulation of systematic knowledge. At higher levels, as in Medical or Law Boards, they ensure that people who make important decisions are competent in their fields. But what does any of that have to do with living an interesting life, or being an interesting person?

Critiques are an entirely different matter. They are unbelievably difficult to understand, and rich with possibilities. Critiques are public conversations, "civic dialogue" as one teacher calls them. They can be open, inclusive, democratic.[1] All kinds of meanings can be at issue. Critiques can mimic real-life situations: they can sound like seductions, trials, poems, or fights. They can run the range from deathly boring to incoherently passionate—and that is appropriate, because artworks themselves express the widest spectrum of human response. But the price critiques pay for that richness is very high. Critiques can come perilously close to total nonsense. Sometimes they just barely make sense.

When you go into a critique, it's good to keep this in mind: a critique is not a test.

The critique's weakness is that it hardly has rules, it there is almost no way to assess or grade it.

The critique's strength is that it hardly has rules, and there is almost no way to assess or grade it.

Use the freedom!

3

Critiques Aren't Just Conversations

One way of looking at critiques is that they are just conversation. In that way of looking at it, there's nothing unusual or somehow *technical* about critiques. They're just talk.

This definition bothers me, because it avoids the strangeness of critiques. Critiques are intensely weird. They aren't just everyday conversations: they take place in settings where young people pay older people to teach them about art. They are very academic: they aren't at all like what happens in the rest of the artworld. After you graduate, if you pursue your art into the world of galleries, residencies, group shows, juried exhibitions, and art fairs, you'll see that there's nothing out there like critiques.

Here's what's normal in the art world: at the opening of your show, someone puts a glass of cheap white wine in your hand. People pat you on the shoulder.

"Great work!" they say, "Really wonderful, fabulous, compelling, *important*."

They ask you easy questions, like "How in the world did you get the idea of putting a watermelon in a baby stroller?"

They say they'll be looking forward to your next show.

"Really great," they say, "congratulations."

And then the opening is over, and that's about it for critique.

In the artworld, people look very quickly at art. At a big art fair, for example, an average glance must be a second or less. People talk a lot about money, fame, and celebrity, and a lot about rents, supplies, and contracts.

I don't mean to sound cynical: the artworld can be absorbing and sometimes very rewarding. But an art critique is an entirely different sort of experience. Art classes may be the only time in your life that people really focus on your work, and try to say all the things that it might mean. Meaning, interpretation, evaluation. Ambiguity, complexity, difficulty. Intensity, confusion, exhaustion. Inspiration, doubt, revision. These are things that happen in critiques.

In the artworld, meaning is much simpler. What's said about contemporary artists in galleries, museums, in short reviews, on television, and in glossy art magazines, is often easy and superficial. Jasper Johns's target pieces are against Abstract Expressionism. Takashi Murakami's sculptures are about consumerism. In art schools and academies, there are mountains of literature about artists like Johns and Murakami. Johns is about materiality, queer culture, and literalism; Murakami is about Japanese kitsch and cuteness. (Murakami has a PhD in art from Tokyo Geidai, where you can go and see his dissertation on file. A page from it is reproduced in the next-to-last chapter of this book.) Things are much more complicated in academia than in the artworld.

It's also said that critiques are like conversations because no one has final authority in the artworld. Contemporary art is pluralist, relativist, and continuously mobile, so there is no authority. This idea also bothers me. It's entirely true, but on the other hand critiques, as an institution, are founded on the exchange between people who think of themselves as learning, and people who are, by general agreement, in possession of something to teach. It's hard to know what to call the function the teachers have: Authority? Expert? Master? What matters is there's an agreed-upon inequality, whether it is real or constructed. (See *The Critique Handbook,* pp. 97–104, for more on these roles, and chapter 33 for more on the "master.")

So whatever critiques are, they aren't just conversations. They are very unusual situations, and it takes a lot of work to try to understand them.

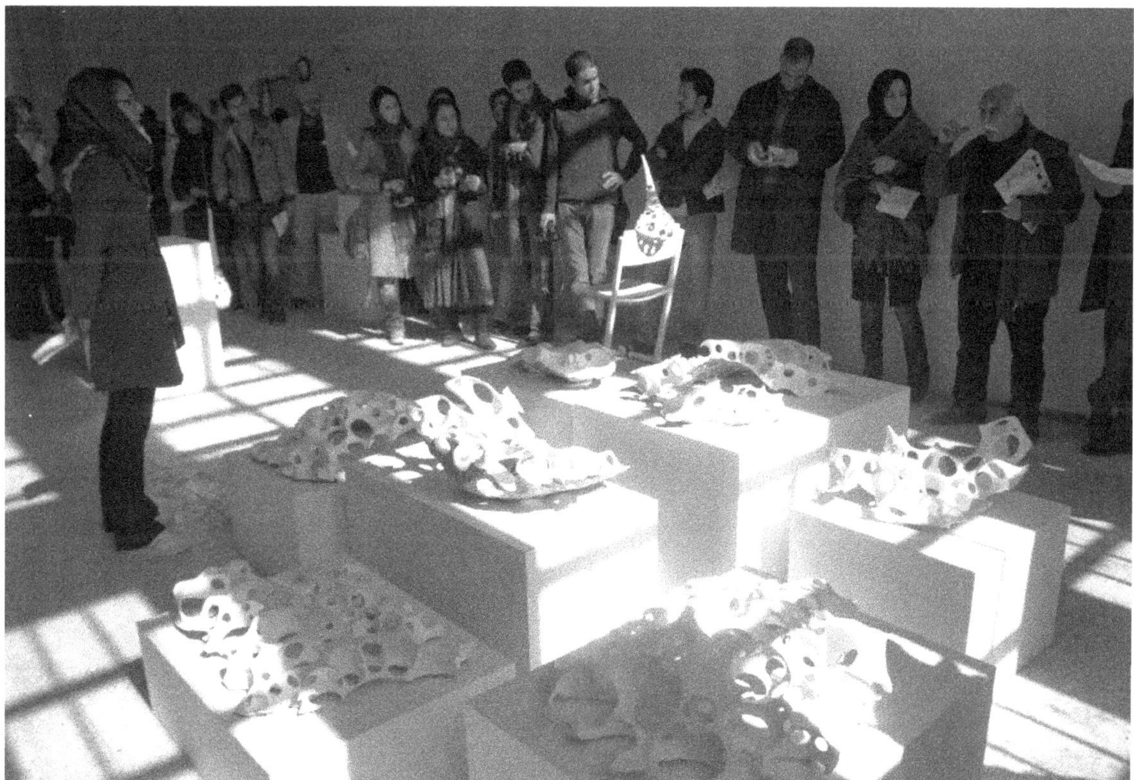

4

Critique Formats

In the first couple of years of the BFA, critiques are usually class discussions in which each student takes a turn saying something. Later on, there may be more than one teacher in the critique. There are many variations in different countries. Here is a chart of some I have seen. This a mix-and-match chart: you can match the columns to find your own critique format.

Time	Number of Faculty	Students present other than the artist
5 minutes	1	0
10 minutes	2	1 (often to take notes)
30 minutes	3 to 5	2 or 3
45 minutes	more than 5	All the student's friends
1 hour to 6 hours	(with faculty from other departments)	A whole class or auditorium

Some critiques have a second part, where the student's progress is discussed in a room away from the work. I was at one critique where the faculty met in an adjoining room, while the student and her friends waited outside. We wrote a report, with a grade. Then the student was called back in. The Chair of the art department showed her the report upside-down on the table, so she could glimpse it. Then the report was taken back and put in the department files!

Critiques vary around the world. The academy in Zürich has a Professional Artist Mentorship Seminar; each week a different professional artist comes to the seminar.[1] In London there's an initiative called Q-Art, a critique group that meets monthly in different institutions and has about 3,000 members (they produced the excellent book *Art Crits: 20 Questions*).[2] Matthew Kolodziej, at the Myers School of Art in Akron, Ohio, has invented a format in which three or four students critique another student's work, and at the same time other groups critique other students;

after ten or fifteen minutes the groups rotate, and eventually other students take turns being critiqued. That way the students hear the same ideas repeated, but not by the same groups, so that the context makes the repetitions interesting.[3] The book *Art Crits: 20 Questions* has a number of other formats used in the U.K. and Ireland. Despite the many variations in critiques—and despite the fact that faculty often think they have unique critique formats—I find that critiques are fairly similar in many countries. Most fit in with the possibilities shown in the chart.

A number of cultures don't have the tradition of harsh open classroom exchanges, making it difficult to get critiques started. In the Nanyang Technological University in Singapore, Joan Kelly helps her shy First Year students save face by asking them to write their opinions on sheets of paper. The sheets are folded and put in containers in front of each artwork, and then read out by the students.[4]

In general, the average situation is this: a BA or BFA critique is about 10 minutes long, and is usually done with a class full of students; an MA or MFA critique averages 30–45 minutes, and is done with more than one teacher present, in a studio, with a small audience. There is no standard form for a PhD critique, but it can amount to a far longer conversation, one on one, lasting several years. (I'll discuss that at the end of the book.)

Here are the average critique formats for the BFA, MFA, and PhD:

	Time	Number of Faculty	Number of students present other than the artist
BA or BFA	10 mins.	1	A whole class
MA or MFA	30 mins.	3 to 5	All the student's friends
PhD	1 hour	1	0

If you're just starting out in art class, you're probably getting brief critiques along with the rest of the class. That means you're at the tip of the iceberg. As you go along, you'll have longer critiques; you'll be expected to speak (or speak more than you have so far); and you'll get feedback from a larger number of instructors.

There's also an idea behind the quick critiques for beginning students: you're just starting, so you don't have many ideas and skills, and your issues are relatively straightforward. Actually I think this is entirely wrong: art is tremendously complex right from the beginning, and I can often see expressive tendencies and character traits in even the simplest life drawing. But that's another story.

5

Skill versus Meaning

About that story I told in the Preface (the one about the student with hairy legs).

The most common subject in beginning critiques is technique or skill. When an instructor gives you advice about how to draw a shadow or paint an eye, that's a matter of skill, technique, or medium. At moments like that, it doesn't seem to matter what the work means, or what mood it expresses, or what sense of yourself it projects. Most first-year critiques are all about artist's techniques, observation, and manual skills.

Somewhere along the line to the MFA, all that changes. In the MFA it is not common to hear criticism about technique or skill. Everything is about what the work means, what it expresses. The most common themes are gender, identity, sexuality, ethnicity, and politics. The talk about that student's hairy legs was absolutely typical of MFA critiques. In a first-year performance art class, the talk would be more about theater, setting, lighting, acting, voice, memory, scripting, and presence—all the technical things that support the medium of theater or performance.

So: generally it's skill or technique first, meaning second.

There is only one problem with this: technique and meaning are entangled, and it is not possible to speak about one without expressing the other. Actually it is impossible to speak *only* about technique, without hinting at meaning; and it is impossible to speak *only* about meaning, without addressing the work's physical presence—its matter, medium, and material

A teacher might be talking about a medium, and thinking about its meanings, or vice versa. A teacher might assume that meanings come out of media, and another might think the opposite. The trick is to listen to the way symbolic and expressive meanings are implied in technical talk, and how media and formal problems are implied in talk about meaning.

If a teacher says, "You need to use Layers in Photoshop less obviously, more subtly: try a new Adjustment Layer and put it at 50% transparency," you may think that you're just getting technical advice. But behind that comment there might be an idea about what makes a photo good, or expressive: maybe your teacher is showing you how to make your image more like a point-and-shoot photo, or a street photo. It is technical advice, but it isn't only technical advice, and in fact it might be aimed principally at what your photograph expresses.

Your teacher may be making the common assumption that it's hard to talk about meaning, so meaning is best discovered through technique. But beware! This way of speaking about technique may itself be a technique to avoid talking about meaning.

Medium and metaphor are mixed. Every artist knows how engrossing technical problems can be, and that is because no technique is without meaning. I think the idea that some techniques are merely techniques, and others have meaning, is connected to the idea that some talk about technique is a way of not coming to terms with one's self. If you believe that techniques are separate from meaning, then you can go on experimenting with them and not be impelled to think consistently or directly about yourself or the meanings you want or need. Conversation about technique is conversation about meaning: it is just a special way of talking about meaning that does not allow the speaker to acknowledge as much.

The problem is how to draw out a teacher who wants to talk only about skill or technique. If your teacher talks consistently about technical matters, it might just mean she thinks she is doing her job. (Maybe she teaches digital video editing, robotics, or 3-D printing—something with a lot of technical issues.) But maybe she has decided—consciously or not—to avoid thinking about symbols or expressive meanings. Perhaps she wants to avoid questions of meaning for personal reasons. Maybe she's lazy, and technical stuff is easier to do. Maybe she has become accustomed to thinking "through media" rather than through ideas. Or maybe she wants to avoid bringing up questions of meaning because she doesn't think you have achieved much meaning yet: maybe you've just been doing classroom exercises, and it's not time for meaning. It's hard to know.

If your critique is about nothing but skill and technique, you might try listening between the lines, to hear what your teachers might be implying about meaning. Or you might just ask them: what do you think this means?

6

Talking About Composition is Easier

Than Talking About Race

Meaning is often about gender, identity, race and ethnicity, religious belief, and sexuality, and those subjects can be sensitive, embarrassing, and even potentially treacherous for your teachers. Talking about composition is easier than talking about race.

Some art critiques are aimed directly at meanings. The talk is all about gender, identity, faith, morality, politics, sexuality, race, and ethnicity. I've been in critiques where meaning dominates the discussion from beginning to end, and the students don't get any feedback on their media, their methods, their levels of skill, or their techniques.

On the other hand, I've been in critiques where the work is obviously about race, ethnicity, religion, or identity, but the teacher has refused to go near those ideas. The talk was all about medium, paint, color, hanging, space, and composition. Over the years I've seen teachers ignore just about every sort of statement of identity: I've seen teachers pretend they don't see feminist, gay, lesbian, and transgender meanings; I've seen teachers ignore work about Chicano, Latino, *mestizo*, Peruvian, Chinese, Serbian, German, Japanese, Indian, and Pakistani ethnicity; I've seen teachers pretend not to see images of Jesus in paintings; I've seen teachers talk about images of war in Afghanistan, Syria, Iraq, and Israel as if they were formal compositions; I've seen teachers ignore work that's clearly about dissociative behavior, dyslexia, compulsions, fetishes, trichotillomania, depression, and even suicide; and I've seen teachers ignore any number of political statements from anarchist to Republican.

There are two obstacles to getting teachers to talk about these kinds of meanings. First, faculty assume they can get in trouble for talking about sensitive or personal themes. That is easy to work around: tell them they won't.

Second, faculty assume they aren't competent to speak about things like ethnicity or faith. Years ago I had a Korean woman student who made large silk screens of the salvation of the world. She was Methodist, and very pious. Her printmaking instructors were helping her with silk screening and keeping a mile away from her images of God. She had to call me in secret to get feedback (I was an art historian, and I wasn't scheduled for a critique in the Print Department).[1] I've also seen white teachers studiously ignore African-American themes in artworks, as if they weren't allowed to comment. I've seen teachers humbly accept lectures on Argentine cultural values, thinking they couldn't say anything. Faculty won't talk because they assume they aren't experts on those subjects. They say their field is printmaking or ceramics or painting, but not politics, faith, or race. They don't want to talk because they feel they aren't competent. This is less easy to work around, but it's possible: just tell your teacher that you'd like some response, no matter how much she may know about your subject.[2]

Once the conversation is underway, you may run into other obstacles. Instructors may tell you that they don't like to work hard to understand the traditional signs and values of your ethnicity, or the codes and meanings of an identity construction. It's an amazing characteristic of the art world that people want art to express different identity constructions, faiths, and ethnicities, but they don't want to have to work to learn the details. In large exhibitions like art fairs and the many biennales, the idea is that you can get an idea of what the artist wants to say relatively quickly, with relatively little work. My advice here is to disregard that custom. Make your instructors work as hard as you would like: make them read, ask them to study what you've done. You should be able to present whatever complexities you'd like: after everything is on the table, then your instructors can help you sort through what works and what doesn't.

Everything I've said in this chapter has to do with getting your instructor to talk. There's another side to this: some instructors won't talk about anything except gender, identity, faith, sexuality, and politics. For them issues of skill and technique are rudimentary, or they are all in service of what really matters. That kind of instructor is less common, and you'll find them more at the graduate level. But it's important to know that the question of skill and meaning is a see-saw: it easily tips one way or the other, and it is difficult to balance.

7

What if You're Asked to Talk

About Your Work?

Teachers commonly ask students to begin by making statements. Sometimes those statements break down. The student runs out of things to say, and begins to doubt herself. She flounders, tries to find more words, but can't. Sometimes the student is very confident, and makes a set speech. Then she just stops and looks around

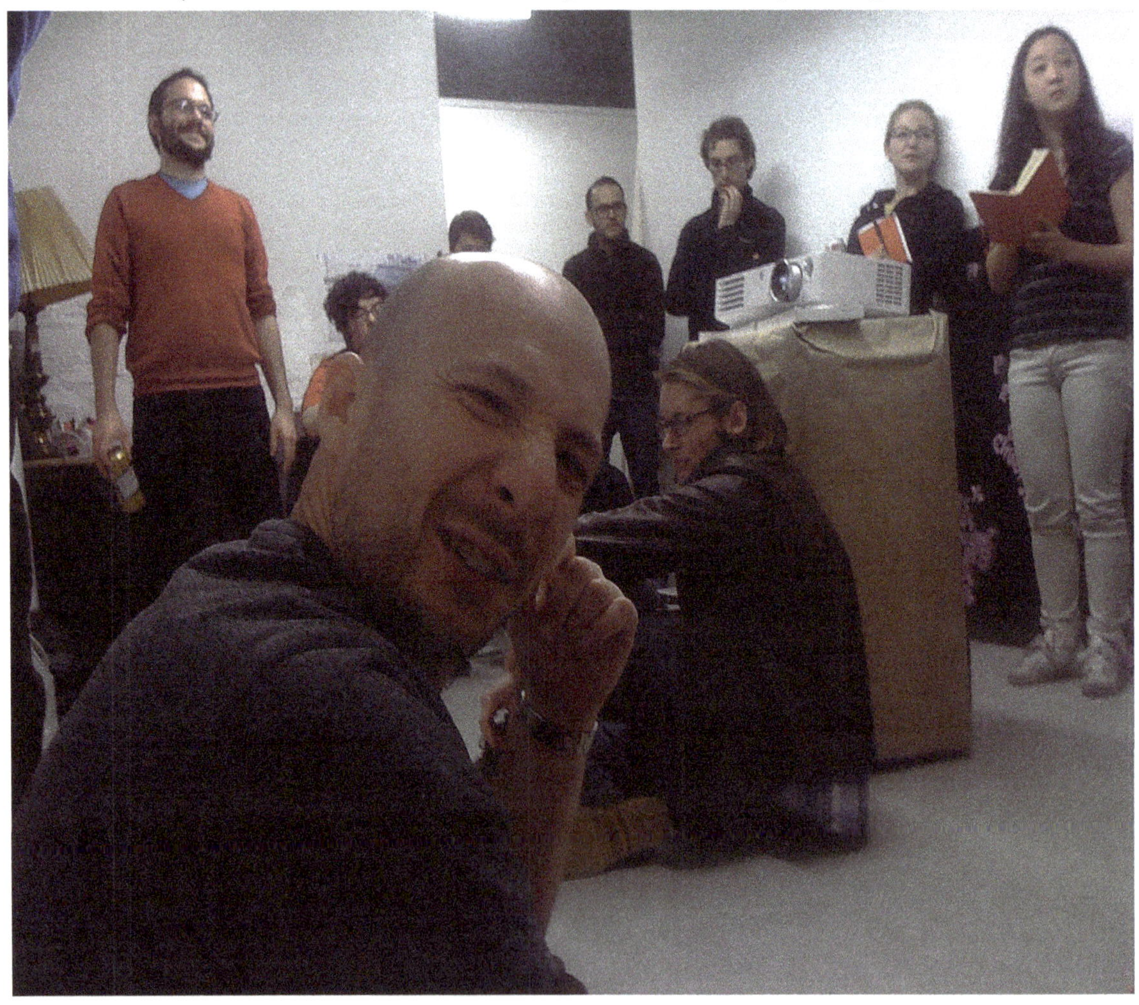

defiantly, as if to say, Try to analyze that. Usually the student prepares some thoughts in advance, but public speaking isn't the easiest thing, and the thoughts might come out too confident, or too confused, or too quickly. The speech might be over before it has started, and then the Silent Teacher might say, "Please, can you say a bit more?" It isn't easy to talk in public, especially if you're standing next to something you've just made, something that doesn't even really make sense to you yet.

If you're asked to give a short introduction to your work, the best thing is to be as informal and honest as possible. You can memorize some talking points, like "Explain the choice of cowboys," "Say something about how my printmaking technique is progressing," or "Describe the idea for next semester." It helps to have a short list of things in your mind. But it's usually not a good idea to prepare too much of a speech. Here are some good things to say to get people started talking:

- I'd like to say a few things about this, and then I'd like to hear what people have to say.
- I can tell you some of my ideas about it.
- If you'd like to hear what I've been reading, I can tell you, or what I've been thinking about, or who I've been looking at…

These are all open-ended and friendly, which helps conversation get started. On Facebook, I asked what some of the worst opening lines are, and got this fabulous list:

- "I'm feeling fragile right now."[1] (It's best not to say this because it puts teachers in a bind, and besides, it's true for everyone.)
- "None of this work is finished," or "I'm just experimenting."[2] (This may be true, but if you broadcast it, you're saying that whatever a teacher thinks won't apply.)
- "I'd like to read this 20,000 word artist's statement that sets out the general theory of my practice." (More on this in a moment.)
- "I'd like to describe a piece I'd like to make."[3]
- "And tell you what else I plan to do to the piece, what I wanted to do but didn't have the money for, and what I wanted to do but didn't have the time."[4]
- "I haven't slept in four days."[5]
- "I ran out of money, I ran out of space, I ran out of paint, I ran out of time, I ran out ideas, I ran out of…."[6]
- "I made this for myself."[7]
- "I am trying to show that painting is not dead."[8]
- "This piece speaks for itself, okay?"[9]
- "You people are not the intended audience for my work."[10]

- "Whatever you see in it is okay with me," or "*You* tell me what my work is about."[11]

Many art departments and art schools offer courses on writing artists' statements. (Some also offer courses on writing manifestoes, which can be great fun.) In some institutions, writing courses are required. By the time students get to MFA programs, most of them have long prepared texts that they use for grant applications, residencies, and juried exhibitions. It can be tempting to bring in your artist's statement and read it in critique, but there's a limit to how useful that is. Teachers will balk at long statements. Some students use statements as a shield, to protect themselves from criticism. They hope the statement will deflect the criticism, and save them from getting hurt. Some students discover art theory, and produce statements brimming with cool theory references. One BFA student began her critique by saying,

"I have just been reading the psychoanalyst Jacques Lacan. I am especially interested in a concept of his, called in French the *objet petit a.*"

A year or two later, that might develop into something more confident, like:

"My work uses Jacques Lacan's idea of the Other, especially the *objet petit a.*"

At the MFA level, the same student might say something even more fancy, like:

"My work interrogates the Lacanian *objet petit a.*"

As you go on through art school, you'll learn how to make art-world and theory-world references more and more smoothly. But there's a danger here, and that is that the instructor might hear your increasingly sophisticated statement as a sign that you're increasingly anxious about what your work is *really* about, and increasingly desperate to keep the conversation on subjects you know. That's why an informal, honest opening statement is always best. If Lacan fits into the conversation later, then fine. But when teachers see the Theory Shield being raised, they're likely to bring on the big Authority Guns.

The standard line about critiques is that it's good to talk, in order to keep the critique on track, steering it toward important topics and away from wild interpretations. Control your critique, people say, and it will go better. (One summer the School of the Art Institute even mailed out letters to incoming MFA students, telling them how to control their critiques, but it only made everyone nervous.) But you might also consider that control is an elusive thing, and the moment when you actually achieve it may well be the moment when you learn the least. In addition, art history shows that artists have been consistently misguided about what they do: the reasons they thought their work was valuable usually aren't the reasons we value their work today.

The lesson art history teaches in this case is that artists need to tell themselves certain stories about their work—enabling stories, myths that let them get on with what they want to do—but that later generations tend to care about entirely different things. I don't mean you shouldn't try to tell your story: I mean that it's sensible to also bear in mind that your version of what you do might be very different from other people's, and that telling people your story might not result in a better critique.

In general: if you're asked to speak, do. It's your opportunity to tell everyone what you intended. In my experience, chances are nearly one hundred percent that people won't have understood your work the way you want it understood, but that is good. As soon as you see the mismatch between your intentions and what people think, you're on your way to developing your art. Some artists never listen, and try over and over to insist on their own interpretations. Sometimes that makes for interesting art, but it isn't the way art usually works, and it doesn't create rewarding classroom experiences. Your intentions are a starting place, a diving board.

And while I'm on this subject, here's a list of things not to say during critique. These are show-stoppers, conversation killers:

- "I just think [*insert name of artist considered hopeless by the teacher, or the name of one of the teacher's colleagues*] is the greatest living artist."
- "I'm not really interested in [*insert the topic the teacher had just been talking about*]."
- "This is all about my private spiritual experience."
- "It means what it means to me, that's all."
- "That's not helpful."[12]

In other words: it's best to be flexible, open, and informal. It's most dangerous to be closed, rigid, paranoid, programmatic, or defensive.

And to be fair to students, here's a list of things teachers shouldn't say:

- "I like the red color you used," or "I like the frame," or "I like the size," or "I like the presentation."[13] (These and a thousand like them can lead to interesting conversations, but they can also be seriously lazy sorts of comments that are mainly intended to fill dead air space.)
- "You really need to read [*insert name of difficult philosopher*]." (This can be fine, provided the teacher explains why that author is pertinent, and gives an exact reference, rather than just recommending all the author's works.)
- "Have you ever looked at [*insert name of artist*]?" (This one is also fine, if you give reasons; but often the student will ask the teacher why she's recommending that particular artist, and she'll say, "I don't know why I thought of her. But you should look at her work.")
- "That is not a painting [*said looking at the student's painting*]."[14]
- "Why did you choose an art career?"[15]

- "Here's the correct way to do that."
- "Okay, just *stop*."

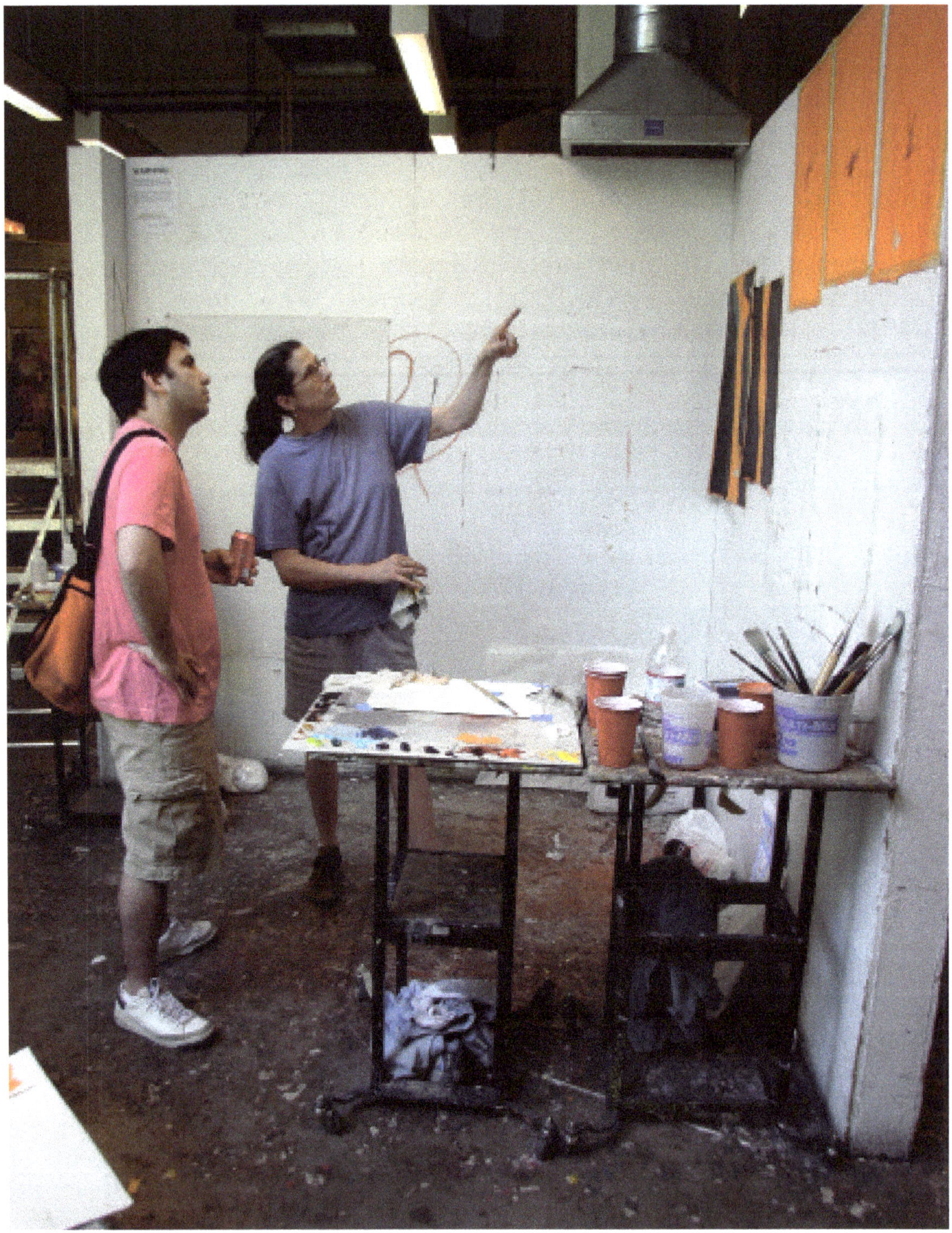

What if You Didn't Put in Much Work on Your Art?

What if you really didn't work very hard on your art, but you have to show it anyway? Maybe you missed class, or you weren't really engaged, or you were experimenting and nothing much worked out. Maybe your studio class is just one of four or five classes you're taking, and you just didn't put in the time. It's a common enough problem.

But then does your work *deserve* 10, 20, or 30 minutes of attention? A student once told me she resented having to spend 45 minutes talking about another student's work that she knew was put together in less than 20 minutes. I'm not so sure of that—after all, it didn't take Duchamp all day to construct his *Fountain*—but it surely doesn't make sense to lavish enormous attention on work that was done carelessly. And from the faculty's point of view, critiquing takes effort, and a good teacher will try to match her interpretive effort to what she thinks of as your effort in making the work. If she realizes she's been putting in the time for no good reason, she won't be happy.

If you are actually trying to get away with minimal effort, you might get some good feedback, and you may even get away with it: but it's also likely that you'll miss the more useful, pertinent sorts of criticism that you would have gotten if you'd put more time and effort into your work.

As a student, the best thing to do if you haven't put in the time is to address the issue directly, right in the critique. That way your teachers will know what kinds of feedback will be most helpful. In some special cases, you could actually ask for minimal or brief feedback. If you're just learning a medium, then a long critique might not make sense, because a lot of what needs to be said will be basic stuff. Likewise, if you're just starting a new project, a long critique might overwhelm you with critical judgments that may be difficult to use.

Teachers Make Their Own Artworks, Different From Yours

In a critique only the student's works are on display. The teachers' works are not, and you may not know what kind of work they make. That means that as a student, you don't always know where your teachers's remarks are coming from.

From a student's point of view, there are good and bad reasons for wanting to know what kind of work your teachers make. A bad reason is to try to weed out instructors whose work seems less interesting or pertinent. (That is a bad reason, because the kind of work someone does has no predictable correlation with the relevance of their judgments.) A good reason is to be able to better understand

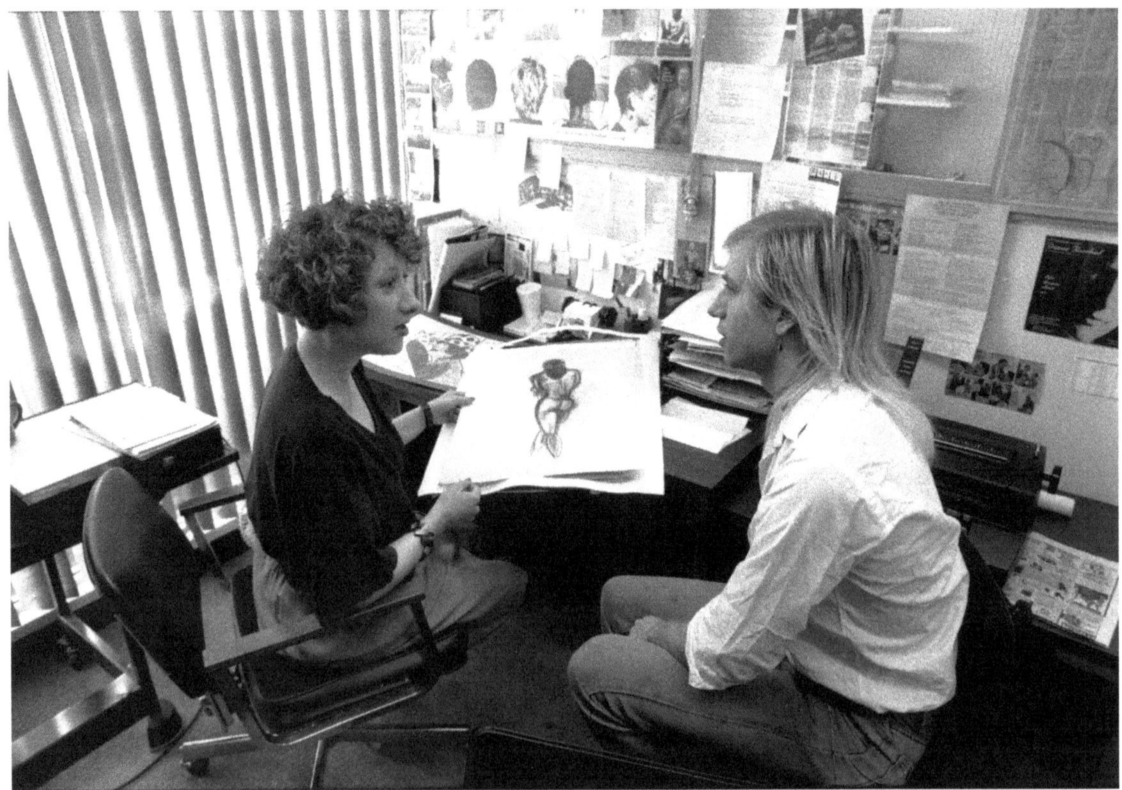

why your teachers say what they say. If a teacher says, "Your editing is too soft. It might be better if it was sharper," then "soft" and "sharp" might have a wide range of meanings. It is easier to understand this criticism if you know that the teacher isn't a filmmaker but a painter, and she paints geometric abstractions. At the same time, it is not helpful to use your familiarity with the teacher's work in order to pigeonhole her remarks. Some teachers have a really astonishing capacity to be empathetic about all kinds of work that does not resemble their own.

(From the teacher's point of view, it is sometimes troublesome to have the students know what you do. Students will pigeonhole you, and they may not take what you say seriously.)

Explaining your teacher's judgments solely by reference to their work can create a false sense of understanding. You might be tempted to think "I can see why he would say *that!*" You may be wrong, but knowing the teacher's work does allow the you to understand what is said a little more *specifically*. The students in Michael Asher's critique, which is discussed in chapter 15, would have a pretty good idea what his silences mean: but really, they would never know for sure. Hard-edge abstract painting evokes a certain sense of "sharp" and "soft," and so you will have an idea what your teacher has in mind and what to ask next. So there is a highly qualified sense in which knowledge of the panelist's work can be helpful.

This is equally true of instructors who are also writers. As a student, if you have a teacher who is also a critic, an historian, or a philosopher, you're well advised to take the time to read whatever you can of your teacher's writings. Often their publications are available in the department offices or in the library. This is not commonly done, perhaps because students think that the written works of historians or liberal arts teachers are irrelevant or overly difficult. But they are no less relevant than studio instructors' works, because in both cases they are what the teachers do: both essays and artworks represent the teachers' knowledge and express their interests. It may be that some publications are too difficult, but the same can be said of artworks in unfamiliar styles. Older studio faculty make works that can be more difficult than the most abstruse piece of philosophic art criticism: simply because the works are old, it can be very hard to sympathize with them. The moral is read and look at everything the faculty does: it probably won't hurt, and it may help.

10

Thinking About the Critique Afterward

There's an art to thinking about your critique when it's over.

Assuming you have notes—you should always have notes!—put them away, and let the whole thing settle out for a few days. Usually what happens is that you'll remember the best thing that was said to you, and the worst thing. You'll probably be a bit obsessive about the bad thing. You'll probably be totally happy about the best thing.

Meanwhile you'll be forgetting everything else.

After a week, or a few weeks—depending on how upset or confused you are—when you feel relatively calm, look back at your notes. It's best to do this in company of someone who was at the critique. You'll find that you have forgotten interesting things that were drowned out by the few very positive and negative remarks. And you'll find that it helps to go through everything slowly, considering each remark on its own.

The most common thing people say about critiques is that they have too much in them; they are confusing, with conflicting opinions and ideas, and basically too much feedback to assimilate. Most of this book is dedicated to minimizing that reaction. I hope that after reading it you will have enough tools to disassemble the confusion and reassemble it in a shape you can understand and use.

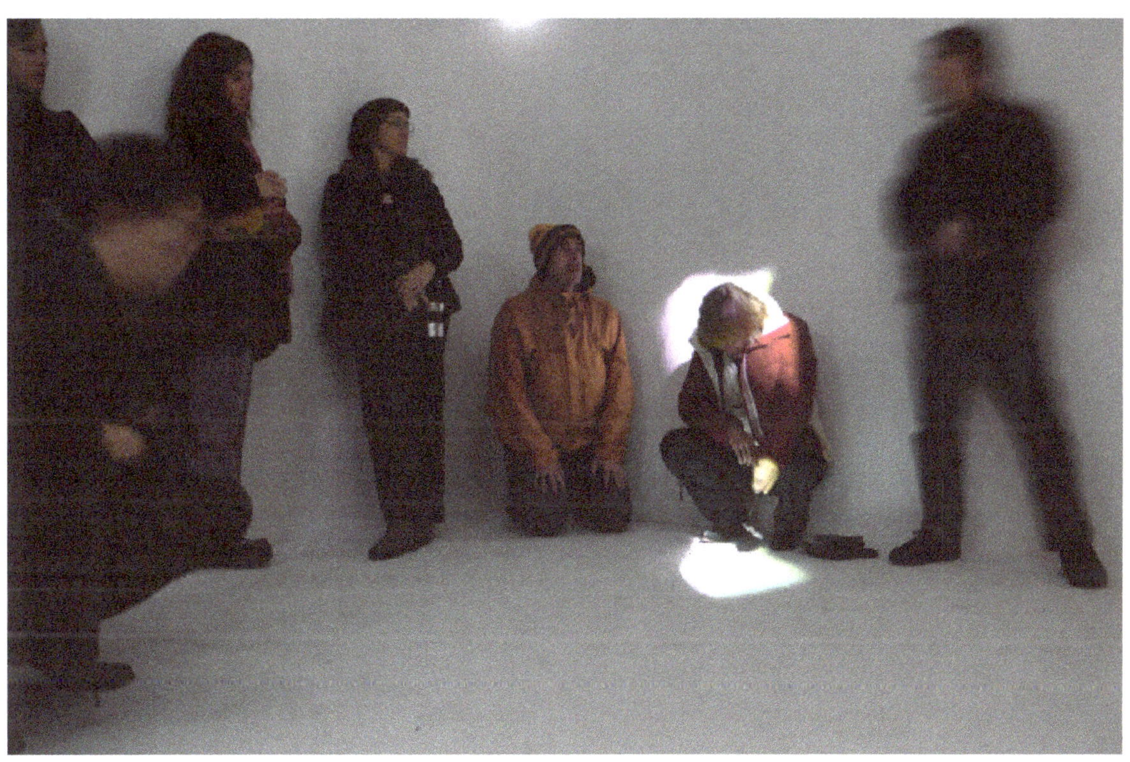

Part Two

BFA Issues

11

A Sample Critique

Critiques have a certain flavor. They are raw and undigested. They are often a bit dull. Inspiration isn't easy, and certainly not for instructors who might be tired or distracted. Sometimes critiques are passionate and even violent, but most are fairly

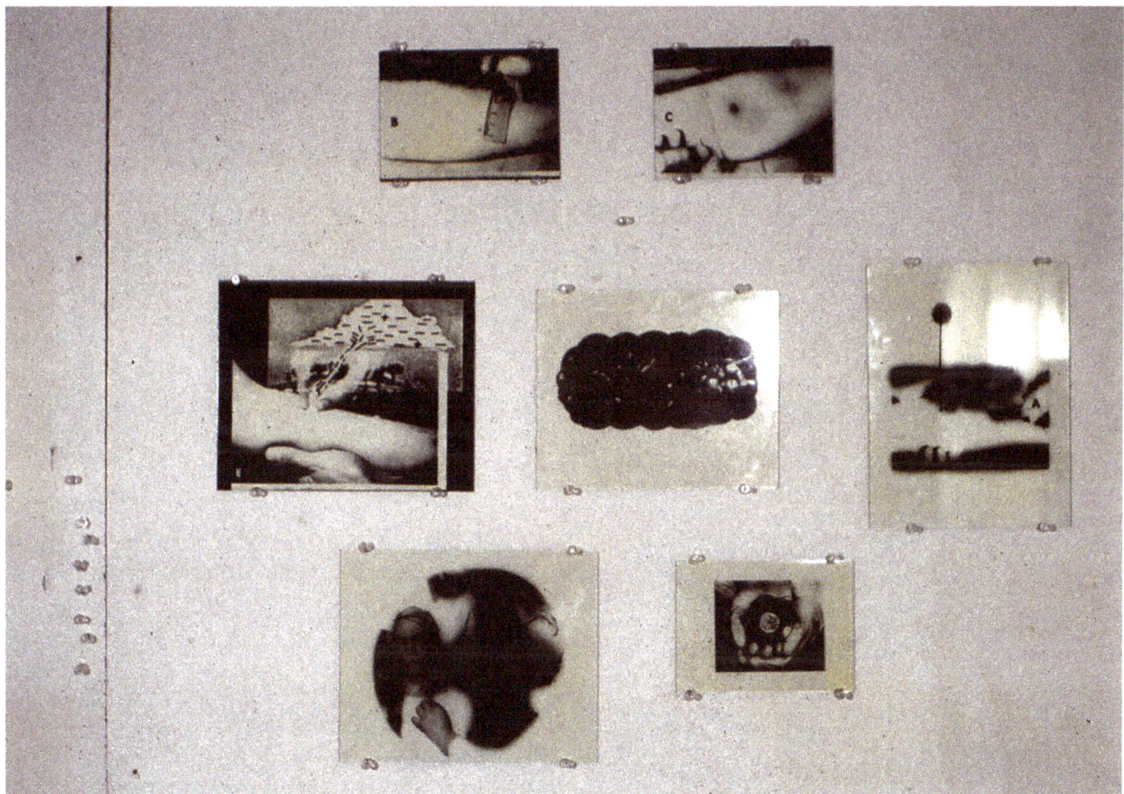

calm. Every once in a while an instructor or a student will say something really memorable, but often the language is a bit awkward, punctuated with gaps and silences, repetitions and obscurities. Occasionally critiques are brilliant: insights spark off each other and stupendous ideas rain down faster than you can hear them.

But most of the time nothing tremendously interesting happens.

It matters that critiques are this way. They aren't Shakespeare, and they are definitely not the professionalized language of art history, art education, or art theory. They aren't philosophical investigations: they're too disorganized and haphazard for that.

I am going to be saying some fairly abstract things in this book, so I want to give something of the flavor of an ordinary critique. This is one that the student transcribed from an audiotape. It isn't the whole critique, but portions of it. I have added some comments.

If it's possible, you should read this aloud in a class, like a play, to get a sense of its tone, its mood, its language. It requires eight students to play the parts.

The artist's name is Andrea Schumacher. She's a painter and sculptor, and you can see her recent work on her website.[1] This was taped when she was a student at the School of the Art Institute of Chicago. There were seven people in the room, most of them faculty. I removed their names, and substituted letters: *R, K, W, J, M, V*, and *Q*. The teacher called *J* is the moderator; she was in charge of keeping time. The faculty saw a group of untitled pieces on glass, mounted together on a wall; three Xeroxes on acetate; and two collages on paper. The first illustration in this chapter is the group of pieces on glass.

The critique begins abruptly, with Andrea's opening statement:

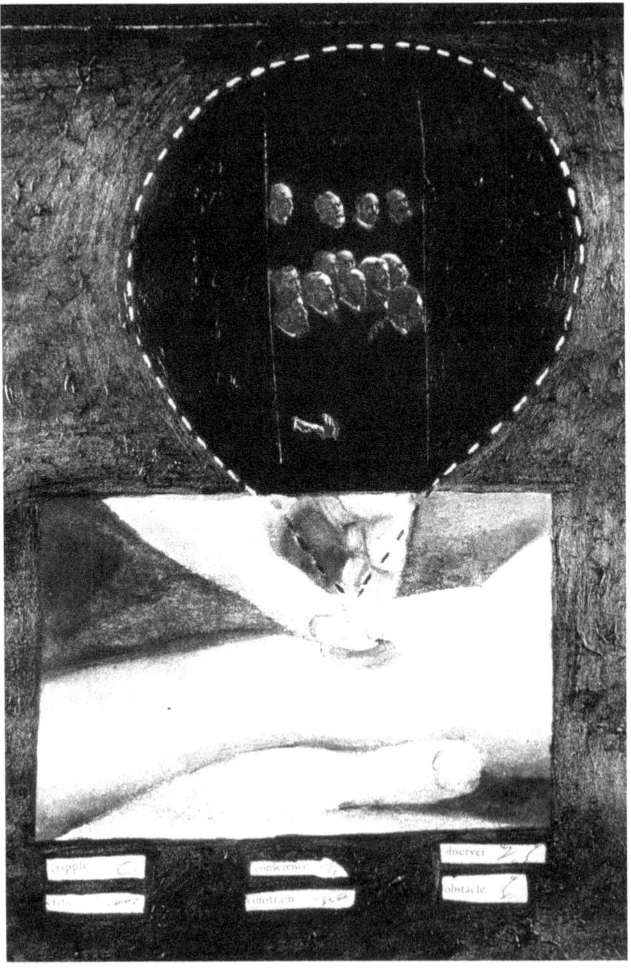

A   This is work in progress, and I just started doing the liquid light on glass, and I'm still in the early stages of working with it. By the end of when I'm working with it, I want it to be presented so that it's either backlit or exposed to whatever ambient light is present, so that one can see through the images. Right now, as they are against the wall, and I'm losing a lot of detail—so it is not the best way to view them, but I wanted just to show where I'm heading.

R   That double image is just a shadow on the wall?

A   Yeah, I mean… they are not… I mean the point of working with transparency is that hopefully that one can have layers of information. Putting these up on the wall is just for practical purposes so that you can see them without handling them. There is more detail in that one… when light passes through it. What I hope to do with the glass is to have many layers, but right now, I'm just working on getting the exposures right. It's definitely work in progress.

I want to interrupt this right here, at the beginning, to make a simple observation. The English is awful. Andrea says "by the end of when I'm working with it," and then she says "right now, as they are against the wall, and I'm losing a lot of detail." Those kinds of errors are ubiquitous in our spoken English, but we don't usually notice them. There are lots of hesitations and unfinished thoughts. Andrea says, "Yeah, I mean… they are not… I mean…." That sort of thing doesn't appear in written texts on art, but it is part of the way people talk about art. It is not easy to talk about art, especially if you're the artist and the work is new: you're likely to be unsure how to speak, or what to say, or even what you really mean when you say something. That is entirely normal, and it is important to attend to it and not try to censor it out. Whatever Andrea's works meant to her at the time, they meant something more than "working with transparency": that was just the phrase she ended up with, after two false starts.

R Will those other layers have other information on them?

A Yeah, that's one of the main reasons I want to use glass—that's one of the things I want to talk about, the aspects of glass and transparency and what kind of connotations you get from it, or if the glass is adding to the imagery or taking away from it. The reason I'm using it is that it was a way to further manipulate the images I'm working with. I've worked with xeroxes a lot and I was getting a little… I was manipulating them in collage and I still work in a collage fashion, but I'd like more opportunity to manipulate the images. These works here [*pointing to three images, one of which is illustrated here*] are Xerox collages on acetate. There are a couple of layers to them, and I've been scraping them and just trying to manipulate these images, trying to put my hand on them to a certain degree. So I went to the glass hoping to find a way to get a little more flexibility—and I think I am going to be working with maybe a low-tech kind of photography so that I can do things that are along the lines of collage and montage. It's a relatively new thing for me, and a lot of work has gone towards using the glass and also about the level of manipulation. Right now I don't feel that I'm manipulating things as much as I want to combining images. I think that I would like to have a certain emotional or expressive content in these images—I don't want them to be purely postmodern appropriations or recontextualizations. I think that I'm combining traditions of expressionism and using something that is more modern or postmodern—using appropriated images and I want to talk a little bit about that—whether that's schizophrenic to take an expressionistic

bent to a more modern practice.
So those are some of the things I'd like to spark interest in.

K   How do you see these being presented, seeing as you are using glass. Will it be a hand-held object? Will it be on a stand? Will it be enclosed in a frame? Will it—

A   I have thought of a couple of possibilities which would be in a kind of a shadow box frame, possibly back-lit, or lights along the sides, or on some sort of a stand with the ability to adjust the space between the layers—maybe enclosed, but maybe not so that the light could pass through them.

Notice what's just happened here, from Andrea's point of view. First she talks some more about her technique—the glass and the acetate. But then, in the second part of her reply, she tries to change the subject. She'd like to talk about content and meaning instead. She mentions a lot of things in quick succession: emotion, expression, postmodern appropriation, recontextualization, expressionism, even schizophrenia! There is plenty to talk about there, and she even says she'd like to "spark interest" in what her work means. But the faculty member, who I am calling "K," either doesn't hear or isn't interested, and the conversation goes right back to technique.

W   Have you only thought of transparent glass? It's that I mean I'm just looking at… when you say backlit. I'm looking at it and thinking of how that would work or why the transparent glass—how would you backlight this? How would it affect this?

A   I don't quite understand your question.

W   Um, maybe I'm trying to—when you keep referring to backlighting it…

A   If it were in a frame and it were enclosed, like in a shadow box there would have to be some sort of light source so that the light could come through the images as they overlapped each other.

W   That's what I'm trying to get at—

R   Frosted light bulbs.

W   —because right now you have the shadows giving that double image, and that's part of the transparent quality of this glass; and you talk about collage and montage, and you are going to get more of that, and if you backlight it, it will eliminate that… but I mean…

Critiques often develop fixed ideas, which get tossed from one instructor to the next, and they develop a life of their own. One of the fixed ideas here is that the shadows of the glass are creating double images. Actually, it is hard to see those double images. They show up next to the letter "B" in the piece on the next page.

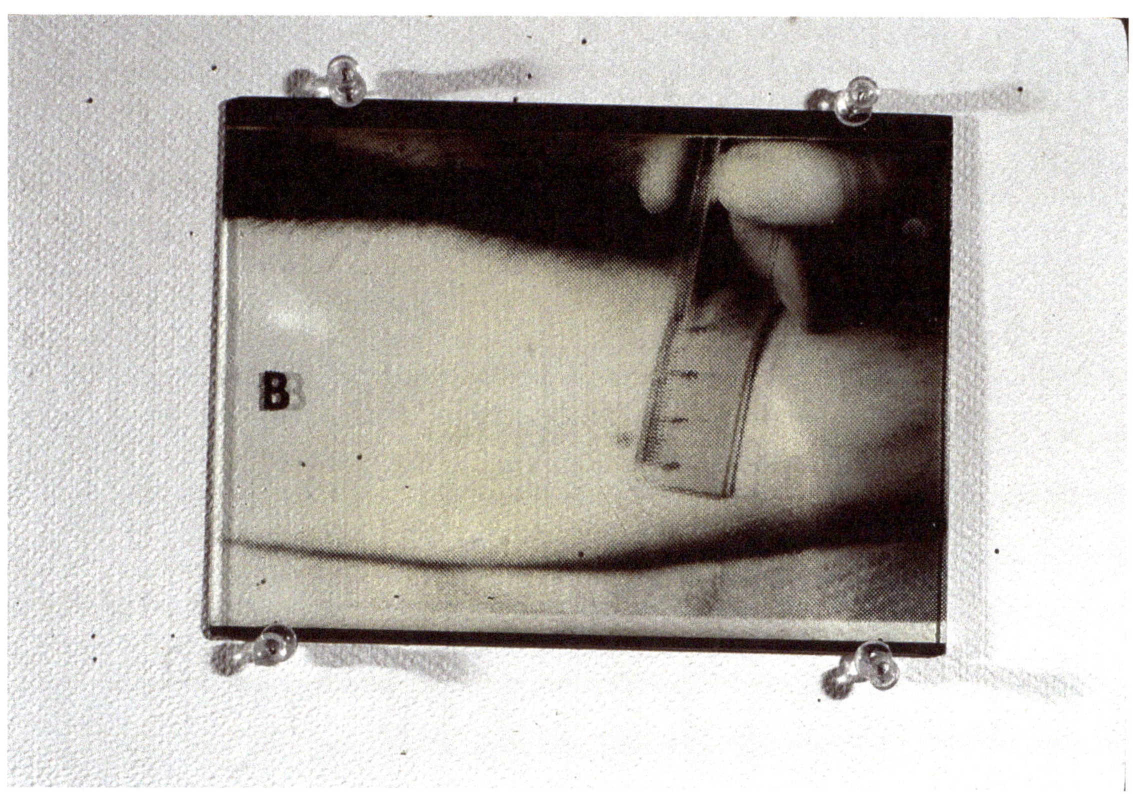

But the plastic ruler already has doubled edges, and the rest of the image is too blurry to make double images. People tend to stand at certain distances during critiques, and as the critique gets underway, it's likely the faculty are all standing back five or ten feet, and they aren't looking closely. That means the conversation can go on about general ideas like glass, acetate, and double reflections.

A   I don't know; I haven't tried one yet. These are possibilities. I have no idea what it will be like—but I have talked to my advisor about having some sort of lit shadow box so that it would be like a light table—that kind of effect.

W   You can print right on the frosted glass—it would do the same thing all in one—and when you backlight—

K   —or any other support that is not, that doesn't have—one of the main connotations that I can think of about glass is fragility or breakability. So I mean, how do you justify its use, maybe given your ideas, given that aspect of that particular material, because it's not a hand-held object and you don't, you know, you don't impose any of these qualities about the material on the viewer, I mean then I would question the use of that as a support.

A   I'm not sure I follow you, but I don't… For me the reason I'm using glass is not for its fragility or breakability, that's not the main quality. It's the transparency, and also I think there are—it has a certain dated quality of old daguerreotypes or negatives on glass—those are the qualities I think about. I'm not really thinking about…

Did you understand what instructor "K" was trying to say? I think she, or he, was saying that there doesn't seem to be a connection between the fact glass is fragile and the way the images are mounted. But maybe the idea is that there is no connection between the choice of glass and the subject matter. Or maybe that the characteristics of glass aren't used in the piece. (I will come back to this speech at the end of this book, in chapter 42.) Andrea tries her best to answer, but she also wants to change the subject: and this time, she succeeds.

W   What about subject matter, in relationship to why you chose glass? Is there any connection?

A   Well, yes, in that much of the imagery is medical. I think there is also that suggestion—of a cell on a slide—or on glass. So far that seems to be the kinds of connections that I've come up with. I mean at this point I'm working on glass, it's the first thing that came to my mind. I'm not sure if Plexiglas would work with liquid light; the chemicals might affect it, and since I don't know silk screen at this point (I'm going to be learning it)… But at this point this is something I know how to do—and glass is one of the materials that liquid light will work on—so that was another reason.

K   Well if you disguise what it is—I mean in a frame or some kind of enclosure—then, then […]
     You know the material itself is significant to the kind of imagery that you are choosing… then it kind of does…

A   I don't know how much it is related—there is some sense of it. That's one of the things I'm wondering now and I want to get responses about… there are a lot of reasons to use glass (the practical reason is that it is transparent), and I can expose liquid light on it, but I'm not sure…

K   I just think that if it was used metaphorically it would be much more interesting than to use it for any practical reason.

A   Yeah, well, I feel like there is a sense of it, but I don't know how far I want to push that and I don't know if there is a different type of subject matter that…

Now subject matter is back on the table. Andrea says her imagery is medical, and she has been thinking of cells on a glass microscope slide. Only a couple of her images look like medical samples, however: most are patients and doctors. She doesn't mention any specific details of her work, for example the "A," "B," and "C" on the glass slides, or the small labels at the bottom of the acetate piece I reproduce here. (The labels say "cripple, conscious, observer, critic, constrain, obstacle," and each one is followed by a little doodle or autograph.) Because she doesn't mention details, she gives the faculty license not to look closely.

J It seems to me a lot of your search has been, this past semester, is the images are… Various ways of searching for the best way to express what you want to express… and glass is perhaps… a long way to do that.

It's very interesting how the glass is very light and transparent and the paper acetate images are so much more heavy and dark. There seems to be a more ominous quality to me (it's so framed in black), and at the same time there is a certain awkwardness about it (in the wrinkling of the paper), and I'm not seeing that same kind of awkwardness in the presentation under glass. It may just be because glass is flat…

A I am just in search of a medium, and I don't know if there is one medium. Or does it involve drawing in different types and kinds of material and continually experimenting and looking for responses to media? I'm using their relation to the images if there happens to be a good marriage between them.

W Have you printed these images on anything else other than glass?

A No.

W I'm only saying that just so you could grasp the difference in maybe the reason why or if even these should even be on glass. I'm trying to look for a way to gauge for the necessity of that glass.

A Well, the necessity of the glass is for layering, and I haven't really explored that to its fullest extent, so it's really hard to say at this point.

W O.K., because glass will allow you to do that, and you say you want to collage things on there, and then you start to get a lot of things happening with light.

A And also with the acetates—there are a couple of layers there and there is a certain amount of patterns, moirés, tints and tones that you can do with layers that are kind of interesting.

W Well, if that's your interest, glass will do it for you and it will do it fairly successfully. I think if you are exploring you should do a lot of things and really work a lot.

A I am.

W And then you know manipulate like…

A Well, as I said, I've just been working on these glass images for only a month. I've got more that didn't work—I mean that just peeled off—or things I did on paper which were kind of interesting.

K You know you should look at those combinations too—of the ones on glass that didn't work and the ones on glass that do work and the ones on paper that either do or don't work and look at those things layered.

W   Is it a material? I just keep wanting to go back to the subject matter.

K   Well, that's important.

W   You know the subject matter, and why there's a lot of interest and investigation of material, and this material can take you twenty-five years of investigation and you still might be investigating what it can possibly do. Glass is very seductive in that way.

You can make thing become three-dimensional just in a single dimension. Fixed point objects come at you by layering them and building up a three-dimensional quality to them and it can be very fascinating. I think it's important to go back and look at the subject matter and find out what's appropriate, what would work best.

I mean I'm curious about the subject matter that's on there. You have these medical photographs on these light… I mean the only connection is that it's like an X-ray sort of, and it's glass and its transparency… I mean the only connection I'm making right there is, [is] there an interest there? Does it go any further than that as far as the imagery that's on glass?

A   I think that again that glass is more practical in terms of layering (this is I think what I said before), and the imagery is all from encyclopedias, and a lot of it lately has been medical, specifically inoculations and injections. I feel that the glass contributes to the clinical sense of the images. Also just, today I was talking with another student who is taking Margaret Olin's class "Theories of Representation," and she said that they were talking about the early photographic inventions such as stereo-optic viewers. Some of the reasons that these machines were made… had to do with theories of representation, scientific analysis of the way people see. This was very interesting to me, I think that the scientific element has something to do with it. I'm using them metaphorically too. I know this sounds kind of jumbled, but…

The transcript goes on like this for another ten pages. This is an average critique. No one is especially inspired, and there's a fair amount of repetition. People circle back to the same themes.

At one point one of the instructors notices that some images are legible, and others aren't:

M   Some of these have a greater degree of readability than others. Can you talk about that? For instance, the one in the center (I'm talking about the ones on glass) the sort of cloud shape is the least readable—the one to the right of it is less readable than some of the others, and the top ones you can see what's going on. So in some cases you are choosing images that are pretty obscure or the process to get them that way, [and] at other times you are pretty visible about it. How does that enter into it?

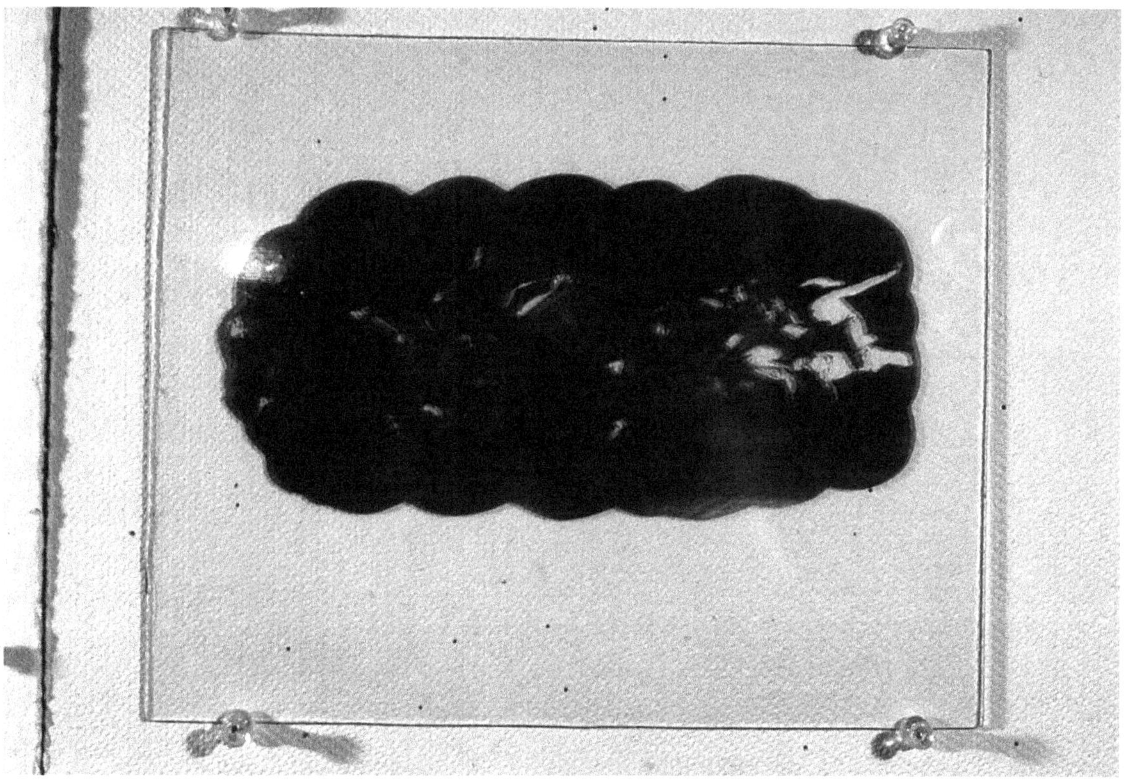

A   That's not—at this point—that's not a conscious decision on my part. That has to do with my ability, and I'm just putting up examples of things that I'm experimenting with, so I wouldn't even dare to say I made a conscious decision one way or another.

K   You can take what you worked with, and even if in certain technical terms one can categorize it as a failure, you can take that thing and juxtapose it against something else. You might conclude that that's exactly the thing I needed to make, so if I were you, I wouldn't necessarily consider anything a failure.

A   Well, these are examples. These are some of the things that have stayed on glass okay, and I've been experimenting with the enlargers and time exposures. I mean I might not have put them up if I really thought that they were… I don't know… I feel like I'm not taking responsibility for them. It's just that they are experiments, examples of—

W   You're investigating glass.

What just happened here? The instructor "M" noticed that some images have clear subjects, and others don't. She, or he, wonders why. Andrea says that she isn't aware of the difference between a blob and a doctor injecting a patient's

arm. If you're not an artist, you might not believe that. But for an artist, it's a common state of mind. You are so close to what you're doing, so engrossed in the glass, or the liquid light, or whatever you're working with, that you lose track of what you're actually producing. After Andrea answers, instructor "K" jumps in to try to make sure she doesn't feel like she's failed. "K" says that it's normal to juxtapose images and ideas, and that doesn't mean the artwork fails. "K" means well, but her speech is also lets Andrea off the hook. Sooner or later, as an artist, you'll need to take responsibility for what viewers might see in your work. This probably wasn't the time to push that problem, and Andrea is relieved to be able to go back to talking about glass, which is the subject she'd tried, at first, to avoid.

This conversation is supportive and generous, but there's another side to things: as you go along toward the MFA level, you will usually be expected to be ready to justify what you do. Andrea would be expected to be able to tell the panelists why she chose that strange organ-shaped blob, why she put labels on one of the pieces, or why some images of doctors measuring and injecting patients are realistic and others are hard to see. On the one hand, it's good for the faculty to acknowledge Andrea's uncertainty. On the other hand, this isn't an especially interesting critique because politeness and supportiveness get the better of the faculty. It's always safe to talk about techniques and materials: no one's sense of themselves ever got bruised talking about glass and liquid light.

I have been interrupting this conversation, but it's important just to get a feel of how drifty and uncertain and circling critique conversations can be, how they weave back and forth from techniques to meanings, from history to media, from personal intentions to free associations, and so I will just reprint most of the rest of it without comment.

A   Again, this is just the beginning and I've just started, so I can't really say, "This is the end, this is all I can think of with glass." I mean, I'm beginning to think about other glass; glass with wire inside, pebbled glass, layers of glass and making the same image and having it recede in space. There are a lot of possibilities and I'm just at the beginning. Those are all thoughts, but it does take a lot longer to achieve that in one's practice. It is a possibility…

W   Yeah, I've spent about six years working with glass, and I got P.P.G. [Pittsburgh Paints] to sponsor me with glass. It's one of those things that the material itself is very seductive, and about the material you can spend a lifetime, and what you can do and what you can say with it. I think that there really could be possibilities. I think that you are right about that.

R   There are ways of working too where you can get a photographic image on and it kind of resists and it resists sand-blasting and you can sand-blast it and frost it, wherever you want. Have you seen that?

W Well I have, like…

R You should get some glass and try some of these things. You may not be able to do all these things yourself. You can go to an industrial source and have somebody work with you.

W You can do photo-etching on it.

A Yeah, because I don't feel confident enough in a lot of technical areas.

R You're confident with this? With the photo-emulsion, right? There are other possibilities you may want to use.

W That same photo-emulsion becomes a repellent if you apply it on thick enough and you can blast right on to it. You can get some amazing qualities with how light transmits through the sand-blasted glass itself, if it's about the material sand. It does things you'd never do with a camera, how it refracts and reflects light, these nuances that… but that's about the material and…

A And I think, as I said, since I'm in an early stage I don't know the extent of the possibilities or maybe connecting the meanings and the images to the material, but it seems like there are many qualities that I've just barely begun to think of, and there is something seductive about it that perhaps maybe could help some of my imagery.

W Do you ever think of glass as liquid?

A No.

Q I immediately have all kinds of non-formal associations with the use of glass to carry photographic emulsion. I immediately have associations with the history of photography, and I also like that the kinds of images you are using could mean all sorts of things. So it does seem to be a very curious decision to use this medium for some reasons other than transparency. Also, that's enhanced by the medical illustrations that you are using, so I get a very keen sense that there is some kind of historical comment here.

A Yeah, and I don't think I'm aware of completely what it is. I wanted to get people's responses.

Q It does seem though, that with the medical illustration aspect of it, those seem… there seems to be something going on there. The one with the cloud, I'm wondering about the juxtaposition of it, especially since some of these illustrations have letters of the alphabet there, a suggestion of order. But the order is not in sequence. You've got B and C at the top and then you have A off to the side and E over there. So there is a suggestion of some connection in relations to the subject matter also that is enhanced by the use of these letters and this cloud. It does seem to imply some kind of center, even though it's not…

But also seeing a connection with your other material not on glass… and also the glass is tinted, that suggests yellowing. These are all conscious decisions, or a sense of conscious decisions.

A   A lot of the images I use I take from old encyclopedias and it's not all medical, it's educational, and talking about a certain time frame in terms of the 40's, 50's and 60's. And there's something about an order. There is an ordered quality to them: there are elements that I want to draw in which are otherwise…

M   Whether you are aware of it or not, there does seem to be a narrative, poetic kind of connotation…

R   I think it needs an external narrative to me, not necessarily something that illustrates, I mean describes, but isn't a narrative. Maybe a parallel narrative, verbal (that is, a language carrier), because you have injection and scales and mutation. All kinds of things are entering this way beyond the medical implications of it, and what I think about the narrative thing is not just something that might come later once this is successful. Then you're going to go to the narrative, but maybe it can't be successful unless you have the narrative, another visual narrative that runs along with this story.

A   I feel also that, in this state, I haven't yet pushed the kinds of statements I want to make, the kinds of juxtapositions I want to make. They really aren't there yet. So it really is hard for that to come out.

I usually have very similar images in another image that is being injected or pushed in, that helps support the connections. Sometimes I'll have some of the same images, only in different combinations that help amplify the meaning, but at this point I haven't gotten those images all together and all on glass, but that has been one way for me to make the meaning additive and help draw the meaning out. I do think they could have another layer on another structure.

K   Yes, because otherwise some of those references are kind of easy. The glass, the glass slides, the references that has to the medical and X-ray is kind of easy. It seems like you just need to get more complicated.

A   You think I need to get more complicated? Because sometimes I feel like I'm being very obtuse, but maybe I've gotten to the other point.

K   Well, there's a difference between obtuse and being ambiguous, so…

A   One or the other, but I have felt in the past that the point I'm trying to make hasn't gotten across, so perhaps at this point I've achieved that and I'm going a little bit too far the other way.

K   Well, sometimes that's what you have to do, I mean to clarify yourself so you can really see it, but then maybe you can start to get more complicated with it so that your references aren't quite so specific. This is "This is this," unless associations are set up, but then you can go past, you can say well…

V   What's your approach in terms of the collage? Sometimes I feel that we are supposed to see it as one total image and I'm aware that it's been collaged and yet in…

In other images its less obvious that you are trying to hide that it's collaged, yet it's coming through…

A   No, [it] hasn't been explored yet. I think that the collaging in layers will take away some of that quality of the obviousness of the way I'm applying the image, although I still do want there to be a sense of my hand in it and to have the choice of image itself be the sense of my presence. When it's exposed photographically, you take away that element of it application.

V   I don't think that you use… Well, I think that the mark is still very… that if you start with something and it's not what you want, you're going to end up with not liking what you do with it.

A   I don't want to take away the quality of my hand, that's not what I meant.

V   Then I feel that I just need it more definite then, if that's what you want—definite marks. I feel that it's too tentative.

K   Yeah, I agree with some of that. It's very much held back.

A   Well in particular… Can you say in a particular piece? I'm kind of going back and forth on how much I want my hand to be there and how much I don't.

K   It's tightly controlled on the one hand, but then on the other hand it doesn't work that well, you know what I mean.

A   I'm not sure what it is that's bothersome, the fact that it's a small element, the fact that…

K   It's the middle of the road, I guess is the best way I can describe it, and I think that's what [speaker V] was saying as well. It's like you want to make the mark. Ugh. Make the mark, you know, don't…

A   I don't know, what I talked about in the beginning was that I do like a certain expressive amount, but I don't want to be, you know, a Pollock painter. I don't want to be a gestural—

K   —Well this does not speak about something particularly expressive.

A   You don't think so?

K   No.

A   What would you view it as, I mean, what is the quality that…

K   That's why I said before I thought it was very tentative. I mean it looks very much like a sketch actually, because the quality of the paper surface and so forth. I mean it looks like a plan for something else, something bigger or…

A   Well, do you think that's a problem in talking about—

K   —In this case I do, because this is a very interesting form after all.

A   Do you think that if you saw that photographically on glass it would be—

M   —You do have that image on glass.

A   Yeah, but it's different.

M   Different image, but it's the same. Just stick arms on that and you have it.

A Yeah, there are figures inside there but what I'm saying is, Do you think that's enough of a change? Or do I still have the same problem there, that it's tentative or…

K It's better, it's better, but it's still hedging the bet, because this [*the cloud-shaped image*] is… that's a very powerful form you know, [it's] God, yet it's [*gestures to suggest doubt, that it's uncertain or wishy-washy*]… The way it's made up, it's just…

A [*Laughing*] That's the way I am.

K I want it to be more…

A Do you think size would be anything to….

K That's part of it, yes. Something about size, something about tools.

A But that's the way that I work, really, I mean I am like [*gestures, moving the brush more with the wrist than the whole arm*]…

K But you have these ideas that are not necessarily coincident with that way of doing it, so you've really got to look at that, you know, and try to… Because you've got some… There are some interesting images here, very powerful—

J —I think it might be time [*to stop*]… Sorry.

K No, no, go ahead, I'm rattling on.

J It might be time for you to step back. I sense a certain excitement with this to go back to the original idea, being that of a strong limiting force, and how to perceive this. Step one is made, and a technique is being learned, but let's do all that. Go back to the original idea and say: This is the idea. Don't get caught up in the image that you've chosen, that the original idea gets watered down or lost. I think in some of these that's been happening. There's a certain struggle in your way. I think that struggle is important but, going back to that piece, because I sense…

A Well, I haven't developed a comfortable way of working with the glass. I don't have enough images yet to start manipulating them as I want to. The darkroom has become my studio, and I'm not really comfortable working there. I'm there in the dark room, and I have the films and I'm trying to do the creative part there.

J But my idea is: be resistant.

K But don't be too clean about it either, you know. I mean look at that [*pointing at the glass skylight*], no I'm… And it's got pieces of wire in it, and it's cracked, and it's got fifty years of grunge on it.

W I bet it would take emulsion.

A No, I don't think so at all.

K It's got a tooth to it.

A No. You have to polyurethane glass before you can ever put emulsion on it, so there's—

W	—or power etch it, or blast it. You need just a little bit of tooth for it to grab.
A	Well, I'll come in and talk to you about it. I know who to talk to now.
W	Well, I've worked with glass forever. I don't work with it anymore.
K	Do you know the *cliché verre* thing too, where you either draw on glass, or you use an emulsion on glass and print that on paper?
A	Oh? No. It's a monoprinting of some sort?
K	It's contact printing, basically. You take one of these [*the images on glass*] and you expose it on photographic paper and you get the results. But what's really interesting about it is the fact that [the glass] has a thickness to it so the way the light goes through there modifies this image to some degree. So you should try that too.
A	Yeah, well I'll have to talk to you about that later, because I'm very open to new—
W	—Well there are a hundred different ways to work with any material.
K	And you can draw on there…
A	And I would really like to have some way of working with it that's freer.
W	That's why it's important that you grasp on to the subject because it's really, really important, because you can get lost with it. The magic of manipulating that material, a hundred different variables, you really have to grasp on to something that you can carry through. And just something that's real to you, something that means something to you, that will keep you moving in that direction of exploration.

Otherwise you can go a hundred different directions and you won't have any foundation for that exploration, and then you're going to have to come up with your system of exploring, and… uh… it's always good to really think that one out personally, with that little bit that you really want, so you can grasp it and say: "Okay, I really feel this way about this image, and then I can try one of those other variables that the glass is going to allow me to do," and then make the connection so you can judge for yourself and see it there, and then have something to grasp. Otherwise you are going to be all over the place, and it'll go, and it'll grow out everywhere, all over the place, and you won't know where to stop.

K	And it will help you to evaluate what works and what doesn't work, because in a certain sense what [speaker W] is talking about is that everything works, I mean it's all so wonderful…
W	And how you look at it—I mean there are a lot of possibilities that the material lends itself to, if you start looking.
M	Ultimately I think that the success or failure of these is not going to rest with the glass as much as with the images.
A	Well, I feel confident that I'm coming up with the images, and it's just their

manipulation and materials that I felt that I really needed to explore.

I mean there are ideas there, there are a lot of ideas that I have, but I need to investigate more a way of putting them out and that's what it seemed to me—

Q   —So do you have definite ideas about the criteria you use for choosing particular images?

A   Well, Yes. Sometimes I'm not sure why I pick something, and then later it will become clear. There are, I think…

For instance the inoculation and immunization images are a very strong and perhaps obvious metaphor for the introduction of foreign bodies or diseases into the body. I was then going to place whatever I felt I wanted to that was being shoved into the body. Some sort of societal force or religion or images that hit a spark for me..

W   I just thought of something you said, inoculation, I think of glass and I think of microscopic transparence, [which] lets you investigate—it's almost like a… like a…

K   A slide—

W   —A slide, a glass slide that gives you all this information, and it makes a lot of sense with that investigation and inoculation, and certain things exist in this little world. Maybe you can use that as a diving board for you investigation.

A   Well, it's been the metaphor I've been pursuing, and there's that kind of educational quality to it, this is the way this is and that is the way that is, tradition, you know, all the stuff that we've had pushed into us through textbooks. Forces that make us up that create bias and limitations on our thinking that are harmful.

Q   I was thinking you might want to step outside yourself and try to focus on some of the choices that you are making…

You don't want [to] make it so simple or so readable… but also explore what happens when [there are] accidents…

A   That's ultimately what… That's how it's meant to be…

Q   That certain kind of focus, in some way not specifying, but focus on the possibilities of connotations for your narrative, that'll help give you control to explore your… Of course that's easy for me to say.

A   Yes, I mean there's the problem of setting up too much to be said, there's no emotional comment or… to a certain extent I'm usually able to comment on some of the reasons why I'm choosing these images… Right now I'm just trying to pair off the images. The combinations haven't happened yet. This is just a sample of images to show where my thinking is at.

R   Excuse me for breaking in, does everyone know where room 260 is? We are meeting back there at one. It's on the second floor and it's somewhere between printmaking and photo.

K   The old fiber room.
A   Are we through? I guess now we are.
R   Usually we would ask you if you've got anything further to ask us, but I think you've done that.
A   Um, yeah, I feel pretty satisfied that we've touched on some of the subjects I introduced, and I'll be talking to you and you about some of these techniques.

A little exhausting to read, isn't it? You can feel the boredom of some of the faculty, and you can sense the difficulty some of them had in trying to figure out what to say. All that is part of critiques. The boredom, the ordinary lack of energy, are the reasons I won't be quoting some very funny parodies of critiques, like Richard Roth's play "The Crit," the video animation "The Crit," or the critique scene with John Malkovich in the movie *Art School Confidential*.[2] They make critiques look entertaining, funny, and absurd: and that's sometimes true, but critiques are a lot more besides, including boring, directionless, slack, and muddled. A film of Andrea's critique might be even more exhausting than this transcript, because then you'd see everyone shuffling and pacing and scratching their heads.[3]

If you were Andrea, you'd probably be a little overwhelmed and confused. It's your job, as a student, to try to make as much sense out of it as you can. Everything, including the boring parts, can be mined for meaning.

12

How Long Should a Critique Be?

A very simple reason why some critiques don't make sense is that they are too short. Even an hour can be barely enough to get acquainted with an artwork. It can take 5 or 10 minutes just to see an average 2-D or 3-D artwork—to walk around and look at it, to find the right angle, to feel it or hear it. (If it's film, video, animation, or performance, just experiencing the work might eat up the entire time allotted to the critique, but that's another problem.) Consider the stages, from the first encounter to the end of the critique. I'll take an average 15 minute BFA critique as an example.

A. In the first 10 seconds—which I'll call the *recognition stage*—a number of ideas fly through the teacher's mind, most of them not very well formed, and the result is a tentative overall verdict. This can happen nearly instantly, in the space of less than a second. If I walk into a critique room, for example, and I see some geometric abstract paintings, I'll form a first impression in the first second or two,

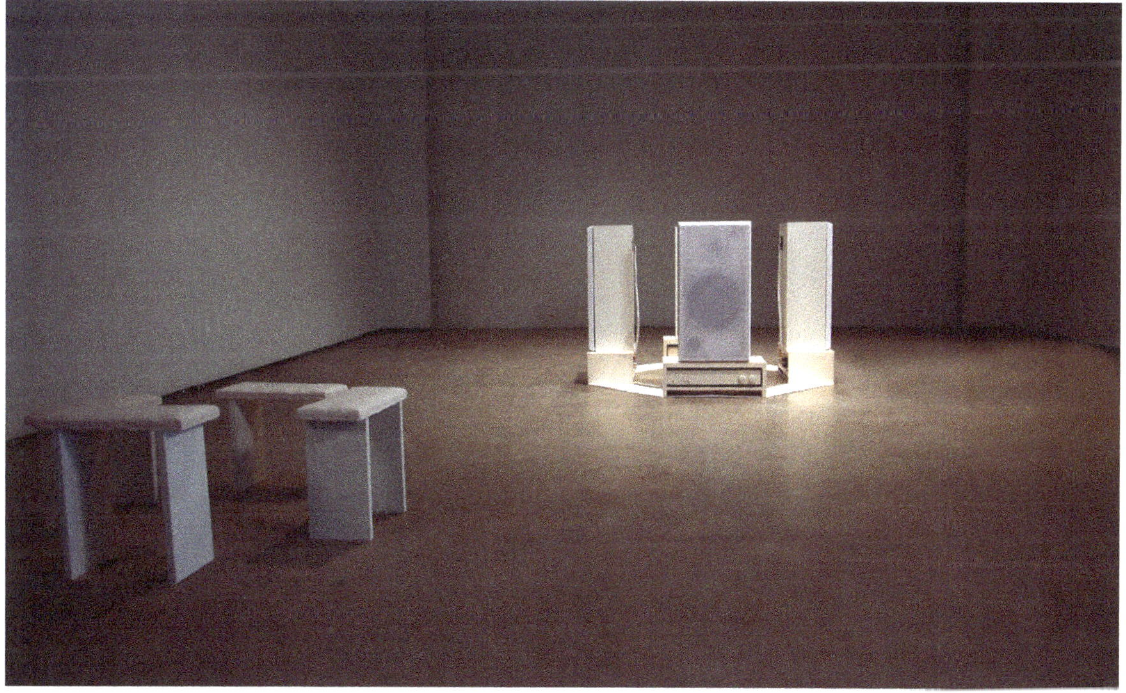

and a couple of seconds later I'll know some of the things we'll be talking about. The first thing a teacher might be aware of thinking is "I like it," or "I'm interested," or "I don't quite get it yet." And then, a second or so later, "That's a pretty interesting geometric abstraction," or "I wonder if the student has done anything else," or "I hope it's not acrylic." Older or more experienced teachers might have all sorts of thoughts in their heads in just a second or two. More on this in the next chapter.

B. *Acclimation stage*. In the next 10 minutes or so the teacher acclimates herself to the work. Some comments are inevitable, and there are things that always seem to have to get said, and that takes some time. If the works are paintings, it is almost inevitable that the teacher will mention framing, hanging, lighting, scale, medium, or color. If the work is an installation, the teacher has to mention the peculiarities or inadequacies of the studio space. I don't know how many times I've heard, "Of course the wall is distracting," or "Ideally, you'd change the lighting." In the acclimation stage, teachers tend to review their first reactions. That means the really interesting, difficult questions are only just ready to be asked when a 15 minute critique is drawing to a close.

C. *Analysis stage*. In the last 5 minutes of a 15 minute critique there is time for scattered inquiries to get underway. But by that time it's often too late, because the instructor may be thinking of ways to encourage you, or wanting you to ask your own questions, rather than pursuing and deepening.

This little schema (*recognition, acclimation, analysis*) is meant to suggest just how difficult it can be to get any really interesting conversation going in a 15 minute critique.

In some kinds of critiques, the students begin by making presentations or introductory speeches, and that can severely cut into the time allotted for comments. In architecture critiques, for example, a group of students might present their work in a sequence of short speeches, taking up a quarter or a half of the entire critique. Because of the nature of architectural projects, there is arguably *more* information to be seen than in some other fields (plans, elevations, sections, models, details, and supporting graphic material all have to be read), and as a result sometimes a smaller percentage of the material is actually understood than in other kinds of critiques.

Time goes by in a critique the way time passes in conversation. Some opportunities for understanding are lost in the silences between statements; some in remarks don't go anywhere; some things only repeat others; some comments have to do with work that is not present, or unfinished, or not yet made. Time is spent on simple mistakes of seeing ("Oh, I see what that is now!"). The best critiques are amiable as well as insightful, and that means another 5 minutes for parenthetical remarks, jokes, and

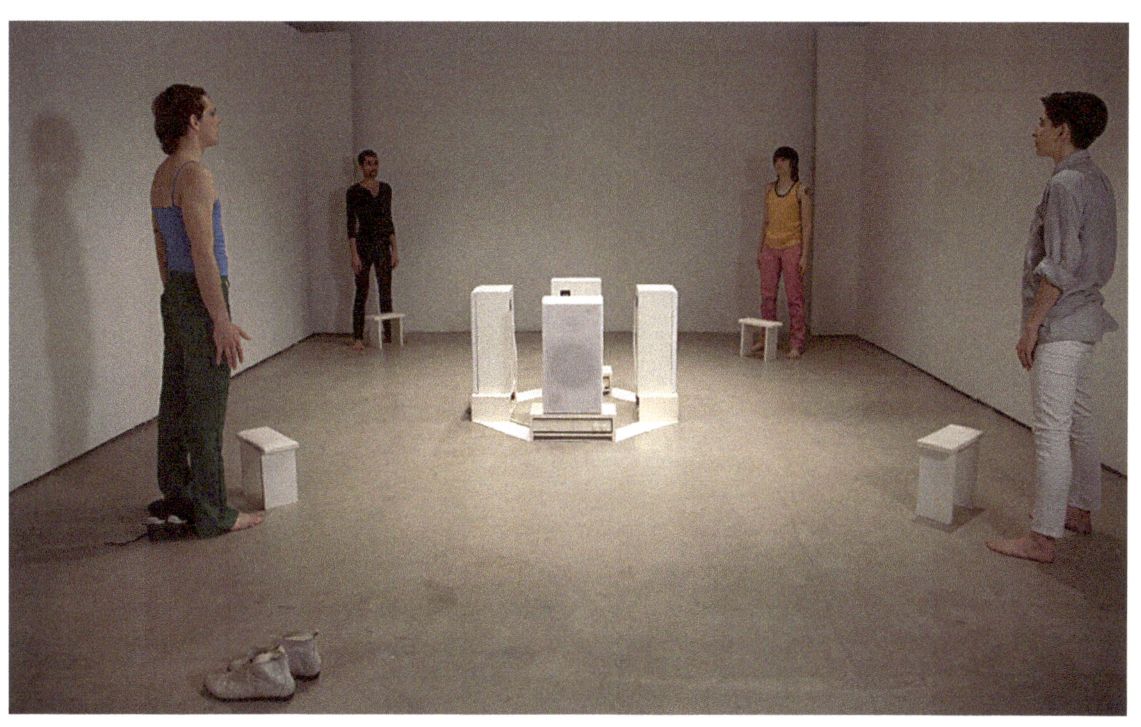

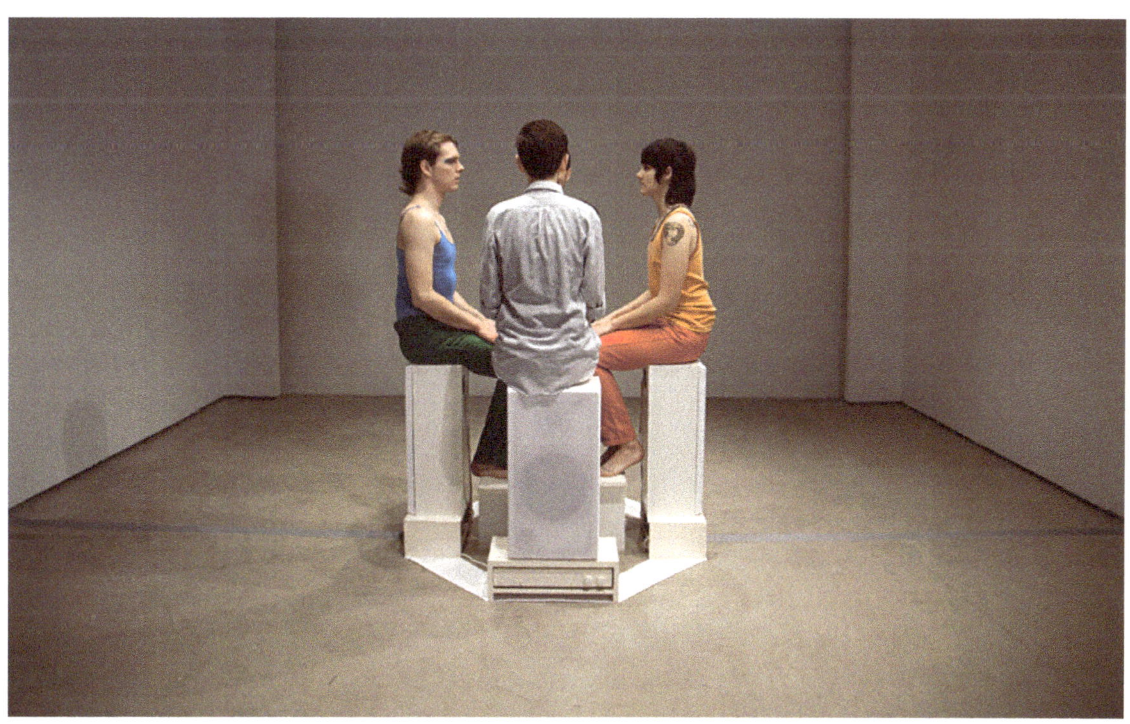

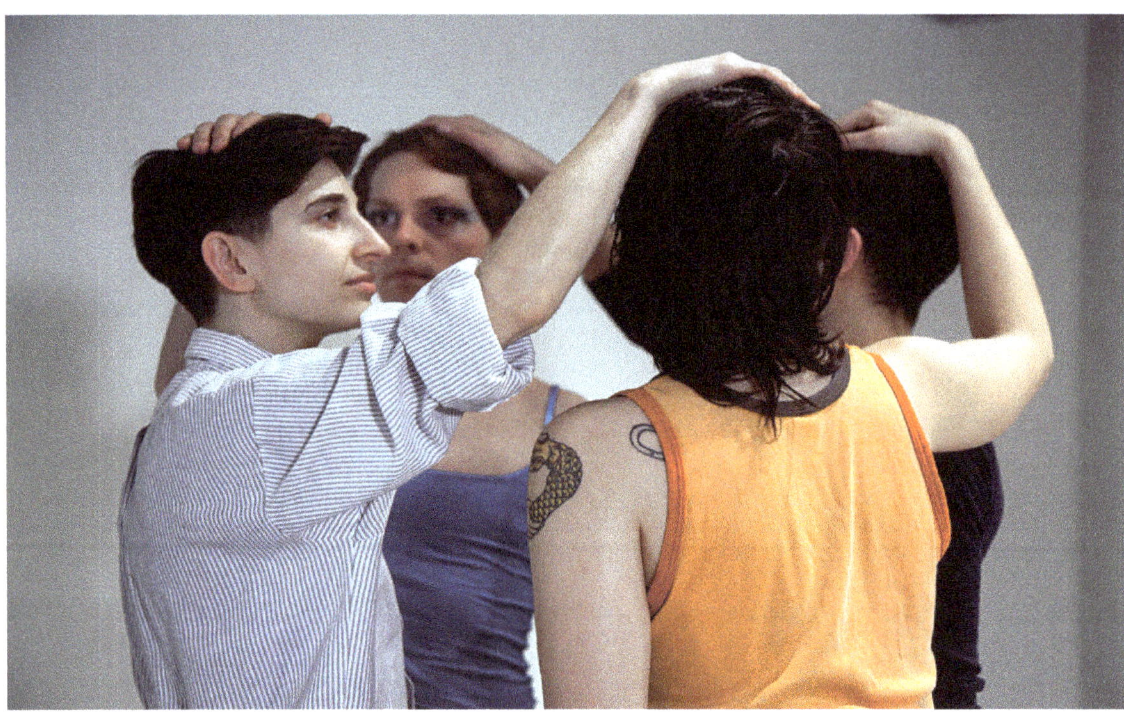

stories meant to ease the tension or to be polite. In a typical critique the acclimation and analysis stages are intermixed, so that people speak at cross-purposes, and that also wastes some time.

It may seem that longer critiques cold solve this problem, but that isn't necessarily true. If a graduate critique is 45 minutes long and there are 5 or 6 panelists, and if no one else speaks, and if each of the panelists speaks continuously, then each panelist has less than 9 minutes—not so different from in a BFA critique where there's usually just one teacher.

Some undergraduate group critiques are 30 minutes long and have 10 or more people participating, which would give each person about 3 minutes. It takes time to discover a work—sometimes, it takes years—and in those few minutes, between silences, repetitions, mis-hearings and mis-seeings, the panelists scarcely have time to adumbrate a considered response.

The illustrations here are of a performance piece by a student named Rebecca Gordon. This was an MFA critique, so she had 45 minutes, but the performance itself would have taken 19 minutes, so she decided to show me, and the other faculty on her critique panel, some video excerpts. *Observants* was a very complex, choreographed performance with a sound component. If we had seen the entire piece, we wouldn't have had time to talk about it at all. As it was, we saw the video, the space, and the pieces she had made for the performance. It took about 5 minutes to get settled, 10 minutes to see the video excerpts, and another 5 to walk around, leaving 25 minutes to talk—a good compromise given the time limitations.

But with work this complex, a critique just can't address anything except general impressions and random details. None of us on the critique panel could remember the details of the video. This may sound unfortunate, but it's typical. A student who makes a 15 minute film has the same issues. The teachers will see the film, but by the end they'll have forgotten lots of detail: no one can remember the sequence of scenes in 15 minutes of a Hollywood film, much less in a complicated experimental film. And these examples are not at all extreme. I had a student who made a 5-hour film, which only a few people saw. Another student made a performance so intricate that it required a wall full of maps and diagrams, which he could only begin to explain. A third student made a roomful of computer-generated sculptures, a tapestry, manipulated photographs, engineering diagrams, a painting, and an entire mythological novel about 300 pages long. (I was that student's advisor, and I didn't manage to get through the novel.)

If your work is complicated, or if it is time-based, any critique will be too short. The challenge, for you, is to figure out how to present parts of it in such a way that you get the best feedback. The usual compromise is to take half the time and show very small portions of the work, but in the best of all possible worlds, you would show your work over several days. If I've seen a complicated work once, I can say certain things; but if I see it again, I can remember much more. Each repeated exposure deepens my response. If it is a film, I may want to see particular scenes again, or see them in slow motion. If it's a performance, I may want to have it repeated several times, with a conversation after each showing. This is in the best of possible worlds; in the real world, I probably won't see or remember very much.

What is the ideal length for a critique? Long enough to let the teachers to revise their initial impressions. Long enough for the teachers to say all those trivial things that seem to need to get said ("Of course the floor is distracting," etc. etc.). Long enough for some real analysis to get done. Long enough for you to say whatever you'd like to say.

13

The First Ten Seconds of the Critique

There is a limited sense in which even a 10 or 15 minute critique is too long. People who have experience in art judge very quickly, and most teachers will have a provisional opinion about a work in the first couple of seconds—in what I called the *acclimation stage*. Teachers, jurors, admissions panels, and interviewers can look at slides very quickly, and that is not simply a matter of callous indifference.

I remember being in an interview for a teaching job in an MFA department, back when I was a painter. The person interviewing me held my slides up against the fluorescent lights in the ceiling, for about a half-second. I was really insulted, but later I realized that might have been plenty of time. (I didn't get the job.)

Teachers can form not just provisional opinions but *final* opinions in those first 10 seconds. Only a few teachers and critics would say that their first impression is not open to revision, but first impressions of visual art are probably more important and lasting than first impressions of a person, or the impression given by the opening bars of a composition or the opening lines of a novel. Visual art can be very unforgiving that way: once you see the shark in formaldehyde, your opinion might be sealed forever.

When I am in a critique I hope to undermine or complicate my first impression. But to be honest that doesn't always happen, and when I am reviewing someone for a grant or a residency, I don't usually get a chance to revise my first impression. That may seem unfair, but it's a fact of the artworld, and it is also simply true that 2D and 3D visual art works quickly as well as slowly. It's also important to know that quick opinions can also be well-informed opinions: just because my student paintings were turned down in a half-second doesn't mean the judgment was wrong. But in critiques, you should get a second chance.

As a student, you can guard against faculty judging you in the first 10 seconds. You can say, "These are just experiments; I don't know much about geometric abstract painting," or "These go along with my video work," or "I don't think of these as paintings," or "This is work I did last semester." Anything like that will throw the panelists off balance just a little, and keep their minds open a bit longer.

14

The Last Ten Minutes of the Critique

On the other hand, it may well take more than 10, 15, or even 45 minutes to change a teacher's first impression. If a teacher doesn't like the work, often she won't say anything right away. Partly that's common politeness, and partly it's because it may take a while for the teacher to find a way to say what she thinks without being curt. Sometimes it is possible to see that dynamic at work: the first few minutes, the teacher will be deciding how to say what she has already decided about the work; in the next few minutes, her opinion will slowly be shifting, and in the last few minutes, she may have time to develop second thoughts.

Because there is no way to predict the speed at which a person re-learns an art work, or erases and adjusts her first impression, the best you can do as a student is to notice when that might be happening, and engage the teacher with questions and new ideas.

The last ten minutes of a critique can also be the best, because people know time is winding down. Teachers will make an extra effort to say something new, and the conversation may suddenly become energetic and unpredictable. This is where both students and teachers should hold the reins, because free association, especially if it ends abruptly, can be more confusing than enlightening. As a student, you might latch on to just one or two remarks, and ask your teacher to follow up on them.

"Since we only have ten minutes left," your teacher might say, "let's talk about what you might do next."

I'm not sure that kind of suggestion is always helpful. More often than not, it means your teacher has just run out of things to say. You can try to make better use of the last ten minutes of the critiques by asking to return to something that was said earlier:

"Okay, but I'm more interested in what you said about my drawings, that they are too fragile. I wonder if you think that's true of all of them."

Anything to bring the teacher's attention back to the place where they got stuck, to provide an opportunity for them to re-think their opinions. (And to work a bit harder!)

15

Five Kinds of Critiques:

A. The Silent Teacher Critique

Starting with this chapter, I'll look at five kinds of critique: the Silent Teacher Critique, the Conceptual Critique, the Boot Camp Critique, the Silent Student Critique, and the Anti-Critique.[1] No doubt there are many more! But if this were a field guide to critiques, these would be five common species.

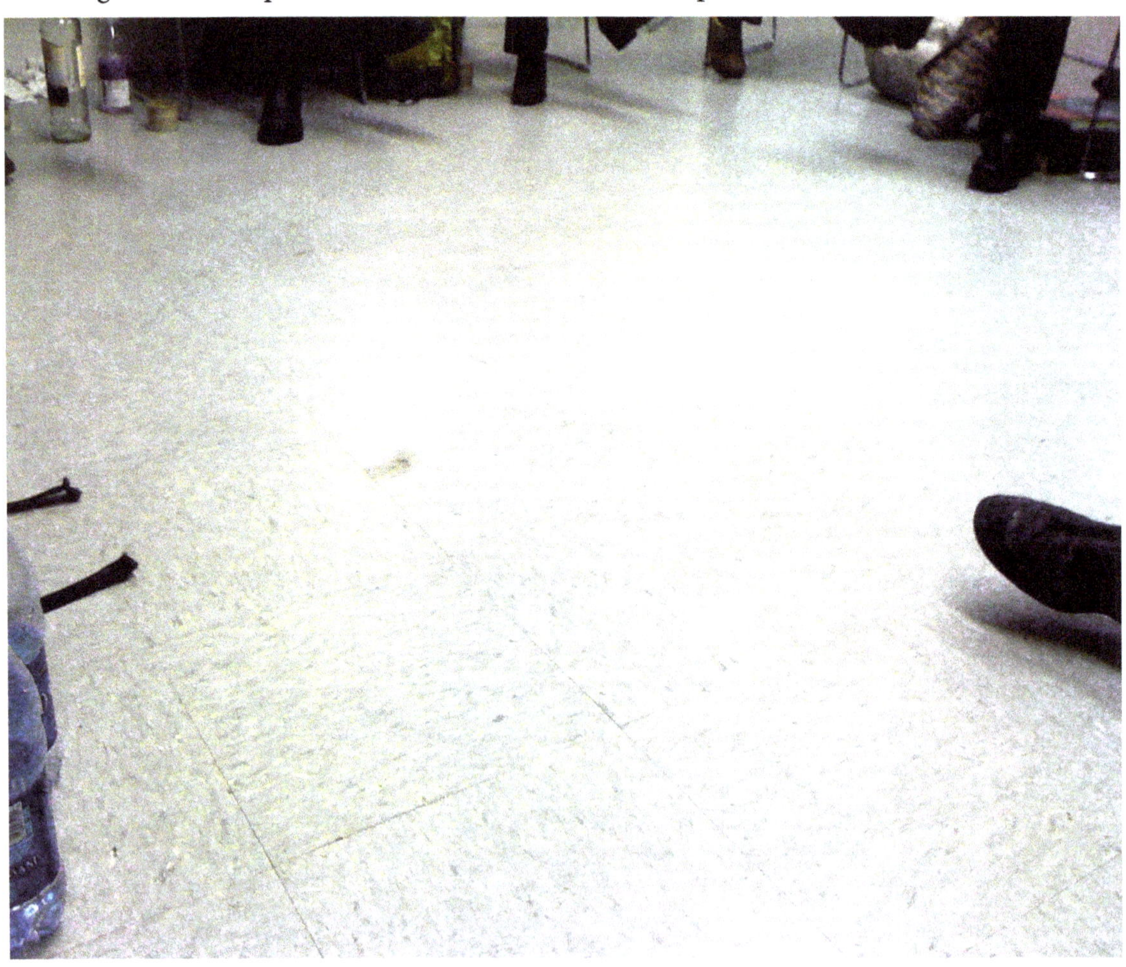

In her book *Seven Days in the Art World,* the sociologist Sarah Thornton describes a day-long critique held at CalArts in 2004 by the conceptual artist Michael Asher. He started at 10 AM and finished at 1 AM, with breaks for food. The class critiqued three students' works, so on average they spent over five hours on each student. I'll have something to say about super-long critiques in a later chapter. For now, what's important is that Asher barely spoke, all day long. The students talked, and every once in a while Asher said something. He didn't speak at all for the first three and a half hours of the day, and then when he spoke it was just one sentence, said to a student who was showing graphite drawings: "Why didn't you enter the project through language or music?"[2]

This is a good example of a sort of critique I call the Silent Teacher Critique. The teacher's idea is that art is something that happens by exploration, not direct instruction. It happens by fits and starts. You never know exactly when a student will be ready to absorb an idea, or to hear something. From a teacher's point of view, it seems important not to preach, not to be an authority figure. The student has to discover or rediscover her practice in the confusion and open-ended forum of public conversation. Thornton quotes John Baldessari saying "students need to see that art is made by human beings just like them."[3]

Here are some pros and cons of the Silent Teacher critique:

From a student's point of view, the Silent Teacher critique can be daunting, because you won't ever really know what the teacher thinks. The Silent Teacher strategy does not necessarily break down the authority of the teacher: in fact it usually builds up that authority to mythic proportions. It may also be frustrating, because you'll be at the mercy of your fellow students: they might be supportive and helpful, but they might also have lots of irrelevant ideas that you can't use. The longer the conversation among students continues, the less it's likely to have any direction. The entire experience can seem like a free-floating exercise in meandering, disconnected free association. You may miss the teacher's guidance, and you may wonder if your tuition money is being well spent.

I heard about a term at Goldsmiths in London, where the tutors decided not to speak at all: that's twelve five-hour sessions of silence from four tutors (teachers). The student who told me this says sometimes it worked, but most of the time the other students spoke in order to score points with the teachers.[4] If you're in a Silent Teacher critique, the best thing to do is be your own moderator: ask your fellow students to elaborate on their thoughts. Follow up on what they say. Ask questions about your work. Don't worry about what the teacher might be secretly thinking.

From a teacher's point of view, the Silent Teacher critique can be a great way to start conversations in a big class. Students who are normally silent sometimes say the most interesting things. I've heard of several cases where teachers take notes instead of speaking—an interesting way of using the silent time, and returning to it later in a different form.[5] It's also worth saying that the Silent Teacher critique is easy: it doesn't require work. Insights come from unexpected places, and especially if you're the lecturing type, who talks through the entire class, it can really help to stop talking and listen.

(My own opinion: as far I am concerned, the Silent Teacher strategy is also an enormous missed opportunity. As a teacher, you can find coincidences and resonances between students' thoughts; you can order and correlate disparate ideas; you can ask the students to develop their thoughts; you can explain their references; you can put order, where it belongs, into the chaos of free conversation; you can distinguish between random thoughts and pertinent ones; you can check students who make speeches, and encourage those who need to speak more; and, above all, you can throw light on the students' ideas, showing where they come from, how they connect to current art, how they might be used. The list of possibilities is practically endless, and they are all given up in the name of conversation: but is conversation that fragile? Will your intervention really spoil the chance of real open dialogue? Even if you don't believe in your authority as teacher, that doesn't mean you shouldn't speak. Authority comes in many forms, and silence is one of the more coercive. At least speaking is always performative, tentative, exploratory. Silence is authoritarian. And one more thing: it's also the case that not all silences are equal. Michael Asher's art practice is itself practically invisible; it's a carefully positioned conceptual art practice, and his kind of silence is not a neutral silence. It's not just anyone's silence. It is itself an art practice, and by putting his practice to work in the critique, Asher is effectively as coercive as the most insistent pedagogue.[6])

16

Five Kinds of Critiques:

B. The Conceptual Critique

Some art departments, schools, and academies are known for being intellectual or conceptual. That means several things. Usually painting is on the defensive or it's excluded entirely, in favor of conceptual art, institutional critique, installation art, or activism—political, social, environmental. Usually aesthetics, beauty, the sublime, creativity, and genius are taboo. Usually the critiques are heavy on theory: gender, identity, psychoanalysis, poststructuralism, deconstruction. (The opposite of "conceptual" institutions is "perceptual" institutions: they privilege realist painting and drawing. Examples include atelier schools, The University New Hampshire at Durham, or the New York Studio School.)

Only a few institutions have been consistent enough so that they are identified with "conceptual" critique, for example CalArts, Goldsmiths in London, and the academies in Frankfurt, Amsterdam, Weimar, and Vienna. According to a faculty member at CalArts, for example, "any artist whose work fails to display some conceptual rigor is little more than a pretender, illustrator, or designer."[1] But most larger art departments, schools, and academies practice versions of the conceptual critiques. Some are called "post-critiques," others "institutional critiques." It's more a matter of the instructors you have than the school you're in, unless you're in the art department of a smaller, regional, state, liberal arts, or community college, in which case it is relatively unlikely that you'll get this kind of critique. Conceptual critiques were a point of pride in some larger institutions in the 1980s, and they continue in various forms.

If you're in such a critique, and you're a painter or printmaker, you may be asked to justify your practice. "Painting is dead" is the cliché cry of this kind of critique, and its touchstones are books on institutional critique, political intervention, and the "post-medium condition."[2] You may be expected to say something about how you're using the conventions of painting to do something different, or how you've thought about the history of painting and decided it is still a workable medium.[3]

It's not easy to generalize about conceptual critiques, because they seep into many settings. What I want to emphasize here is that they privilege *language*: you are expected to be able to speak clearly and with insight about your practice, and to put as much as possible into words. Whatever is inarticulate should be articulated. Whatever is just a feeling should be made eloquent. Whatever is "purely" or "simply" visual should be brought into discourse. To some degree, this happens in all critiques, but in conceptual critiques, eloquence and self-reflection are at a premium. What's excluded is feelings, awe, wonder, or anything so deeply subjective that it can't be spoken. What's privileged is language, rigor, self-analysis, introspection, eloquence, articulateness.

People who don't like conceptual critiques have two main complaints: they say that visual art should be about the visual, and not about language; and they say that good art is not necessarily correlated with eloquence. After all, history is full of wonderful artists who were not at all articulate about what they did. People who practice some form of conceptual critiques have two responses to those two complaints: they say that teaching can't happen without language; and they say that interesting contemporary art is, in fact, correlated with ideas, concepts, and thinking.

This book isn't the place to resolve that! But as a student, you should be aware from the start that this is a fork in the road. One path leads to art practice that might or might not be able to justify itself. You work, you feel something, you work some more. People see your work, they respond, and perhaps they speak. Visual art is about the visual and the feelings, emotions, and other mental states it produces. The other path leads to art practice that is self-aware, where you can say what you're trying to do. You read, you consider other people's art, and then you produce work. You might do research, you might experiment, you might even write theories about your work. This second path leads on to the MFA and the PhD.[4]

Needless to say, the two paths meander, and often get entangled. And it's entirely reasonable to say that mixtures of the two are, in fact, the usual state of the artworld.[5] But there is a basic question about orientation here. Do you enjoy knowing as much as you can about your art? Its history, its philosophic ideas, its claims on the world, its position in contemporary criticism? Or do you enjoy losing yourself in your art, immersing yourself in it, working without thinking of all the precedents and parallels? You can choose instructors and schools using this kind of criterion. If you find yourself in a conceptual critique, and you're not sure if it's doing you any good to be articulating everything about your own practice, I would recommend trying it: knowledge isn't usually poison. If your instructor presses you to try to understand the historical or philosophic framework of your art, I'd go along, to see if it might help to bring more of what you do into language.

On the other hand, if you're a very verbal person, interested in theory and history, you need to keep a constant vigilant watch on your work, and make sure it doesn't just illustrate your conceptual interests. Some highly conceptual art is just that: uninteresting visual examples of interesting theories.

Five Kinds of Critiques:

C. The Boot Camp Critique

Once, when I was a student in an MFA program, another student showed an installation piece in his final critique. It was a table, and on it was a board, propped up like a piano lid. Between the board and the tabletop, the student had piled garbage he had found around the studios, including discarded sculpture by other students. From somewhere inside the heap a radio was playing a random station. Everyone stood around in silence for a few minutes. Then one teacher said this (mostly while he was looking at his feet):

"Well, I'd like to be able to say this is an embarrassing piece. I mean, I'd like to be able to tell you I'm embarrassed because the piece is so bad. I wanted to say it's badly made, it looks bad, it's not well thought out, it's been done before, it's been done a million times, much better, with skill, with interest…

"But I realized I can't say that. I'm not embarrassed, because the work isn't even bad enough to make me embarrassed. Obviously it's not good, and it's also not bad enough to embarrass me.

"So I think that the piece is really about embarrassment, about the way you think you might be bored, or you might blush, and then you don't, because you don't care. About the way you maybe think about being embarrassed, when you're not. (Or maybe I am embarrassed because I'm not embarrassed.)

"So I think you should think about this: I mean, ask yourself, 'How can I make a piece that will be just a little bit embarrassing? Are there different kinds of embarrassment?' Stuff like that."

When he finished, he sighed. He was just too overcome with boredom to go on—or perhaps he was affecting to be bored in order to drive his point home.

It may seem surprising to people who haven't been to art school that such things can happen. But they are not at all rare. At this particular school, critiques were held in front of all the students and faculty, and it was not uncommon to have the student cry in front of everyone. One visiting student from another department called our critiques "psychodramas." A fellow student of mine was told, in front of a roomful of people, that she wasn't an artist and that she should be barefoot and pregnant in the kitchen. I was treated to some pretty sadistic critiques myself, and that was the reason I wrote the book *Why Art Cannot be Taught*. Some of what happened to me was funny—the Chair of the department handed me a letter one time informing me I was on DOUBLE SECRET PROBATION and I should bring a sleeping bag into the studio and work until I had done something good—but most of it wasn't funny at all. I know just how dispiriting it can be to hear harsh, negative criticism. It happened to me in my MFA program, and also in a year I spent at the Boston Museum School of Fine Arts, where I filled a large room with my paintings and walked out an hour later convinced I should give up painting.

The Boot Camp critique is rare, but hurtful, and if you're the victim, you won't forget it. Here are some others I've collected, mostly from people on the internet answering my question, "What's the worst thing that ever happened to you in a critique?":

• "I was all of 18 years old, in a Sophomore paintings class; we were assigned self-portraits. I came to class with mine half-done and the 'professor,' puffing on his cigar, looked at the painting, looked at me, and said 'You flatter yourself,' and walked away."

• "We had a poor, tenured, sad-sack who would spend the length of a critique discussing the place on a wall where I wiped my brush clean."

• "Did your dog make that painting?"

• "That's the ugliest shirt I've ever seen."

• "There is nothing interesting about your work."

• "I had a guy tell me my piece reminded him of when he had found human remains (bones) hidden in the wall of an apartment building he was having remodeled."

• "I was in a Sophomore in a painting class and made a landscape and the instructor looked at it and laughed at me, for a long time, with no comment, and shook his head and walked away."[1]

• "Your wood has such agency. I mean your wood has a lot of agency!"

• "The most interesting thing about your studio is your crock pot."

• "Is this series inspired by your parents getting divorced?" (The person who posed this added, "that's how I found out"!)

• "You seem like an individual with a temperament best suited for an occupation that is less taxing on your narrow abilities and imagination, like perhaps retail sales."

• "Did you make this yourself?"

• "My professor told me that I was the type of person who might end up in a hotel room with a gun to my head."

• "I remember Richard Tuttle coming as a guest artist to the School of the Art Institute. A fellow grad student put up her work for his critique. He stared quietly at it for a long time, occasionally holding up his hand to block some aspect out. Eventually he asked her if some smudge on the wall was part of the piece."[2]

• "One of my undergrad drawing professors... talked for about twenty minutes about how [the student] should go to the supermarket and buy every manner of produce and then go home and defecate on a piece of paper to make a better piece of artwork than what she had brought to the studio that day."[3]

• A student who had made a personal film started to cry under pressure from her teachers. One of them said, "I'm trying to make you hate me."[4]

• "I was in a group studio critique in a life drawing class at Long Beach back in the 1980's... the teacher walked up to a very meticulously rendered drawing of a nude woman, tore it off the wall and ripped it in half. There was a gasp and the student, of course, started crying."[5]

• "If the teacher thought the work was particularly bad, he would just hand the student a book of matches, with one match bent forward. No commentary, just the matches. Hee."[6]

• And to end on a slightly lighter note, I got this anecdote from Jane Fine: she was invited to a critique with Leon Golub. "I was making small paintings that looked to be one thing at first, but each had a hidden face. Leon was happily surprised as he noticed the faces, pointed them out to everyone, said how much he liked the work. I was in hog heaven for about thirty seconds. Then he said, 'Unless they were intended. Were they? Yes? Oh no, then I don't like them.'"

I quote these partly because they're outrageous, partly because quoting them is a stock in trade of writing on critiques, partly because they show just how ruleless and irresponsible critiques can be, but mostly to make a point. No matter how far you go in your career, chances are you'll always remember you worst critique. Even famous middle-aged artists remember bad things they heard as students. For teachers, this should be a warning: be careful what you say. For students, there is an easy moral and two harder morals. The easy one is: a lot of what gets said is just irresponsible and inaccurate, and you should try to move on. The first hard moral is: sometimes there is a kernel of truth in the negative judgment, and if you think there might be, then you should try to pay attention to it even if it's painful. Some of the lines I've quoted have no redeeming virtue. But others might. In my MFA program, a teacher once said that my paintings weren't paintings, and that my drawing was "dead." One day, he took the charcoal himself and tried to draw the live model. He failed, and he said something like, "Hey, this life drawing thing is harder than I thought." For a couple of years I consoled myself by saying he couldn't draw, so I didn't need to listen when he said my drawing was dead. But later I realized there is a sense in which my drawing was *dead*. (It was lifeless, dry, and fastidiously accurate.)

And here's the second hard moral: if you can't often trust the bad things you hear, you should also be careful not to get too puffed up by the good things you hear. We all need praise, but over-the-top praise might not be any more accurate than indefensibly awful negative judgments. Think of the sum of all the things people have said about your work as a bell curve. The really awful stuff is off to the left, under the tail of the curve. The ordinary, everyday comments you get are the

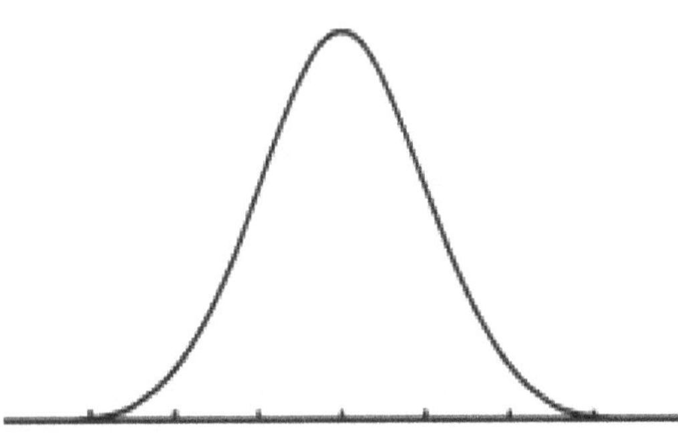

main part of the bell curve. That's the average reaction to your work, the consensus opinion. The bell curve suggests why you probably shouldn't dwell on the bad things. But the bell curve also implies that you shouldn't pay too much attention to the really amazing things people have said about your work: those comments are off on the right of the bell curve, and they are just as unusual, statistically speaking, as the unbearably awful things. The bell curve teaches a hard lesson: if you ignore the worst things people have said—and you probably should—then you should also ignore the best things.

The usual justification for the Boot Camp critique is that it prepares students for the real world. We were told that in my MFA program. One instructor said something like, "This will toughen you up so you can survive in the artworld." In *Seven Days in the Art World*, Sarah Thornton quotes the filmmaker William E. Jones as saying that tough critiques prepare art students for "negotiating interviews, conversations with critics, press releases, catalogues, and wall texts." The Boot Camp critique, Jones says, helps students "develop thick skins," so they can "see criticism as rhetoric rather than personal attack."[7] It's true that the art world can be harsh. But that is uncommon. The real pain of the artworld is being ignored, being forgotten, not getting shows, not selling, not becoming famous. *That* is pain, and it isn't helped by being bashed around in school.

Another justification for the Boot Camp Critique is that it's a teacher's duty to upset the students' assumptions, to shake them up, to wipe the slate clean, to rid them of unexamined assumptions, to help them rethink their work from the ground up. I'll say more about this at the end of this book. Basically, this idea comes from the Bauhaus: it's a modernist notion, born of the Bauhaus's loathing of academic art instruction. But in the 21st century, how does a teacher know the student's working assumptions are all in need of revision? And who can take an inventory of her own, or other people's, assumptions? More on this in Part Five.

I don't think the Boot Camp critique is justified: I didn't believe it then, and I don't believe it now.

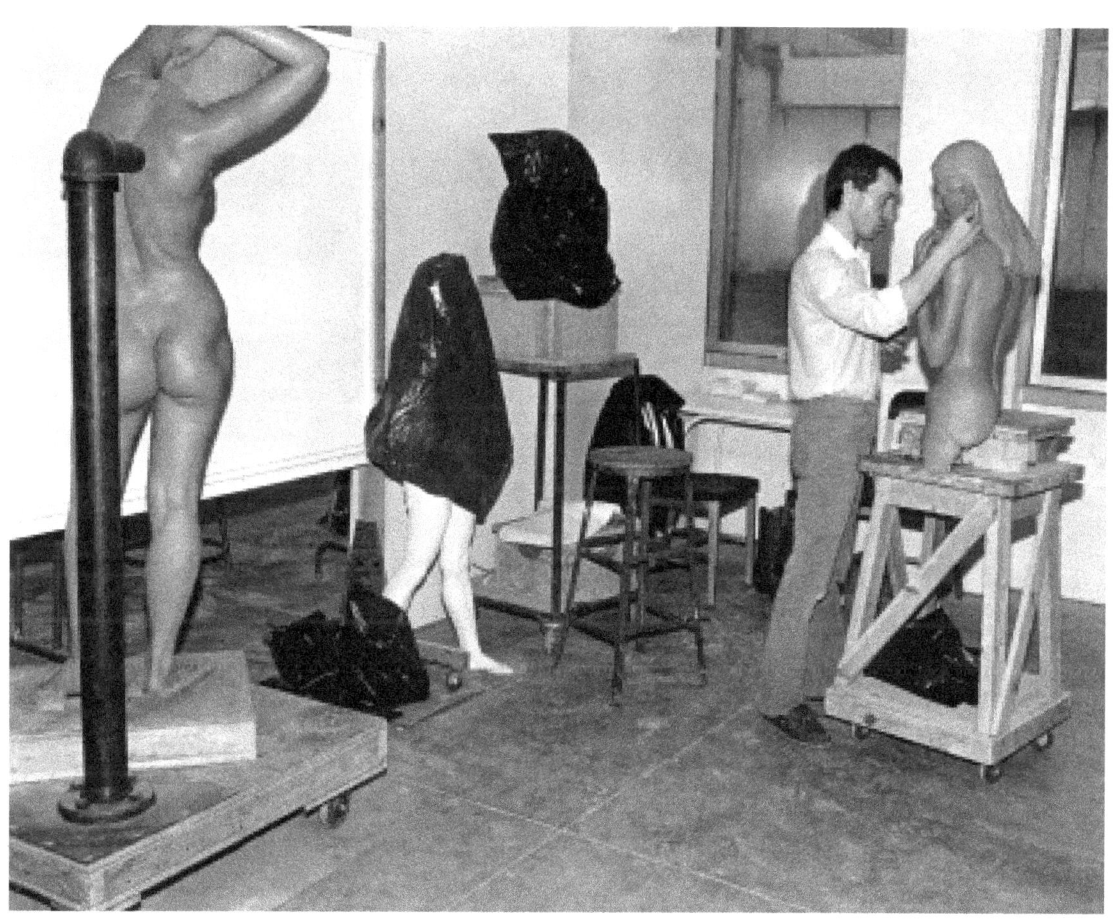

Five Kinds of Critiques:

D. The Silent Student Critique

Occasionally you might find yourself in a critique where you're asked not to speak. Or you might decline to speak. (Both are also called "cold reads.") There are several reasons this may happen, so I've divided this chapter into two parts.

A. *Reasons why students sometimes tell their teachers they'd rather not speak.*

(1) The usual reason students ask for a cold read is to see how the work will play out in the world. I am not in favor if this for beginning students. If you ask for a cold read, you'll get dozens of different responses, and most of them won't have anything

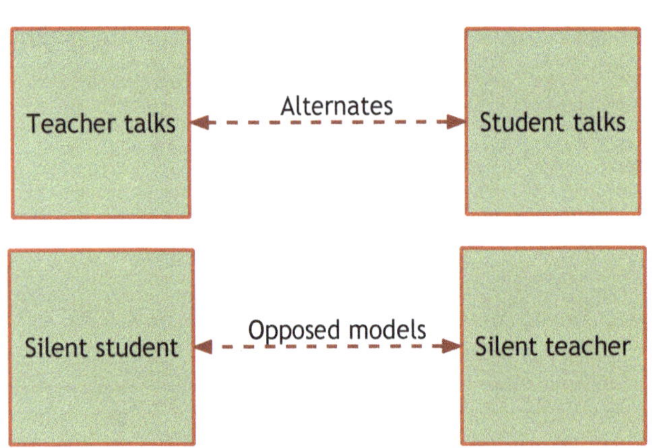

to do with the issues that concern you. Your cold read won't help you articulate and develop your themes, because it'll be all over the place, and mainly entirely off topic. If you're a beginning student, it's usually much better to give your teachers a hint, at least, of what you'd like to talk about.

It's a different question if you're about to graduate with an MFA and go out into the art world. At that point it may be useful to have a cold read, but for a specific purpose: you'll need to be sure people are getting the general idea of what your work is about, and that you have effectively controlled your work in such a way that the many crazy, off-the-wall opinions you used to get are no longer part of the picture. As the artist Gaylen Gerber puts it, a cold read "should be reserved for mature students who are in command of their language and are at the point where they need to witness the reception their work without defending it." As Gaylen says, when students ask for cold reads they are often ready for whatever comes, so they often "don't 'hear' what's said because they're strategizing their defense."

In short, the cold read should mainly be reserved for students who are close to the end of their education, and who have a good idea of what their practice is and how it communicates, who have thought about the odd reactions they have gotten in the past and figured out ways of avoiding or minimizing those reactions. For most art students, a cold read wastes critique time by introducing many problems other than the ones you're struggling with.

(2) The Silent Student Critique also happens for an entirely different reason: you might just refuse to talk. Maybe you don't have any clear ideas about your work, or you're shy, or critiques are new to you. My advice here is: try to talk a little. Just admit whatever uncertainty you have. The danger of just not talking, or not talking much, or not replying when your teachers ask questions, is that you'll turn your teachers against you. When a student refuses to talk, I am always suspicious. What's the issue? Is the student always shy, or is something going on? Has she put effort into figuring out how her work might appear to other people? (I think everyone should put in that effort.)

Here's a story Gaylen sometimes recounts in critiques, to get silent students to talk:

> The story I normally tell around the request for a "cold read" is related to something that happened a few years ago during critique week. In the spring semester we conduct interdisciplinary panels and I'm often the moderator of at least one panel. That was the case that day and in the early afternoon we were scheduled to meet a young photographer in his MFA exhibition for his final critique. I arrived a little earlier than my panel and had an opportunity to see the exhibition. The work was clear, a little clever, but otherwise well realized and I thought it might be an easy afternoon. As we congregated in the space to begin the critique, I asked the artist if he would introduce himself and say something about his work. In a strident, arrogant manner, he declared that he would not say anything but instead asked for a cold-read. There was a feeling of a dismissal and challenge in the tone of his request and the feeling in the room immediately changed from one predisposed towards the work to something more adversarial.
>
> I remember thinking that we could rhetorically dismantle him but that would be counterproductive. I did want to address the change in atmosphere that had been created in a moment's notice. I started by saying that I thought there had been a misunderstanding. He thought that we were here to help him, to critique his work. We thought that he was there to help us, to set the stage for our conversation, to create a context for the work that would allow us to have a conversation that felt relevant to him. He had had a lifetime with his work but we're just being introduced to it. If he took a moment to

point us in the right direction, to suggest his intentions, there was a good chance that we might spend our time together well. He thought about it for a moment and decided to say a few words, the mood immediately shifted and a genuine and more productive conversation followed.

It's usually best to tell people why you don't feel comfortable speaking, and then to provide just a little information to get people started. It's likely your critique will be more useful, and also more congenial.

B. *Reasons why teachers sometimes tell their students not to speak.*

I've encountered two reasons why teachers ask students to remain silent.

(1) Mary Kelly, the conceptual artist, led critiques in which the artist wasn't permitted to speak. That decision came from a conviction about the relation between intentionality and art: the artist's intentions—what they think they're doing—are only loosely related to what they're actually producing. So for Kelly, what matters is how viewers think about artwork, not what the artist thinks. Note this is very different from (1): the idea here is that what you wanted to make doesn't matter. In art history, this way of thinking is called *anti-intentionalist*. It means Rothko, for example, had only a muddled idea of what he was making, and it fell to the next generation of critics and historians to elucidate the work's historical importance. His painting wasn't about religion, tragedy, and profound emotions, as he thought, but about the history of painting, self-referentiality, and representation.[1] An expression for the sum total of viewers' opinions is *critical field*; some people call it the *discursive field*. Rothko's work may have been made in a postwar atmosphere of troubled religious convictions, but it entered the discursive field of poststructuralist art criticism and theory, and that body of writing is what has given Rothko his current place in art.

If you are in a critique where you're not asked to speak, make the best of it by attending to everyone's comments together. See if they form a consensus, or if there's a general set of questions and themes that keep coming up. If you had the ideal audience (say, the world's best art critics on their best day) those repeated themes, ideas, and concerns would be the critical field. At first you might not recognize it at all. You may want to resist it, and say "I didn't intend that at all." But you might also begin to see that this is how your art will make its way through the world. If you wish to change the terms of the critical field, you may have to change some basic things about what you're making and how you're making it.

(2) The book *Art Crits: 20 Questions* mentions another common reason for the rule that the student can't speak: as Sean Kaye, at the Leeds College of Art puts it, some students are very persuasive, and the other students just listen and say "Oh yeah, I can see that now." It's a good point for lower-level critiques. At the MA or MFA level students wouldn't be as likely to buy into what the artist says.

This topic, the Silent Student Critique, is complicated. The "Mary Kelly critique," where your teacher tells you not to speak, might be based on a number of other assumptions. *The Critique Handbook* has a paragraph that lists some of the things you may hear. "Instructors may refuse to hear about your intentions," they write. You may hear such things as:

"Your ideas are getting in the way."

"The artwork speaks for itself."

"You're all caught up in the ideas and not in the work."

"I don't care about what you think you're doing, you don't know what you're doing." [p. 89]

Notice these are different. Kelly might subscribe to the second, and she might also agree with the first part of the fourth. But the first one, "Your ideas are getting in the way," points to a different philosophy of art. The idea there is that some artists have lots of ideas—theories, usually—and those ideas stop them from thinking about more central or difficult themes. (See chapters 7 and 39 for more on this.) The third one sounds to me like a teacher who is against some theory, or just in favor of spending time in the studio without books. Either that, or a teacher who thinks your work is too much driven by concepts. And the last clause of the fourth sentence— "you don't know what you're doing"? That sounds like a teacher who has no confidence in your ability to understand and describe your work.

The point is: all these attitudes call for explanation. Ask your teachers, politely but persistently, why they say such things.

Now I've mentioned the Silent Teacher Critique and the Silent Student Critique. There is also such a thing as the Totally Silent Critique, where no one speaks. Decades ago, the School of the Art Institute had a teacher who supposedly never spoke: she went from one student to the next, painting or drawing for them, on their own canvas or paper. That's a radical solution if you mistrust language.

One person on Facebook wrote, "Francesco Clemente sat with me in front of my work… and didn't say a word for thirty minutes. We sat in silence." And she adds that it was "super helpful."[2] I was once in a day-long critique, involving five faculty and five MFA students; one of the faculty was a world-famous painter. I didn't keep count, but I think he didn't say more than five words the entire day. In one of the critiques the student was also nearly silent. It's part of the strangeness of critiques that silence can be meaningful and helpful. Needless to say the Totally Silent Critique isn't common![3]

19

Five Kinds of Critiques:

E. The Anti-Critique

Critiques are nearly universal in art instruction up to the PhD level. In the United States, the most visible exception is the critic Dave Hickey, who dislikes group critiques. It's his "*one* rule," he told Sarah Thornton. Critiques, he said, are "social occasions that reinforce the norm," imposing a "standardized discourse," and for that reason they "privilege unfinished, incompetent art."[1] This is part of Hickey's anti-establishment rhetoric: for years he's railed against art education. When he came to the School of the Art Institute in 2003, he told a packed auditorium full of art students that if he were a prospective student, he'd pocket the $200,000 in student loans he'd need to get his MFA, and spend the money on a De Kooning drawing. That comment caused a lot of trouble in my seminars the next week, because students were anxious that such an influential critic thought their educations were worthless. Hickey was in Chicago on that occasion for a panel discussion on art criticism, which has been published; and if you read his contributions to that, you'll see he is hardly consistent in his anti-establishment line.[2] He once taught MFA students at the University of Nevada; their studios were rented stores in an unused strip mall, and they looked out across a parking lot at the back of the Liberace Museum. That's about as far from academia as you can get (as he said at the time), but it was still in academia, still connected to the art world, still mobilized by the community of students. What he means by his anti-critique rhetoric is that it is vitally important to follow your own interests, and find your own voice.

Hickey also told Thornton that he thought there was "undue pressure on students to verbalize." Hickey said he doesn't care about the artist's intentions; he cares only about the work. That's part of the anti-conceptual position that I described under the heading "The Conceptual Critique." Hickey loves sensuous qualities in art—the feel, the visceral impact. In that he is very consistent, but it isn't a reason to avoid critiques.

I take Hickey as an example of a teacher who wants to avoid critiques. In each case I know, the teacher either prefers not to evaluate work at all, or chooses one-on-one conversation instead of group critiques.

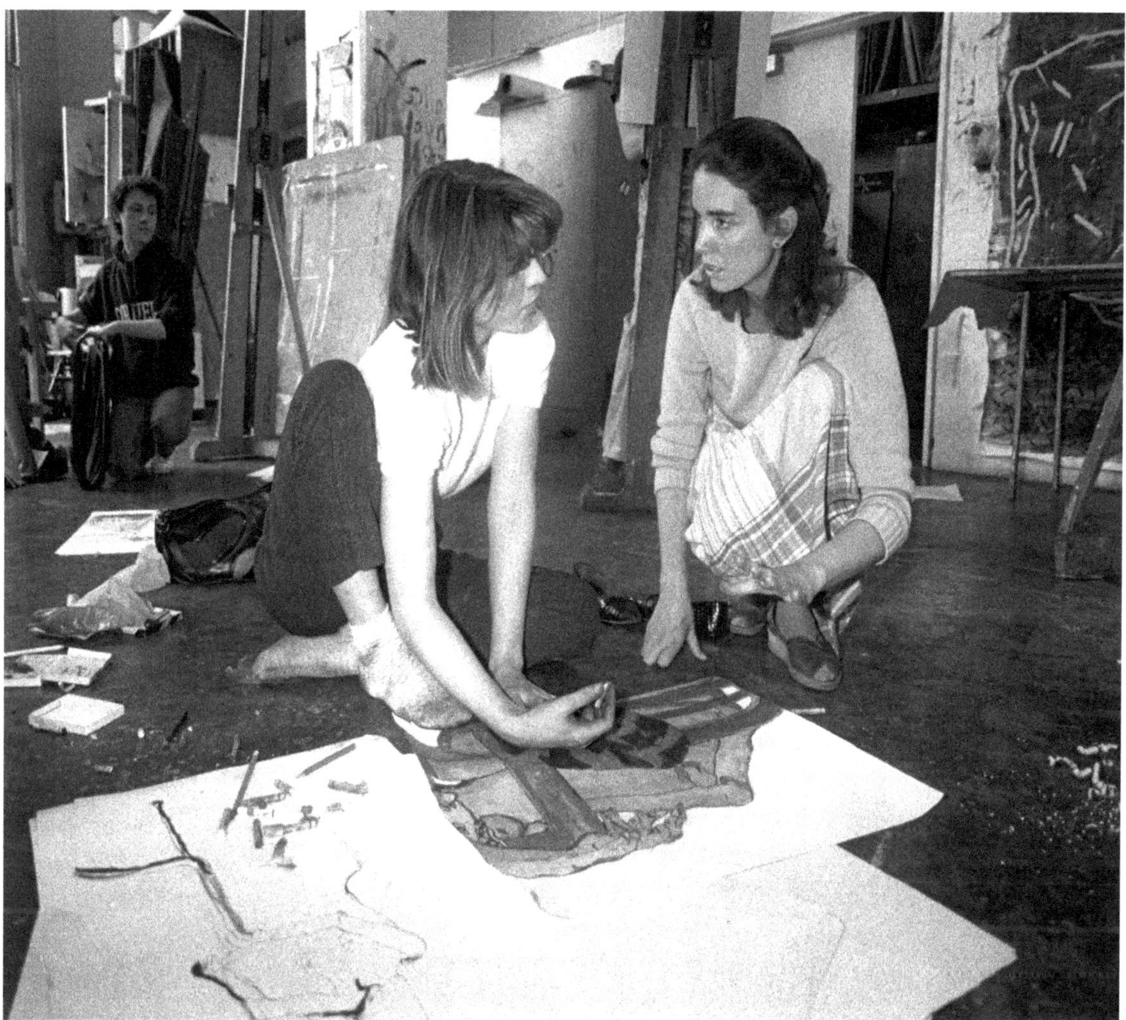

A. *The idea that art shouldn't be evaluated.* This is a radical form of the anti-conceptual stance. At the Savannah College of Art and Design, I saw row upon row of students, filling several floors of a large converted warehouse, each student bent over a monitor, learning techniques of post-production effects, titling, or video editing. Classes like those are necessary to teach technically complex subjects, and they often push evaluation of the work off to one side.

B. *The idea that one-on-one conversation is better than critiques.* This is the commonest workaround for teachers who don't like group critiques. It has a very interesting drawback, which is that the one-on-one conversation goes back to the German Romantic period, when art instruction broke away from the previous academic model. I'll discuss this later: for now, I just want to note the fact that a one-on-one lesson is fundamentally not modern, or postmodern: it's premodern.

Student + Teacher + Artwork = Confusion

Consider three hypothetical scenes: *A*, a teacher wanders into your classroom or studio when you're not there, and sees your work. *B*, you walk in, but you don't say anything. *C*, you start explaining your work.

A. *Teacher + Artwork.* An artwork implies a creator. As viewers we construct— often without trying, or being aware of what we are doing—entire personalities for artists based on what we see of their works. It's not necessarily that we try to picture how the artist works or what kind of a person she is when she's at home: it's that our response to a work involves a story of some sort, a story we tell ourselves, about the kind of person who would make such a work. After poststructuralism, people have been wary of saying they care too much, or know to much, about what the artist intended. But art that doesn't give us *some* sense of the artist's intention will seem random, irresponsible, or unaccountable. Some philosophers of art say that an artwork without a notion of the maker's intention cannot even appear as an artwork: it will look like a random configuration of marks.[1] Whatever guesses we make about the artist's thinking are probably wrong, but that is what enables us to understand work to begin with. What I mean to emphasize here is that a version of the artist is *already* present in every teacher's mind when she looks at an artwork, even if she hasn't seen the student who made the work.

B. *Teacher + Artwork + Student (no sound).* The situation is complicated when the teacher sees you, because it is a natural human reaction to form an idea of a person even before she speaks. Just by looking at you, your teacher will immediately have some sense of you as a person, and even a vague notion of what kind of work you might make. In a critique, when it's clear you made the work, your teacher has to square her notion of you with the sense of you that she gets from the artwork itself. Two implied personalities that have to be correlated: the one implied by the work, and the one you project just by being in the room. It is simpler, by comparison, to look at art in a museum, because then you only have one kind of intention to think about, the one apparently embodied in the work. The artist isn't usually around to confound your assumptions. It's a cliché to say that the impression you have of someone based only on their appearance is bound to be wrong: but the fact remains that we all have such ideas floating in our heads. It's the same with point *A*: I know that my notion of the kind of artist that would make a work is bound to be wrong: but without some notion, I can't actually continue perceiving the work as an artwork.

This can also happen in reverse: the teacher meets you first, and then sees the work. A few years ago I was in a critique with a very quiet, neatly dressed student, and I guess I had a kind of idea about the work he probably did. I had seen some of his pictures based on paint-by-numbers kits, but they didn't prepare me for the work he showed, which was Polaroids of toilets in the men's rooms of gay clubs. He hadn't even taken those pictures himself—he had loaned his camera to men who were on their way into the washroom, telling them to photograph whatever they chose. The studio was full of large pictures of toilets, some of them full. The student was clean and quiet. When there is a strong disparity between the student himself and the kind of person implied by the work, it can be difficult to get a good critique started. Unconsciously, we all require at least a minimal sense of a single, coherent personality—an intentionality—behind the work. (In that case, it was easy for me to tell myself a story about the repressed, button-down person I saw in the studio and his gross-out artwork.)

C. *Teacher + Artwork + Student (with sound)*. So it can already be confusing for a teacher when you don't seem to look or behave like the person whom your teacher thinks might plausibly make your work. In addition students usually *speak* in critiques. The moment you say a few words the critique is decisively changed. Your teacher then has *three* versions of you to contend with: the reconstructed intention implied by the works, the persona implied by your appearance, and whatever explanatory narrative you offer. When the critique gets underway the situation is compounded by the fact that everyone in the room is working with slightly (or wildly) different ideas of the kind of person who would make such an artwork, of the kind of person who would look like you do, and of the kind of ideas you're actually expressing.

Everything in a critique matters. It matters where you stand, how you look, what tone of voice you have. In addition to what's actually said, there are all the subliminal accompaniments of speaking—your offhanded gestures, your sighs and nods, your pose and attitude. I've even seen dancing and miming in critiques: gestures enrich the critique—after all, they're nonverbal elements of communication, just like the visual art that is under consideration.[2] (Critiques aren't the same as reading or listening to a lecture, and all the differences count.[3]) A shy artist, for example, might make panelists gentle and earnest in their reading of the work, or it might make them think the work itself is antisocial. An artist who speaks about family relationships will make panelists think of their own family relationships, and might prompt them to bring in themes and images from family life. I had a student a few years ago who painted lovely landscapes, interiors, and vases of flowers. One of his paintings was a lesbian couple making love. It was obviously lifted from a pornographic magazine. The student insisted it wasn't pornographic, but just a lovely composition with two blondes. When he said that, my whole idea about him fell apart: I realized I had to rethink my idea of him as a person, and also reconsider my interpretations of his other paintings. For a teacher it can be hard enough to achieve a coherent sense of the student, her words, and her work.

I don't mean to say you have to script every word you say and choreograph every move you make: you couldn't do that anyway, and even if you could you couldn't predict what a teacher would make of it. My moral is simple: critiques are a heady mix of invented and projected meanings, and it helps to be aware of just how complicated that mixture is.

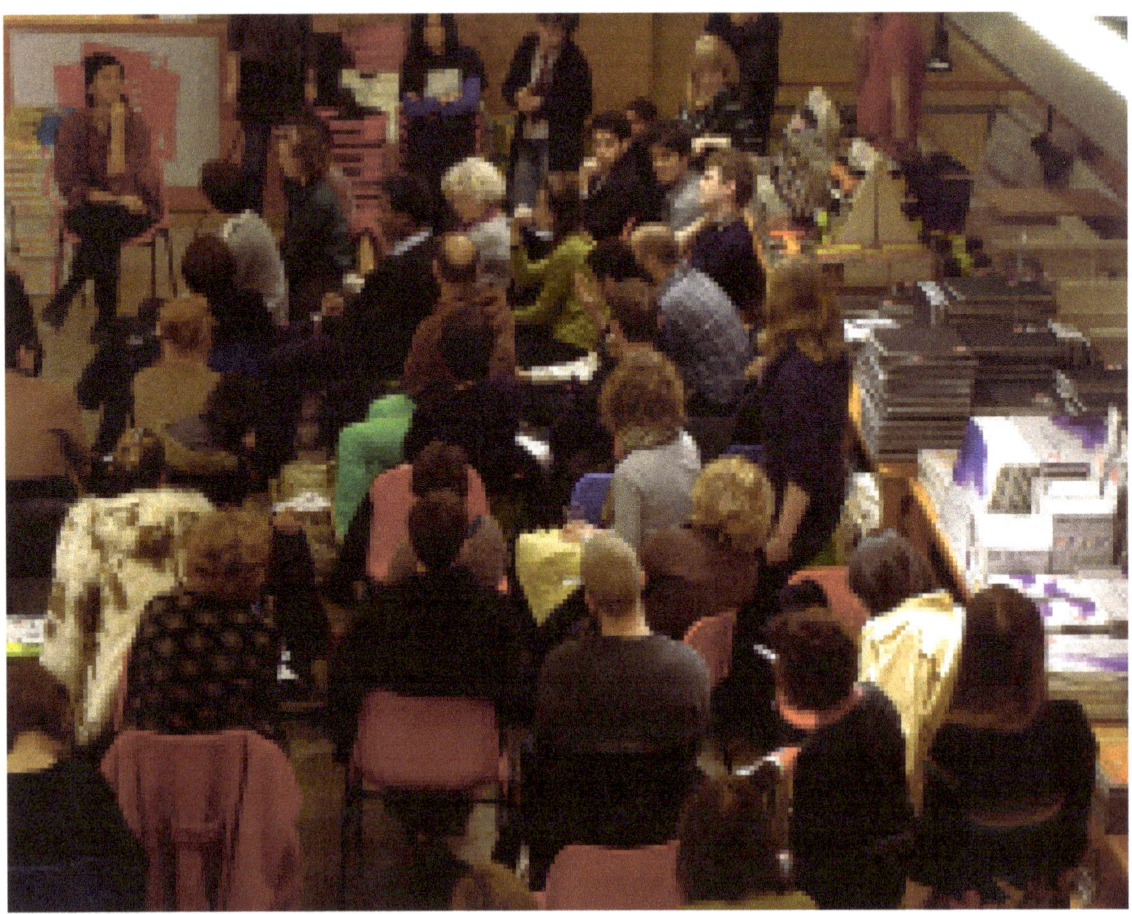

21

All the Ways to Fail

Failing is something everyone does, simply because every artwork is not a masterpiece. But the words that tell you that you've failed are never easy to hear. Here are some I gathered at the School of the Art Institute. It's a long list, just for fun:

Didactic
Anachronistic
Fancy
Pretty
Merely pretty
Vague
Just fun
Easy
Almost insulting
Boring
Bland
Dull
Painfully dull
Unintelligent
Stupid
Trite
Doesn't make sense
Has useless additions
Uninvolved
Dishonest
Immoral
Stupidly, gratuitously immoral
Unreflective
Over-controlled
Uncontrolled

Impersonal
Careless
Makeshift
Thoughtless
Been there, done that
Poor composition
Maudlin
Melodramatic
Too sci-fi
Schlocky
Garish
Kitsch
Not close enough to kitsch
Its only thrill is how close it can get to
    kitsch
Not kitschy enough
Unaware it's humorous
Distracting use of medium
Obvious
Blunt
In your face
Gratuitous appropriations
Obscure
Obscure, bordering on obtuse
Condescending

Weak
Thin
Odd
Not odd enough
Too much
Self-serving
Too amiable
Simple
Simplistic
Literal-minded
Corny
Ridiculous
Awful ("bloomin' awful," etc.)
No motivation
Sexist
Silly
Too light
Too dark
Finicky
Unstable
Neither accessible to all,
 nor accessible to none
Colors dissonant
Colors too harmonious
No congruence between artist,
 aim, and result
Cute
Too cute
Cutesy
Sweet
Campy
Stale
Mismatched styles
Half-hearted
Disengaged
Less than overwhelming
Too overwhelming
Just too much
OTT

Heartless
Repetitive
Incoherent
Too satisfying
Plays to the audience
Manipulative
Looks lousy
Commercial
Overly commercial
Subject matter and idea
 are disconnected
Form and content are disconnected
Too serious
Too corporate
Too manly
Unfocused
Pointless
Aimless
Hopeless
Senseless
Mindless
Painless
Apathetic
Lacks apathy (too committed)
Wash-out
Unconvincing
Unconfident
Waste of time
Hypocritical
Happy
Amiable
Easy
Funny, but so what?
Self-censored
A one-liner
An ad
Too slick
Cheesy
Smooth

<table>
<tr><td>Cultish about the avant-garde</td><td>A cliché</td></tr>
<tr><td>Looks like art</td><td>Propaganda</td></tr>
<tr><td>Too trendy</td><td>A slogan</td></tr>
<tr><td>Wrong medium</td><td>A message</td></tr>
<tr><td>Propaganda</td><td>Intrusive</td></tr>
<tr><td>Illustrates a theory</td><td>Heavy-handed</td></tr>
<tr><td>Too systematic</td><td>Contrived</td></tr>
<tr><td>Formulaic</td><td>Merely aesthetic</td></tr>
<tr><td>Makes no sense, but seems like it should</td><td>Not aesthetic enough</td></tr>
<tr><td>Just tossed off</td><td>Tries too hard</td></tr>
<tr><td>Badly done</td><td>Lost</td></tr>
<tr><td>Mystical</td><td>Naïve</td></tr>
<tr><td>Spiritual</td><td>Cloying</td></tr>
<tr><td>Not spiritual</td><td>Sentimental</td></tr>
<tr><td>Intentions unclear</td><td>Romantic</td></tr>
<tr><td>Intentions too clear</td><td>Romanticizing</td></tr>
<tr><td>Meaningless</td><td>Just plain ugly</td></tr>
<tr><td>Empty</td><td>Junky</td></tr>
<tr><td>Bullshit</td><td>Offensive</td></tr>
<tr><td>Lets the critics dictate its meanings</td><td>Disgusting</td></tr>
<tr><td>Implies a meaning, but has none</td><td>Not disturbing enough</td></tr>
<tr><td>Not in control of possible meanings</td><td>Not extreme enough</td></tr>
<tr><td>Indecisive</td><td>Not weird enough</td></tr>
<tr><td>Not sick enough</td><td>Derivative</td></tr>
<tr><td>Fake-o psychotic</td><td>Interesting</td></tr>
</table>

Notice the last word on the list. Even interesting work can be a failure! You've probably heard a line like this:

"Hmm, yes, that's very interesting."

You can hear the boredom. It might mean, "I have next to nothing to say about this," or it might mean, "Hmm, no, that's not really interesting at all," or it might mean, "That's just interesting, not really compelling," or it might mean, "God, I wish I was at home watching TV," or, if you're lucky, it might mean, "I can't see much in it at the moment, but you've got my attention. I might think of something in a while." Philosophers know that "interesting" is an especially interesting word, because it tends to replace older aesthetic criteria such as "good" or "successful."[1] It's value-neutral. But in this context, it's less a matter of what in the world "interesting" might signal in relation to aesthetic, as it is a matter of what it might cover up.

In 2011, I posted this list of failure words on the internet, asking if people had any to add. I got lots more:[2]

<table>
<tr><td>Sucks hard</td><td>Too uptight</td></tr>
<tr><td>Depraved</td><td>Anal</td></tr>
<tr><td>Risqué</td><td>Doctrinaire</td></tr>
<tr><td>Jejune</td><td>Doctor in the house?</td></tr>
<tr><td>Over-ambitious</td><td>Academic</td></tr>
<tr><td>Under-ambitious</td><td>Stiff</td></tr>
<tr><td>Arch</td><td>Stuffy</td></tr>
<tr><td>A knock-off</td><td>Stolid</td></tr>
<tr><td>Predictable</td><td>Oppressive</td></tr>
<tr><td>Shambolic</td><td>Out of touch</td></tr>
<tr><td>Traditional</td><td>Need to stand back</td></tr>
<tr><td>Conventional</td><td>Need to get a life</td></tr>
<tr><td>Counter-productive</td><td>Need to settle down</td></tr>
<tr><td>Esoteric</td><td>Need to apply yourself</td></tr>
<tr><td>Mild</td><td>Frivolous</td></tr>
<tr><td>Complacent</td><td>Immature</td></tr>
<tr><td>Safe</td><td>Dabbling</td></tr>
<tr><td>Insincere</td><td>Amateur</td></tr>
<tr><td>Savvy</td><td>Unsophisticated</td></tr>
<tr><td>Cynical</td><td>Over-sophisticated</td></tr>
<tr><td>Plagiarized</td><td>Knowing</td></tr>
<tr><td>Lacks rigor</td><td>Negative</td></tr>
<tr><td>Lacks discipline</td><td>Neurotic</td></tr>
<tr><td>Lacks commitment</td><td>Nice</td></tr>
<tr><td>Artsy</td><td>Self-indulgent</td></tr>
<tr><td>Too artsy</td><td>Perfunctory</td></tr>
<tr><td>Not artsy enough</td><td>Provincial</td></tr>
<tr><td>Doesn't sing</td><td>Chocolate-box</td></tr>
<tr><td>Hackneyed</td><td>Cod surrealist</td></tr>
<tr><td>Ham fisted</td><td>Bourgeois</td></tr>
<tr><td>Sloppy</td><td>Twee</td></tr>
<tr><td>Cold</td><td>Dated</td></tr>
<tr><td>Tone deaf</td><td>Prolix</td></tr>
</table>

(The last few of those are very English.)

The list of words for failure is bewilderingly miscellaneous: it seems to have no rhyme or reason, as if anything, anytime, can be called a failure for any reason whatsoever. Basically, that is true. When you hear criticism of your work, take note of the words that your teachers use. At first they may seem as miscellaneous as this list is. They'll seem endless, unpredictable, and subjective. But the artworld is not as complex as it seems.

It is true that after the end of modernism, styles and manners and media have multiplied, and now the artworld is comprised of an uncountable number of different practices. Each one, in theory—if they could even be numbered or separated from one another—has its own criteria for success and failure. So it is true that there are many more criteria than there were, say, in the 18th century art academies.

But it is crucial to realize that does not mean the list of ways to fail is infinite, or that is has no potential order. Actually there are a relatively small number of ways of thinking about art that have grown up since the beginnings of modernism in the early 20th century. Most, if not all, of the terms on these two lists belong to a relatively small number of ways of thinking about art and media. The challenge is to begin to see order in this apparent chaos. In Part Five of this book I'll develop this theme. As a practical matter, if you start a list of critical terms people have used to describe your work, you will find after a while it starts to show repeated patterns. At the beginning of your BFA, the list may be chaotic. By the end, it should reveal tendencies and patterns, and they can be assigned to different modes of artmaking over the last century. Often your art history classes will suggest where certain words come from, and if you keep working on the list, you should be able to explain most of the things you've heard.

There's am unexpected surprise here: if I make a list of words used for successful work, it turns out to be much shorter than this. I will explain that later in this book.[3]

22

Being Close to Your Work,

Being Too Close to Your Work

One way of thinking about the point of a critique is that it's an opportunity to put a little distance between yourself and what you have made. One of the biggest differences between people who make art and people who look at it is that if you haven't made art, you will have no idea what it's like to be so close to what you've made that you can barely see it. Art historians (people in my field) are notorious for this, but so are philosophers, and so are some critics. (If you're reading this, and you haven't made art, trust me: you have no idea what I'm talking about.) When you make a work of art, no matter how successful it is, it can be very very close to you, as close as your skin. You won't have a good way of talking about it: you won't have words, you won't have distance. A critique can help pry you apart from your work.

"Distance" is not at stake in what the faculty do: they begin and end at a comfortable intellectual and emotional distance from what they see. They just want to say something insightful, partly because they feel an obligation to you, partly because they love art, partly because usually they have been in your position and they understand how strange it is, and partly because they know their colleagues are listening.

The most effective teachers in critiques are artists, or have made art; they are the ones who can understand it when you can barely articulate what in the world you've just made. Conversely, the academic faculty (art historians, philosophers, liberal arts people, etc.) can be like a splash of cold water: they can snap you out of your hypnosis very fast, just by talking as if you had always had an idea what you were doing—or else you *should* have had an idea what you were doing.

A sympathetic teacher will know when it is not appropriate to say something abstract like "These marks subvert the innocuousness of that gesture," and when it is better to say instead, "Well, don't worry, the first semester is always the worst." As a student, you can appreciate the teacher's interest in explaining everything. That you will know when it is better to say "I think that's too intellectual," instead of "What the hell do you mean, the marks 'subvert the innocuousness'?" On both sides there's a give and take, as the art slowly comes apart from you.

The images in this chapter are a nice example of being very close to your work. The student, Diego Gutierrez, showed a half-dozen paintings. Some of them showed a small-sized man. There were two large paintings in which the small man was apparently trying to help a woman lift a pole. In another, the small man and ordinary-sized woman (it was clear from other paintings he was diminutive, and she was normal) worked together in a large landscape.

What were these? we wondered. Diego said the man was Noah, and the woman was one of his daughters, and they were building the Ark.

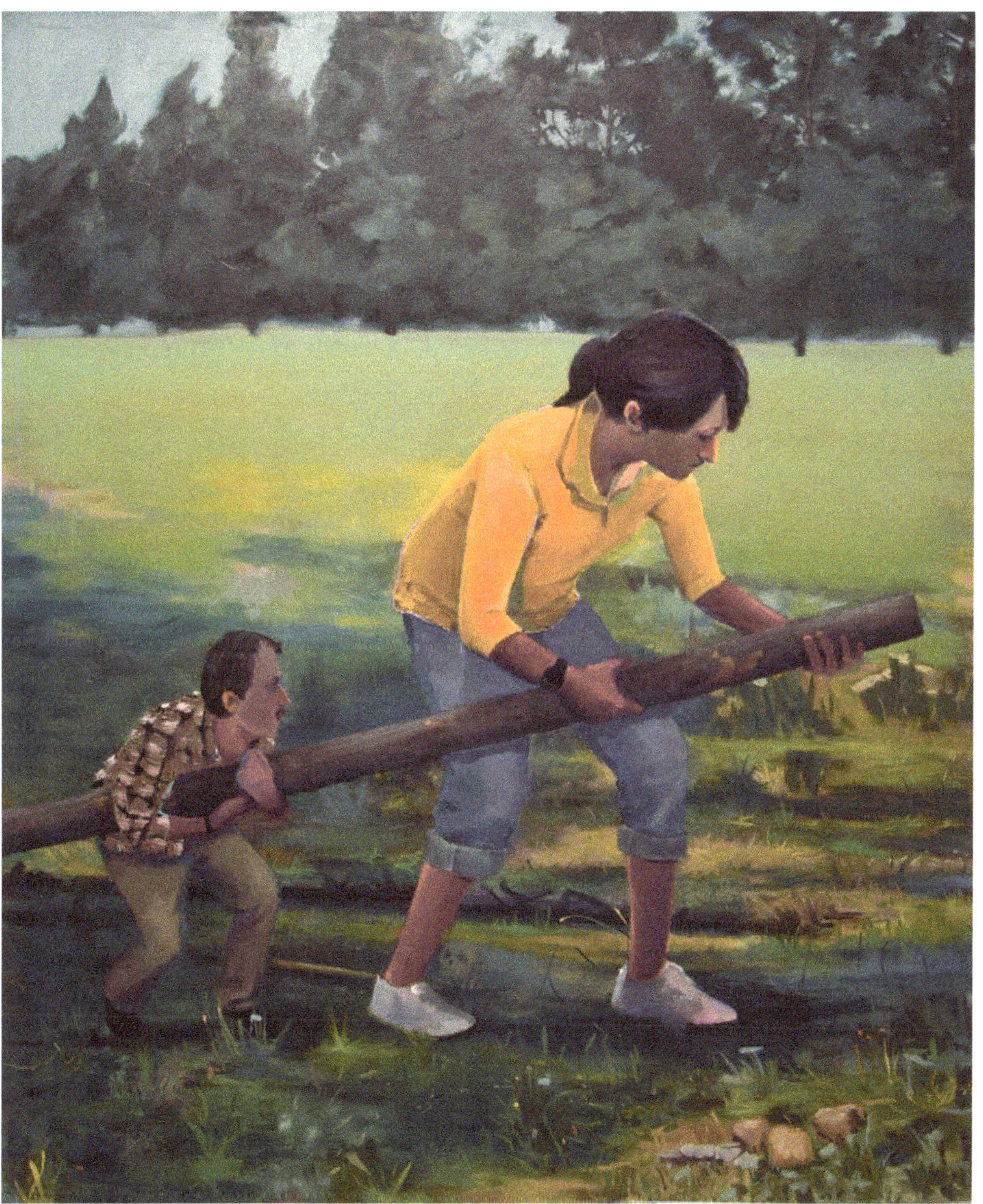

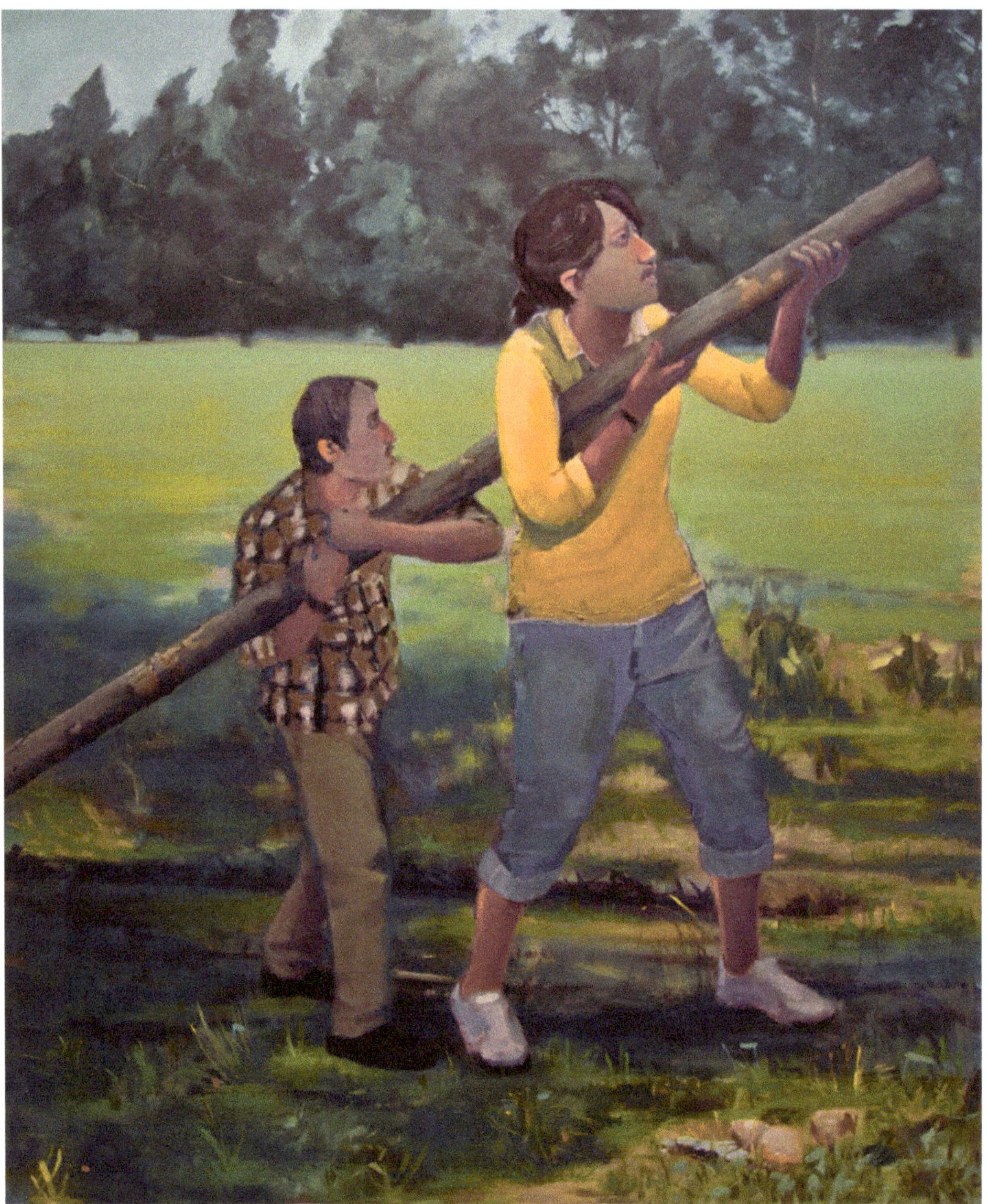

"How would we know that?" I asked.

"I am not sure," he said.

I noticed that Noah apparently had only one daughter helping him; that there was no ark anywhere around; that if they had trouble lifting the first pole, the ark might never get built; that in the Bible, Noah isn't especially short; and that Noah and his daughter have flaming red noses and ears.

"Yes, I am working on all that," he said, or something to that effect.

It was a great critique, because the story the student had been telling himself about his work was so weird and counter-intuitive. After a while the other teachers on the panel wandered into other subjects, and that was probably just as well.

As far as I could tell, this was the first time the student had been asked to talk about what he'd been thinking. For him, it was a surprise that the story didn't seem to fit what he'd been making.

This is the entirely normal, absolutely common experience of making art. People who haven't made art can barely understand it. A good teacher will bring out the differences between the student's story and the viewer's story as gently as possible. As a student, you should be ready to have the thoughts in your mind gently pried apart from the appearance of what you have made.

23

Does Your Teacher Like The Other Teachers?

Here's a diagram of some of the orientations that feed into critiques. I'll be talking about all of them in this book. Notice what's in the upper right. In any art department, there's office politics. I have been to hundreds of art and art history departments, and I have yet to find one that is really, genuinely, totally happy. Some have great chemistry, but there's bound to be a problem somewhere. Usually some faculty dislike other faculty. In a average-sized art department of six or eight teachers, it's likely that one will be a total annoyance to the others, and several more will be routinely ostracized by the rest.

Why does this matter? Because as a student, you may have to consider that some of the faculty are actually talking to one another, and not just to you. When a teacher says, "I think your work is great," hopefully that means she thinks it's great, but it might also mean, "I think your work is great despite what my idiotic colleague Professor X thinks."

There isn't an easy way for a student to negotiate these faculty relationships. My general advice is: don't obsess about it. Most of the time, most of the faculty really are speaking to you.

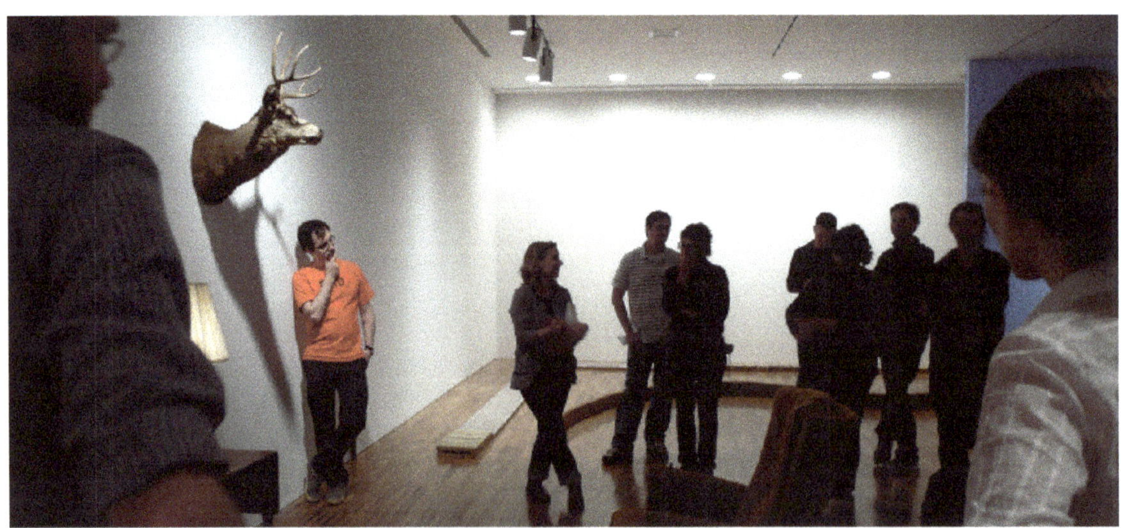

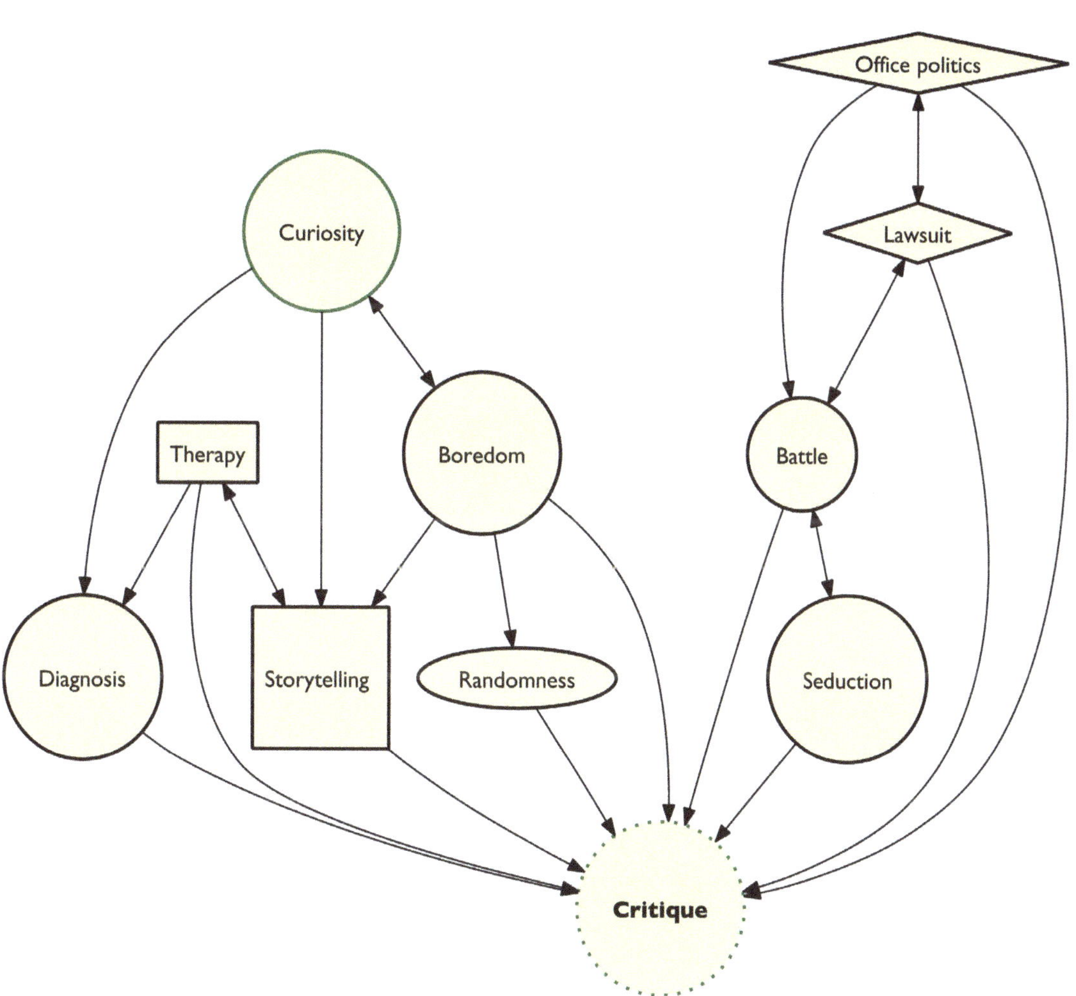

Office politics
Lawsuit
Curiosity
Therapy
Boredom
Battle
Diagnosis
Storytelling
Randomness
Seduction
Critique

24

Therapy

The diagram in the previous chapter also includes Therapy. In an abstract sense, critiques are therapies because they are meant to help you make better art.[1] In a not-so-abstract sense, critiques often involve personal advice, as in my opening example about the student who had hairy legs. All that is okay. But in a concrete, real-world sense, critiques sometimes *become* therapy sessions. That can be a frightening experience.

I was in a critique once where a student said that one of his art practices was to write to large companies like Kellogg's, saying how much he liked their products, and hoping to get a personal note in return. He said he'd always gotten form letters back, until recently, when he'd gotten this amazing postcard. He showed us the card, which he'd framed and put on the wall. It said, in blue felt-tip pen, "Thank you! We're so glad you liked Kellogg's Corn Flakes!" He said he had treasured that card, until he had noticed that in the lower-left corner of the postcard, there was a small line in blue print—the same color as the blue "handwriting"—that said "FORM C-6."

Everyone in the room laughed. But the student wasn't laughing, he was tearing up.

He said, "I have tried *so, so* hard to get someone, just anyone, to write me back."

He had furnished his studio so it looked like his bedroom, complete with his bed. He reached under the bed and pulled out an enormous wooden open-top box, completely filled with thousands of form letters that different companies had sent him. He stood there, crying.

"No one will write me," he said.

The whole room full of faculty and students were stunned and embarrassed. It was clear that what he needed was therapy, not art advice. He had issues that weren't being solved or even addressed by his art.

This is a clear example of a moment when all the therapeutic sorts of talk that are common in critiques become empty and useless, because people realize that art is no longer the point. You might think this is a special case, requiring a trained nurse or therapist. But where is the line between a critique that is mostly therapy—for which no one on the faculty is trained—and one that has a lot of therapy in it—for which all the faculty think they're adequately trained?

Here is a second example. I was in an MFA critique with four other faculty members. The studio was completely bare. In walked the student, with a ball of black yarn, knitting needles, and a bundle of fabric he had knitted, about fifteen inches wide and maybe 20 feet long. He sat down and started knitting. One of us on the faculty asked what he was making, and he said, "Nothing."

Someone asked how he worked, and he said, "Every day I get up, and I go on some public transport, usually a bus. I knit all day long."

Then we thought it was a kind of performance art. Someone asked if he taped people's reactions.

"No," he said.

Someone asked if he talked to people.

"Not usually," he said.

I asked if he was making something.

"No."

I asked what happened when the thing he was knitting got too large.

"I wrap it around myself," he said, "and if it's too big to carry I just start unraveling it."

I said I didn't believe him: I thought he was pretending not to make something, but he secretly was making something. He started unraveling the thing he'd knitted.

Gradually we realized that this student was not making art, or even thinking about art. He had a simple activity, which he did all day long, day after day, for no reason he could name. He apparently had no social life, and no other interests. We looked around the empty studio.

The thing is, this student wasn't *simply* in need of therapy. He knew what he wanted, which was to talk about what he did *as* art, to pretend or hope that it was art. So we, the faculty, did have a job, and for the rest of the critique that's what we did.

I'm making a difficult point here: critiques always involve some therapy, because they are intended to help you with your art, and that often involves personal advice. But occasionally, critiques are almost all therapy, and that is clearly a problem because few studio art instructors are trained therapists. Yet we, the teachers, don't often think of therapy as a deep problem in critiques, because we generally think we can keep therapy out of the mix most of the time. But the truth is more difficult: art critiques *are* a mixture of therapy and talk about art, and no one knows how to manage that.

25

Critiques Don't Always Build on One Another,

But Start Again and Again from Scratch

As you go along through the BFA, you'll accumulate experiences of critiques, and you'll probably begin to notice some repetition. It doesn't help that time is often wasted going over topics that you have already talked about with your teacher. Typically you will have talked about some things before your critique, and if other teachers come to your critique, then it's inevitable they will repeat some of those same themes. If you have been working hard on some issues, the new teachers' thoughts may seem somewhat simple or unhelpful, and you may want to talk at a higher level.

This is another fundamental difference between art critiques and tests in other disciplines. Isn't it reasonable to assume that students can not only *accumulate* knowledge of their work, but *build* knowledge from easier to more difficult or complex problems? In physics, for example, a student may be asked about Newton in Freshman year, but she won't be asked again in Sophomore year and again in Junior year. Science, social science, the humanities—they all try to build, maybe not systematically or programmatically, but they try to move forward from year to year.

In studio art classes, you will probably revisit some themes over and over, as long as you stay in school. It's common to have to explain yourself again, from scratch, each time you have a critique. In part that's normal: everyone has to be able to present themselves to new people. But in part it's frustrating, because if you're working on a theme, or a set of formal problems, or a complicated project, then you probably don't need to go back to square one every time you show your work. I've had this experience from a student's point of view, and also as a teacher.

I've advised students who have difficult, complicated projects, and I have shared in the students' frustration as they have to explain the simplest parts of their work, over and over, each semester. It's as if an astronomer had to explain what a telescope was, again and again, instead of being able to talk about what she was actually doing with it.

Two assumptions in art schools work against the slow building-up of knowledge, and ensure that every new conversation begins from scratch.

A. It is thought that art is a *non-hierarchical activity*: that it needs to question itself fundamentally at each encounter, rather than building up patiently and rationally from its different starting points to more intricate kinds of practice and expression. (See the chapter on the Boot Camp Critique.) Very often art is non-hierarchical in that sense, and a lot of modernism and poststructuralism is built on assumptions like that. But it is not always true. Sometimes art practice is hierarchical, and understanding, knowledge, and expression build from year to year. PhD programs are structured like that, but BFA and MFA programs are usually a mixture of hierarchical and anti-hierarchical teaching.

B. It is said that the spontaneity of critiques allows for unexpected opinions that the student might not otherwise hear. Though that is certainly true, it is also the case that our thinking is not as inventive as we sometimes take it to be, and that many thoughts repeat other thoughts that have been articulated before. Often enough a student gets the same kind of critique semester after semester, as her teachers discover and rediscover the same qualities in her work. This kind of repetition is a self-fulfilling prophecy, because the conventions of spontaneous commentary do not promote the kind of teaching in which an advisor sits down with a student to research meanings and build on previous conclusions.

In Part Five of this book I will consider a kind of critique that tries to *build* meaning, but even in ordinary critiques there are various ways around this problem. You might begin your critique by listing some themes you have been considering, or things that you and your teachers have already covered. Then, if one of the themes appears in the conversation, you could say, "Yes, I have discussed that with my advisor, and it seems to us that your observation leads to the conclusion that…," and then you might add a request: "What *we* were wondering was…." That way you help people build on ideas you've already thought about. Without some sense of building, a critique can easily end up going over old territory. If you work with just one teacher, your conversations will move along (possibly not forward, but at least they'll move!), but if you have a new teacher and audience for each critique, you may have to do some work to make sure you're not reinventing the wheel each time.

Critiques Drift From Topic to Topic

During a critique, your teacher (or teachers) may skip unceremoniously from one subject to another, so it is not clear when one topic is finished and the next is underway. Some of the best exchanges drift in this sense, because people's thoughts evolve as they look; and it can be argued that some the best artworks inspire exactly this kind of wandering, metamorphic, "nomadic" thinking.[1] Nevertheless some drifting is inimical to rational argument. In particular there is a difference, crucial for the clarity of the critique, between a kind of drifting where your teacher divides her thoughts one from another and reports them in sequence, and a kind of drifting in which your teacher discovers her thoughts in the course of speaking. In the former, her thoughts may shift rapidly, but her sentences will be remade to fit their content. In the latter, half-formed ideas will overlap in sentence fragments, and her contributions may become hard to follow.

I call the first *reporting thoughts*: it's when you think of something to say, and then you say it. I call the second *discovering thoughts*: it's when you sort of know what you're going to say, and you launch into your speech, and find your way toward your thoughts while you're speaking.

The second kind of speaking is common in critiques because everyone is struggling to say the most interesting or insightful thing they can. In such an environment the contrast between *reporting* and *discovering* thoughts becomes unnaturally crisp. The difference is present in these two statements, both from a single critique:

A It seems to me that this is the first one of your pieces that's about incomprehension, or that leads me to incomprehension. There might have been, in some of the prints and earlier works… there might have been pieces on the left and the right that looked a lot like those. But in the middle one, there would have been a "third term" which you're invited to read as music, or a sentence, or as a class in a foreign language that you only understand when the class is over. And everything in between the first time and anything of yours that I've seen seems to say, "You will never understand this." Of course there's always the possibility here that you might.

B   I'm not quite sure what you're doing, how much of it is playful, how much of it has to do with the person. It seems to have all those qualities. I don't know how much you want to pin it down… a commentary on a tree, or…

Both speakers are groping for insights that they do not quite possess; but the first continues to speak as his thoughts form, and the result is nearly incomprehensible. The second speaker's thoughts are also changing, but each grammatical unit contains and expresses a comprehensible idea, even if it is only a hunch or a declaration of confusion. You can see this if you read one sentence at a time: speaker *B* makes sense, and speaker *A* doesn't. Speaker *B* has said something that can be immediately understood and built upon by subsequent speakers. Speaker *A*'s kind of drifting is really detrimental to the minute-by-minute sense of the critique.

Like most of the quotations in this book, this is a transcription of an actual critique at the School of the Art Institute of Chicago. I was speaker *A*, and when I first saw my words transcribed onto the page, I couldn't understand them myself. In a minute I remembered what I had been trying to say, and I could see how I was thinking ahead to something new while I was still talking about a previous thought. I'm sure what I said was totally useless to the student.

If this were all there is to the problem, it would be enough to say you should listen to see whether your teacher's thoughts come out in discrete units or all chained together. But it's more complicated than that, because a speaker who composes his thoughts while he speaks might say something that *sounds like* a complete thought, but is really a kind of rough draft for some other thought that is still not quite comprised into sentences.

In the following example one instructor seems to be asking a single question, but as the exchange progresses it appears that she is drifting from one subject to another, working out her thoughts as she goes. Her first question seems pretty clear, until it becomes apparent that she didn't really mean it—or rather, she meant something larger, and the first question was just a way of starting out. I have annotated the critique in the right column to show how the topics shift.

The work they're discussing is a group of gestural abstract paintings by a student named Chris Fennell.[2] (In this transcript he is speaker B.) Here is one of his paintings:

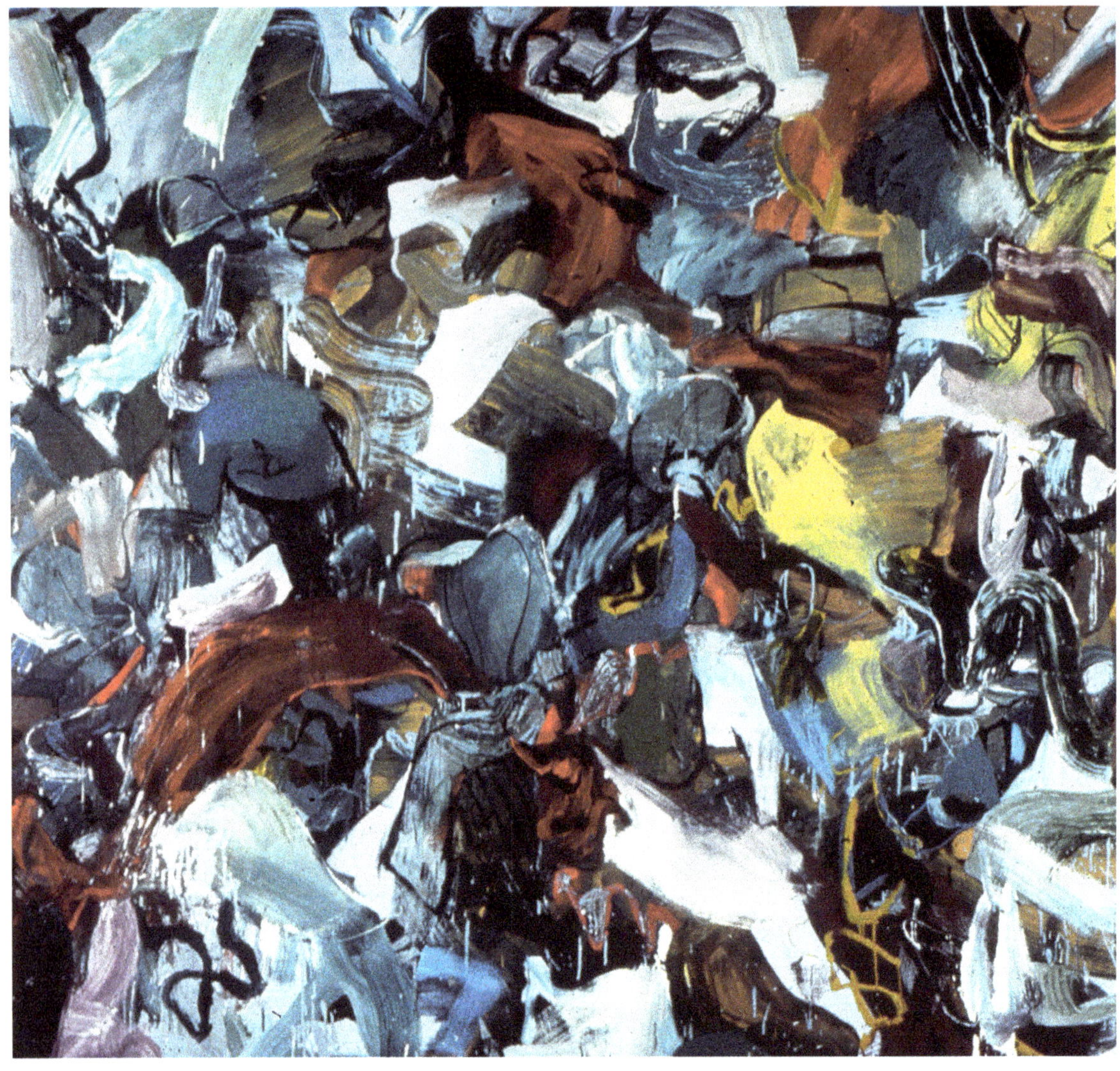

A	Do you give titles? Individually or as a group?	*At first the question seems to be a straightforward request for information.*
B	No, not yet.	
A	Will they, though?	
B	Eventually, probably. Eventually, I mean that's more associative, I'll just sit down with my wife, get a six-pack, and start thinking about it. […]	
A	I'm curious… the reason I ask is, how do you see the attitude of the paintings? There's a sort of temperature, or an attitude to them. It is like—maybe I'm not making my question clear—I'm speaking of temperament, how do you see the temperament of the paintings.	*Now it seems as if the question was loaded, and the teacher is really wondering about something she saw in the paintings. That "something" is not at all clear, it seems, to the teacher herself. Perhaps it is an "attitude" or a "temperament" that might be explained in a title.*
B	Probably pretty much like myself. Hyperactive. Sort of hyperactive, but analytical in a way, in terms of the—	*Chris, the student, does not address the teacher's implication that the paintings are double-entendres, that they might not be straightforward and serious. He is just explaining his character.*

A	—Are they ironic at all? Do you see them as ironic?	*The teacher asks again, this time implying more forcibly that the paintings have an "attitude": Do you realize that your paintings are ironic?*
B	No. I can see where they have elements of that, perhaps. Sort of [...] in juxtaposition [...], especially the irony of a certain kind of stroke, and then you have this real artificial stroke, like in that one, the sort of candy cane aspect—	*Chris has a specific answer for the question of irony: to him it means a contrast of "artificial" and natural marks.*
A	Yes.	
B	—of the silver [paint]. But I—	
A	But my question revolves around the use of materials, and attitudes that seem very preconceived, a [will] of the painting, so to speak, as opposed to a painting that wound through the landscape, a sensuous aspect of it. [...]	*The teacher is not speaking of that kind of contrast. It now seems (if the student had time to think back to the previous comments) as if the words "temperament" and "attitude" were attempts to describe something "preconceived" and rigid in the paintings, which is contrasted against something exploratory and "sensuous." Her questions are doing two things at once: seeking to clarify (perhaps to herself) the nature of the "temperament," and asking if its is intentional.*

	I'm just asking a question, wondering how you're thinking about your paintings.	*This is what is really important. Not precisely what is going on in the paintings but whether the artist is in control of those qualities.*
B	I don't think I feel that ironic about them; I'm not trying to make a statement about the futility of painting or something. That would be—	*Chris has reinterpreted the word "irony" in light of the teacher's last remark about the "will" of his painting that won't let go in a "sensuous" way. Perhaps he is thinking that she means painting is futile unless it will let go.*
A	I meant more perhaps in a more humorous—	*The teacher redefines her position, and substitutes humor for irony and the other terms.*
B	You mean like Lichtenstein, like the Lichtenstein brushstroke?	
A	A little bit.	
B	Humor, I think, is an aspect of it, because I think there are elements of these that are funny.	*Though Chris agrees...*
A	Yes.	

B	Because there's really something, if you think about it, stupid, about making this gestural brushstroke and then this preconceived thing next to it. But I think those things give each other a kind of vitality that's hard [to top] within the painting; that's really why I was doing things like that, and it's not—	*…he explains by citing the same example he had used as an example of irony in his painting.* *—perhaps this would have continued, "not a matter of 'irony' or 'humor'."*
A	Is that pretty much a process in your painting, that there will be something more spontaneous, and then a response to it? A more literal response to it?	*The contrast is reformulated again, this time as "spontaneous" and "literal."*
B	Definitely.	*This particular exchange ends far from where it started. These latest terms do not resolve or include the many intermediate concepts.*

This dialogue is between one faculty member and the student; the more common, and more confusing, exchanges occur when several teachers are talking in succession, interrupting each other as they discover their own meanings and those of the other instructors.

Drifting is inevitable whenever people have not thought out their reactions in advance of the moment they begin a sentence. It can be creative, and also difficult to understand. Your best bet is to take notes, or record the critique, so that you can review it afterward and try to distinguish *reported thoughts* from *discovered thoughts*.

That Critique Room

Everyone who spends enough time in art critiques and artists' studios knows they can be really awful. A typical critique room is either a classroom, with rows of work tables or desks or chairs; or else it's a "crit space," a dedicated room with sheet rock walls and metal frames for hanging things from the ceiling. Usually the floor is industrial hardened concrete, spattered and stained. The light may be natural, but it

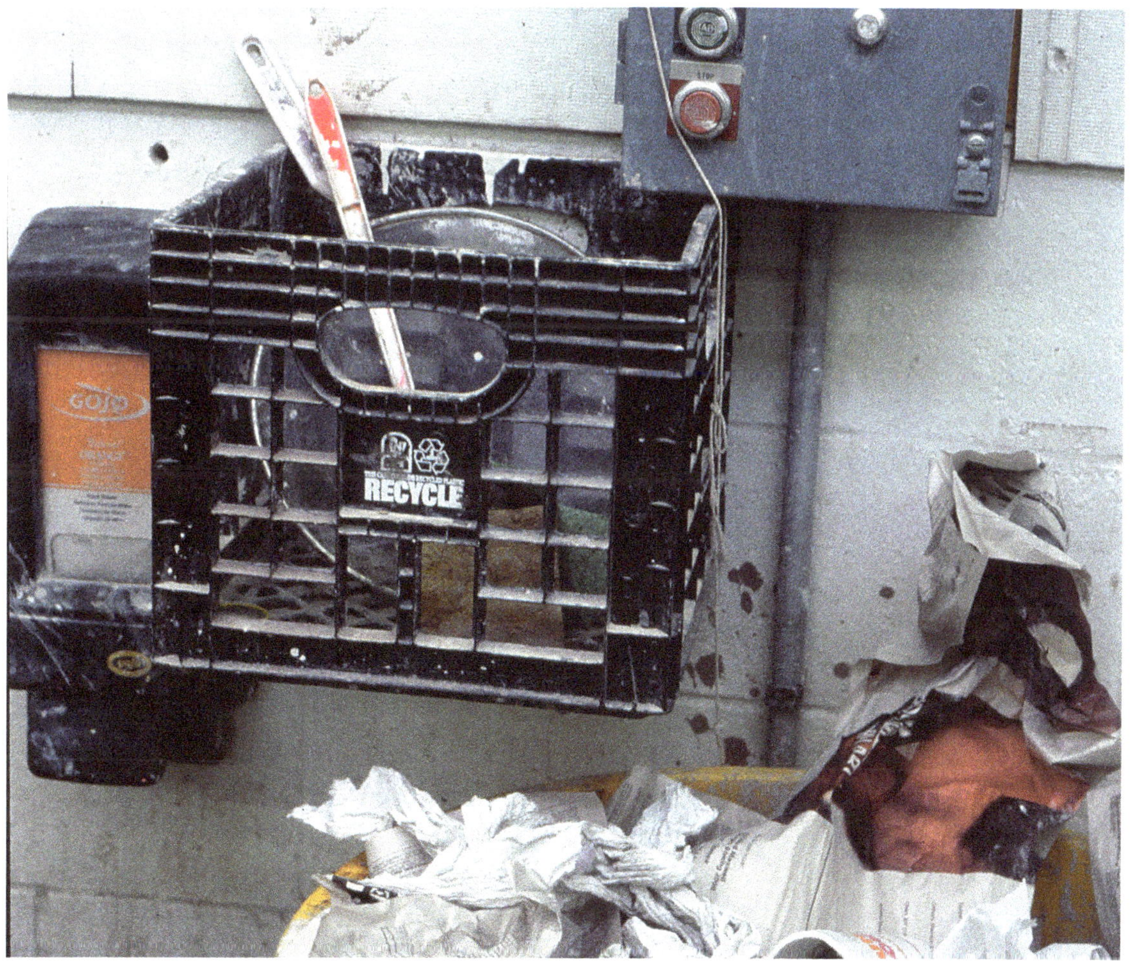

isn't always, and it's often bright and harsh. The walls have dozens of coats of white paint. If the critique space is a common area, like in a ceramics studio or a painting studio, there will also be pots, paints, overflowing sinks, stained curtains, rickety easels, and all sorts of supplies in boxes and shelves. Dust will be everywhere.

Why do I mention this? Because the room isn't irrelevant. In art, everything counts. Take note of the light in the room: see where it's coming from, and whether it is warm or cold. Have a look at the walls: can you pretend they're fresh and new, or will you have to ask your teachers to ignore them? A depressing room will affect your work and the critique, and it is probably a good idea to just come out and say it. An industrial-looking room will have a subtle effect on people's idea of your work, and so will a room that looks too domestic, or too capitalist, or too neat.

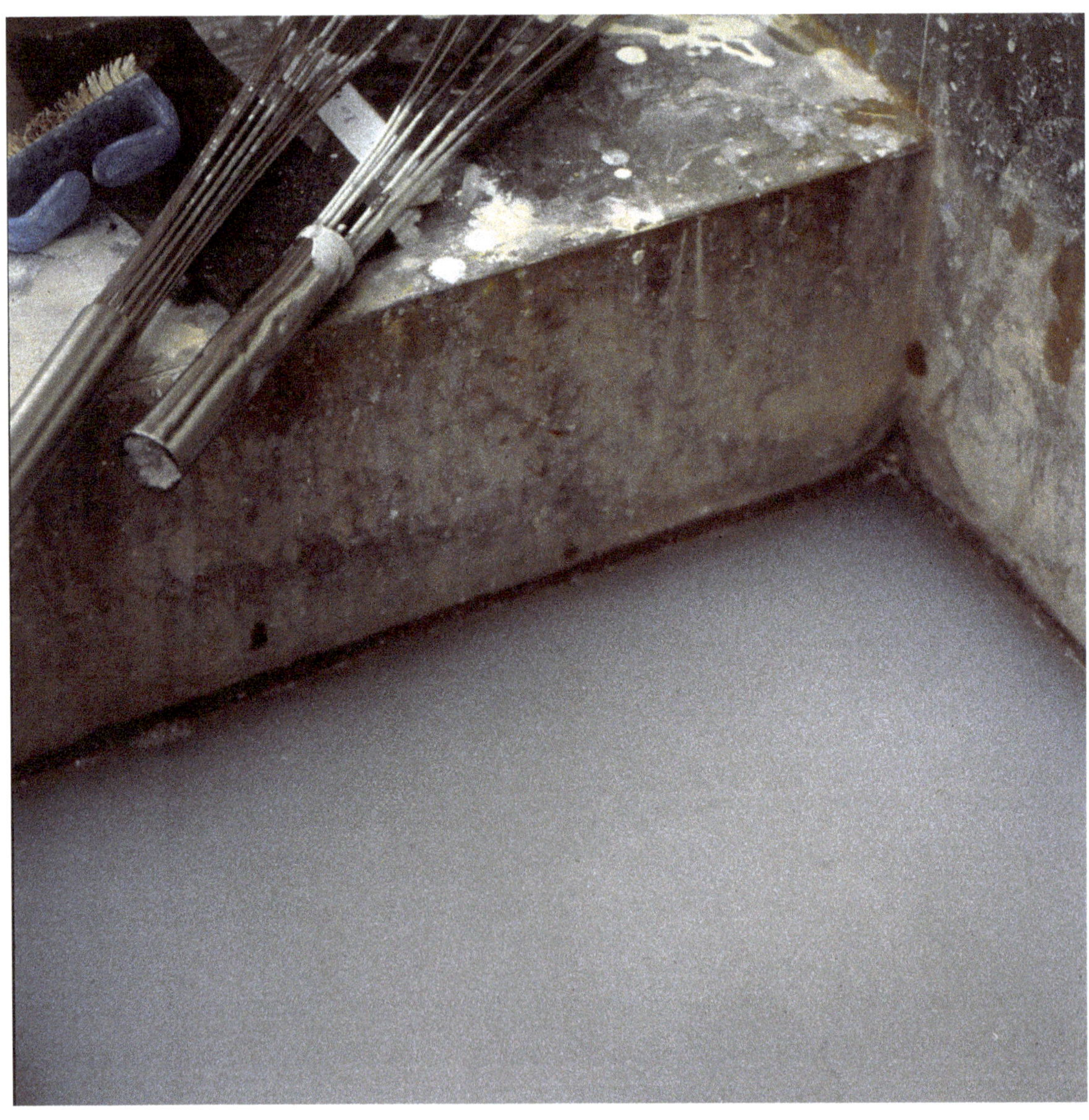

And don't forget to think about where people will sit or stand during your critique. If you're being critiqued in a classroom, everyone will be comfortable, but that is not necessarily a good thing: it usually means people will be sitting a good distance away from your work. They will be less animated, and more likely to behave like we all do in big classes. Personally, I don't like critiques in classrooms. There's something odd, I think, about the idea of people sitting at desks looking at artwork—as if art was some bureaucratic or administrative project that could be judged by office workers. It is best if everyone is in a small studio space, or a cleared-away area, and people are encouraged to walk, stand, and even lie on the floor. The space should be as dynamic as the conversation. Chairs are for church.

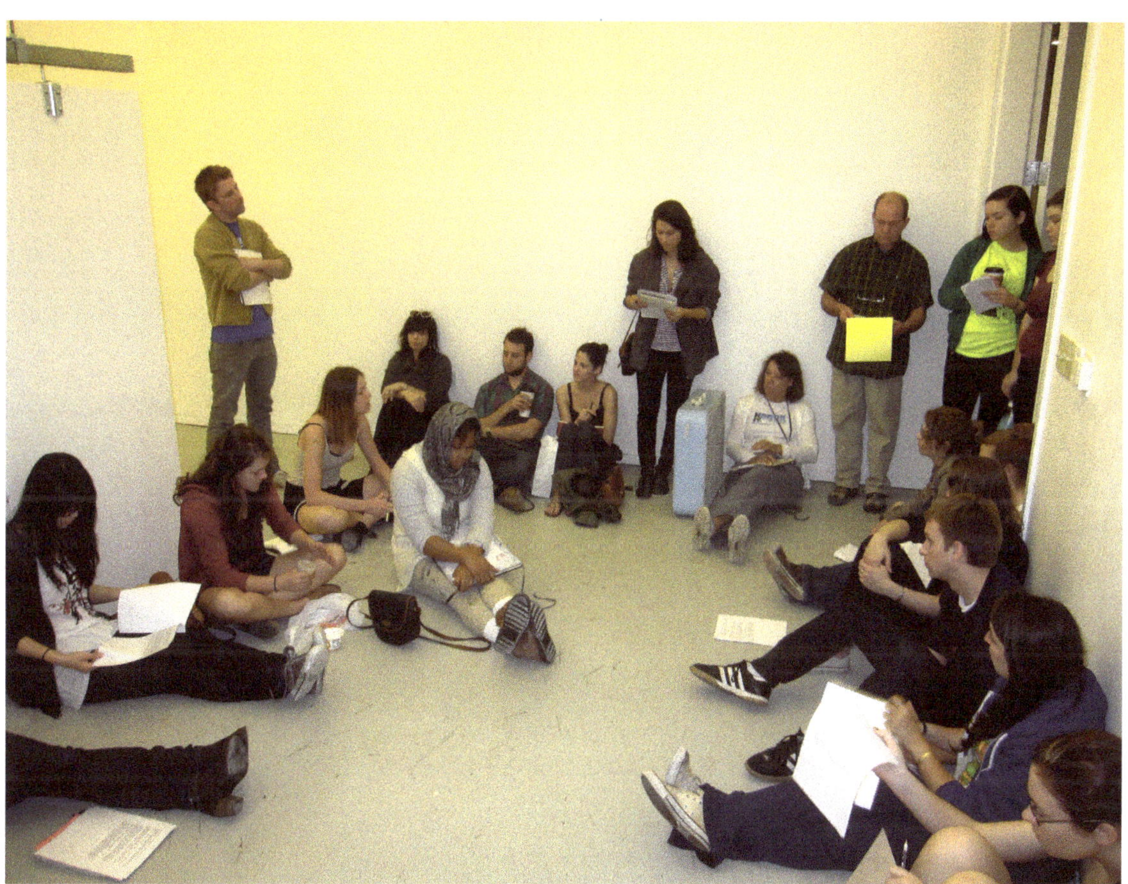

And that's all I have to say under the heading "BFA Issues." As I said at the beginning, there is no clear distinction between BFA and MFA critiques, so there is no way to round up the issues that pertain only to the undergraduate experience. But these, I think, are among the most common.

Part Three

MFA Issues

<h1 style="text-align:center">28</h1>

What if You Make Very Different Kinds of Work?

You make life easier on your teachers if you have just one style of work. That generally helps them focus on the differences between individual artworks. It's usually much harder, from a teacher's point of view, to deal with work that is very diverse. A student named Chris Campe showed four different kinds of work in her critique. First, she showed architectural drawings, like the one below.

She had made these extremely carefully, without using a straightedge. If you looked at them very closely, you saw they were freehand, and they seemed tremendously skillful. They were also empty, and somewhat sad, and very impersonal.

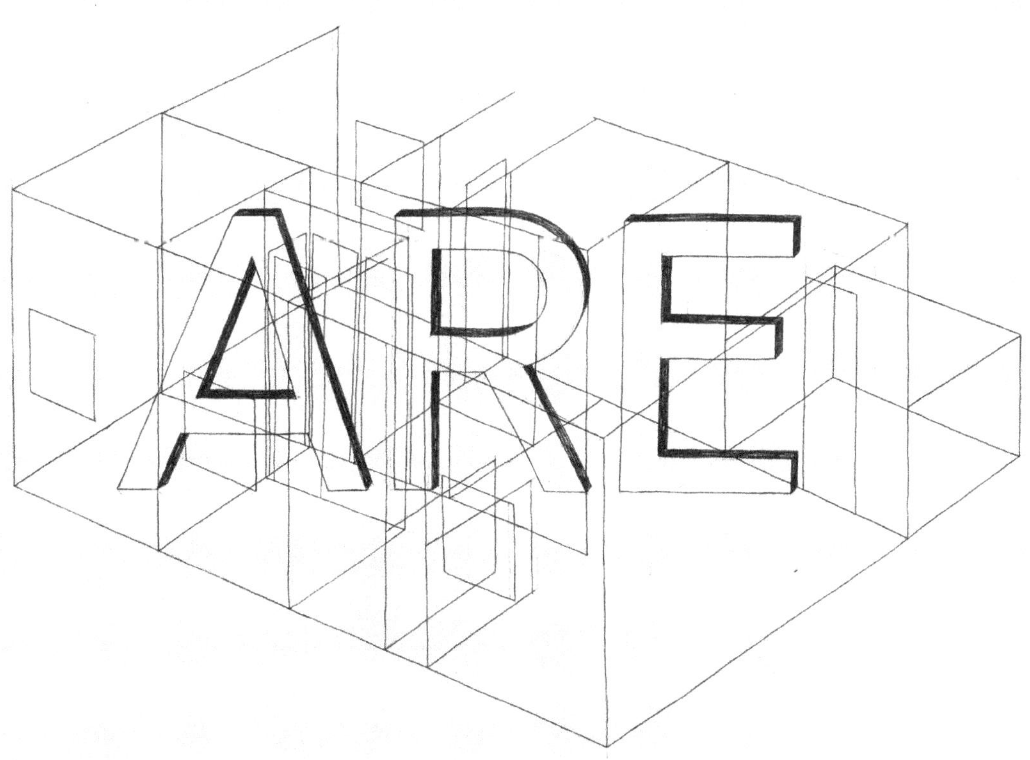

She also showed some life drawings, most of them done on small sheets of paper, about five inches high. She said she could only draw people when they were around, and she also made drawings in seminars and classrooms.

On another wall she had put up complicated drawings full of words and images. These drawings had all sorts of things going on: diagrams, parts of sentences and slogans in English and German, and life drawings. Chris was excellent at drawing fonts, and the drawings mimicked everything from signage to handwriting.

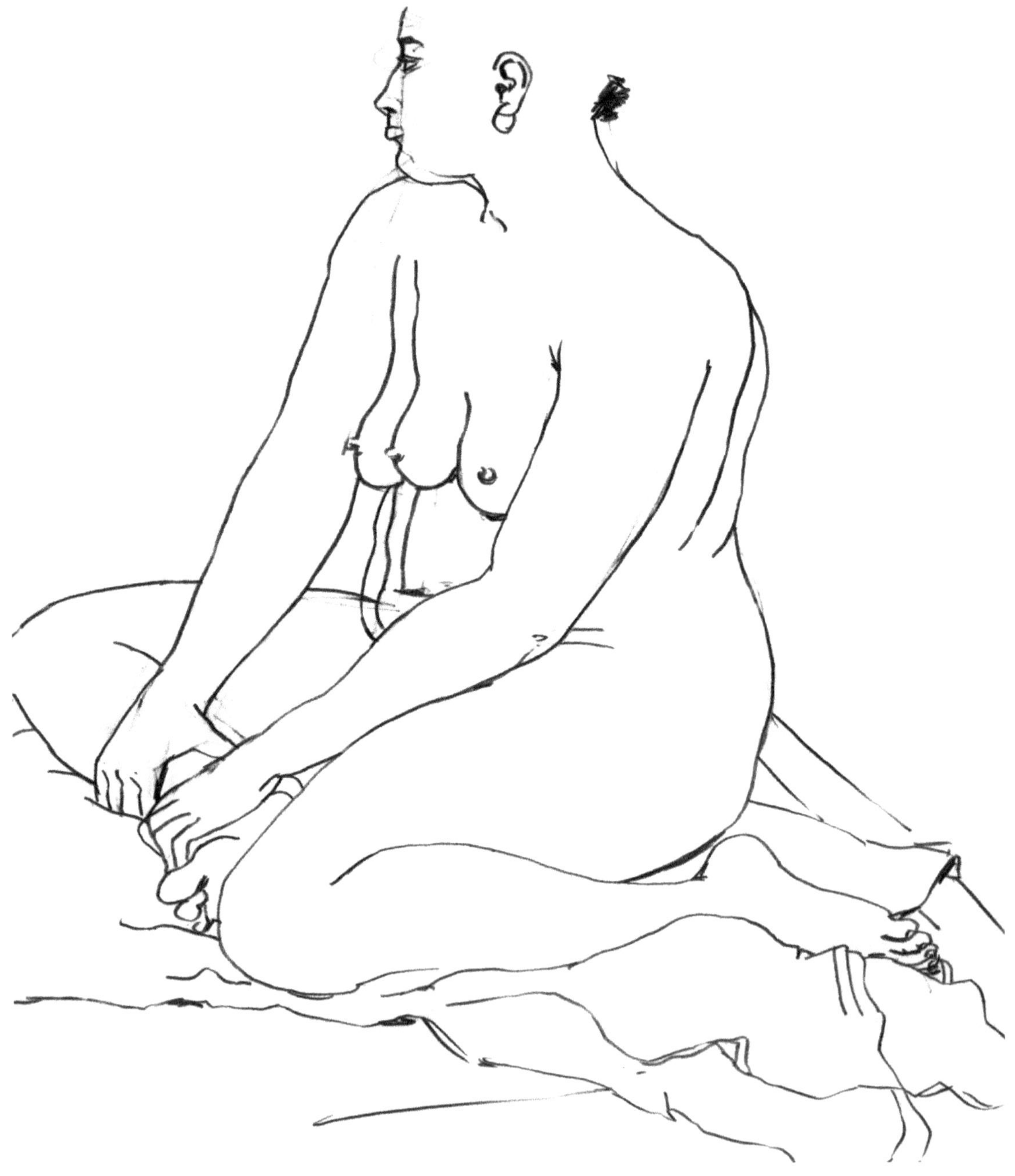

As part of another critique, she read an academic paper she had written, asking whether or not there is such a thing a queer life drawing. She had gone to a "Radical Queer Semaine [week]" in Montréal, and she had participated in a queer life drawing

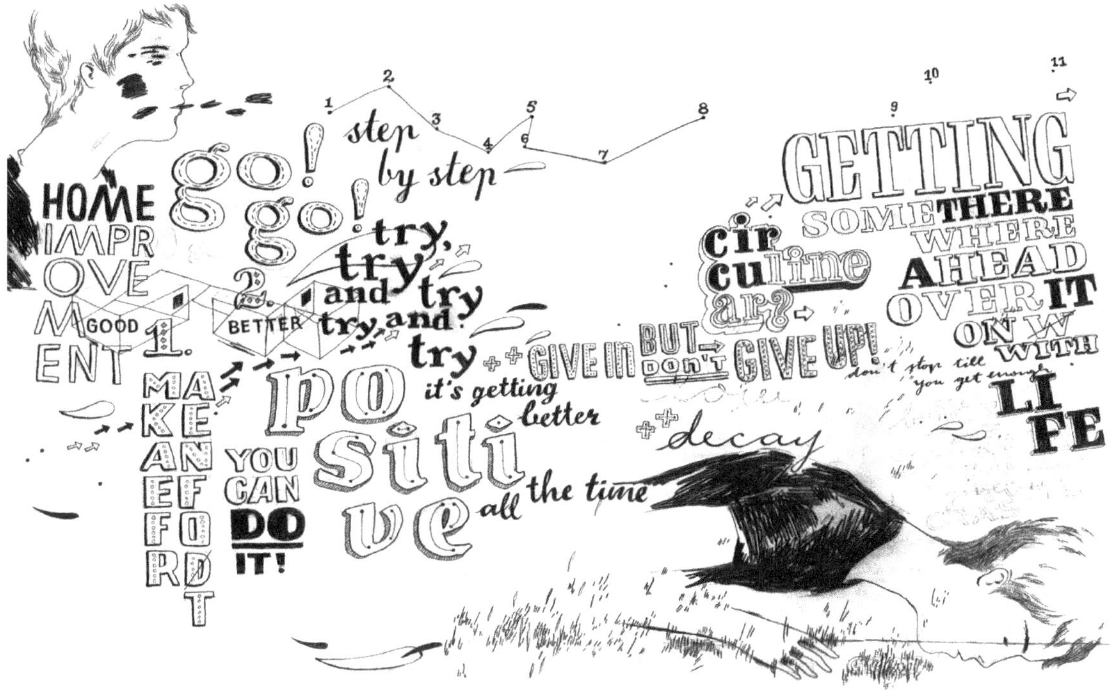

class. She did not think that class was queer in any interesting way, and her paper was a meditation on what might queer the institution of life drawing. "One of my drawings," she wrote, "shows a female figure with three breasts—for the simple reason that the first two were not in the right spot. So, is that a representation of a queer body? Or is it just a lack of drawing skills? My inability to get the proportions 'right' made me wonder whether technically bad drawings are in fact queer drawings." It was a meditative, open-ended paper, full of historical and theoretical research, and it changed the way I saw the life drawings.

So: four kinds of work, each different from the others. Chris is hardly an extreme example of this. Over the years, I've seen work so diverse that I actually, literally didn't believe that a single student had done it all. When things get that extreme, the faculty may mistrust the student, or wonder if the student has psychological issues that cannot be adequately addressed in a critique. Chris is a more average example.

If you show some work that is quiet, austere and nearly abstract, and other work that is loud and full of forms, then the faculty will have to work to create a story about you that will encompass both modes. If, in addition, you also write, sing, or act, then the divergence becomes even greater, and the faculty might be even more challenged. (Sometimes very diverse work really does hang together, and then the critique can be easy; I am thinking of times when the work doesn't seem to cohere.)

Why is a diverse body of work potentially a problem? Because one of the deepest ideas of the critique, and also of art instruction at the college level and beyond, is that the teacher's responsibility is to help the student artist find a voice, a manner, a style, a mode, that is all her own. The very idea of a critique is founded on a notion from nineteenth century Romanticism: an artist's work is an expression of her sensibility—her perspective, psyche, subjectivity, identity. The entire point of artistic practice, from a Romantic standpoint, is that the artist is a single cohesive spirit, and that the artwork expresses that spirit—that singular mind, that sensitivity,

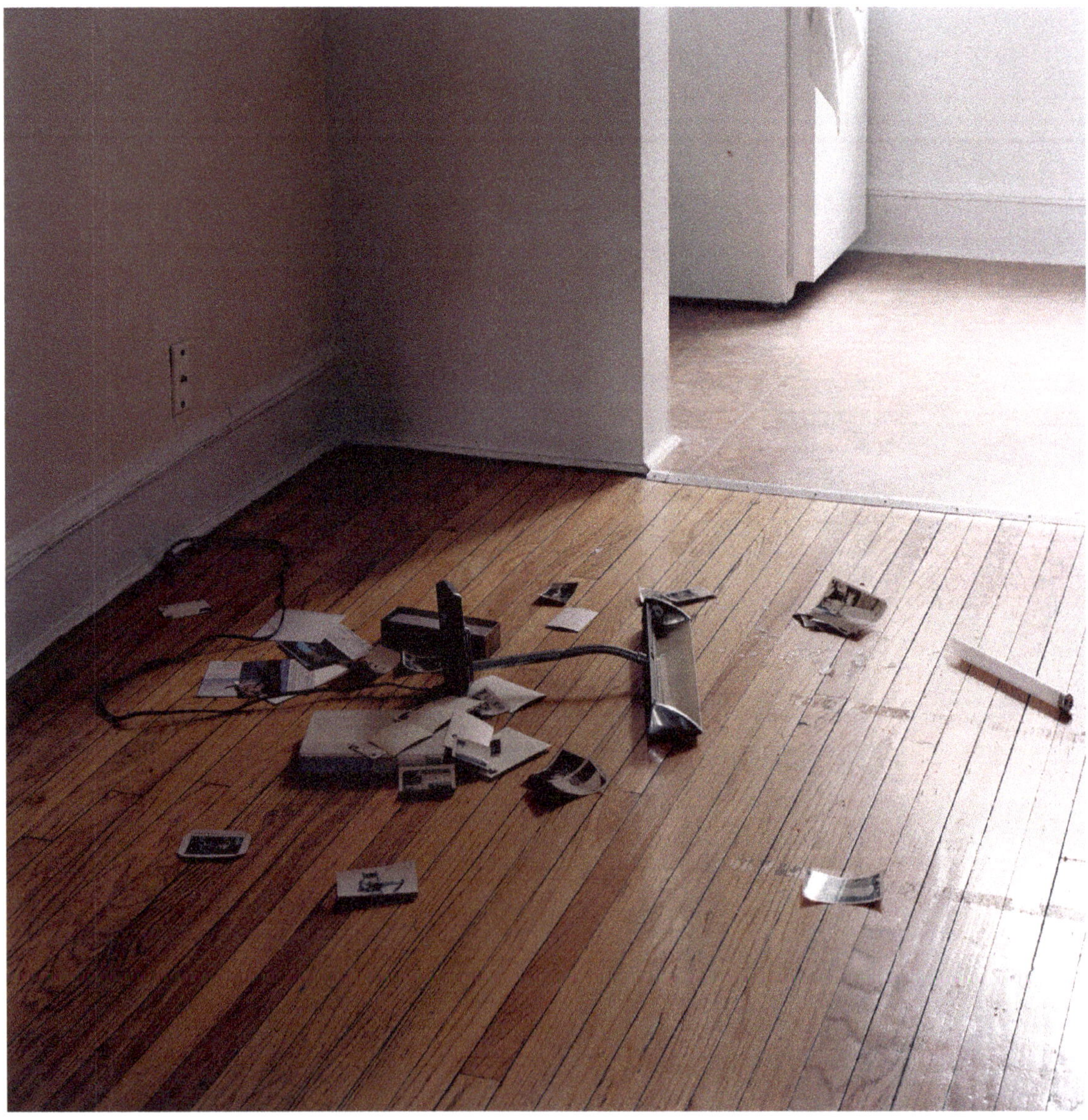

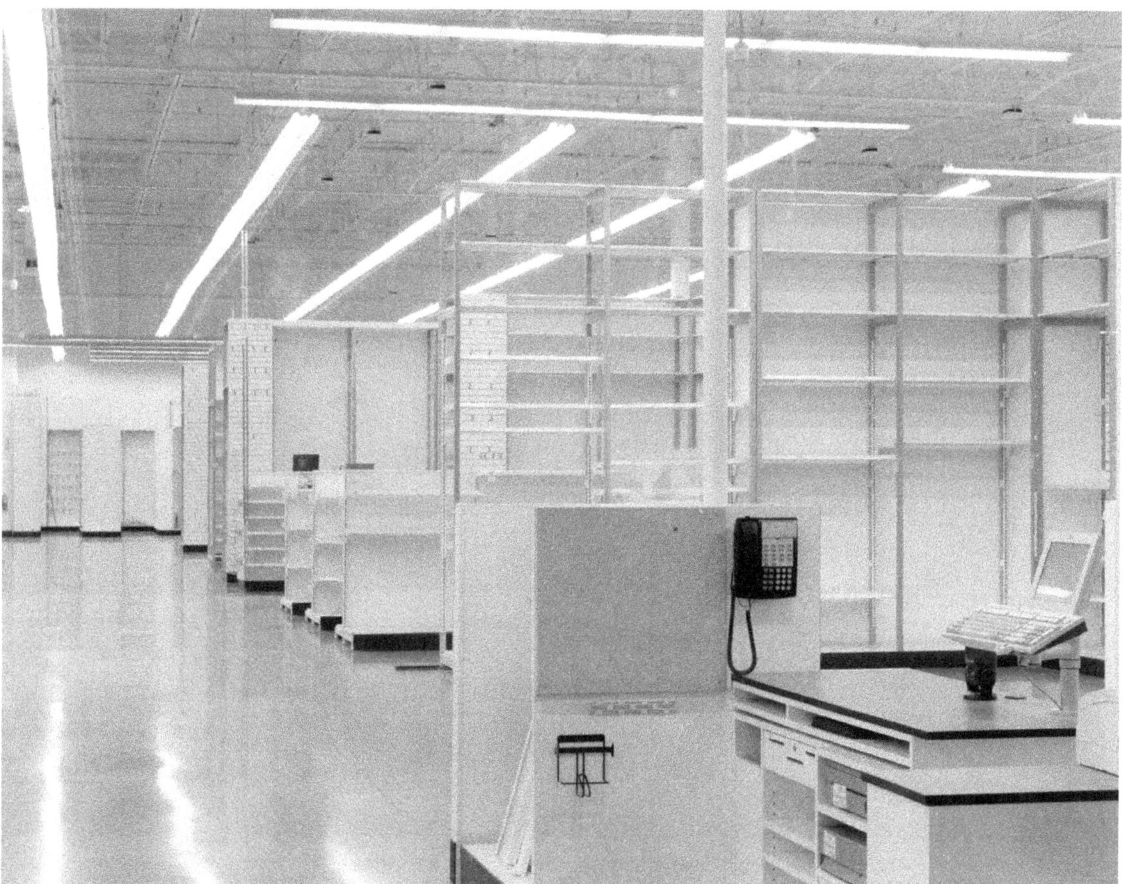

that sensibility. (This is a fundamental point about art education, which I'm only touching on here: German Romanticism is the origin of the one-on-one critique, the master class, and much of the MFA.[1]) Therefore a body of work that seems to be doing different things presents severe difficulties in the critique setting. (Sometimes a diverse body of work is just what the instructors are looking for. If a student's work has been too narrow, then evidence of experimentation is great. But I am not concerned with those possibilities here. The deeper goal, especially as the work progresses toward the MFA and PhD, is to help the young artist find her voice.)

In Chris's case, the instructors who were in the critiques with me focused on one aspect of her work or another. Naturally, some responded to the austere architectural drawings, where no human life—and no shadows, and no furniture, and no color—interrupts the silent emptiness. Others responded to the themes of queer identity, and others liked the busy and lively experiments in typography and handwriting.

If you are working in several different modes or styles or media, you might consider several possibilities:

1. It might be that one of your styles or media is close to what you really care about, and the others might be things you do just because you have time, or you can,

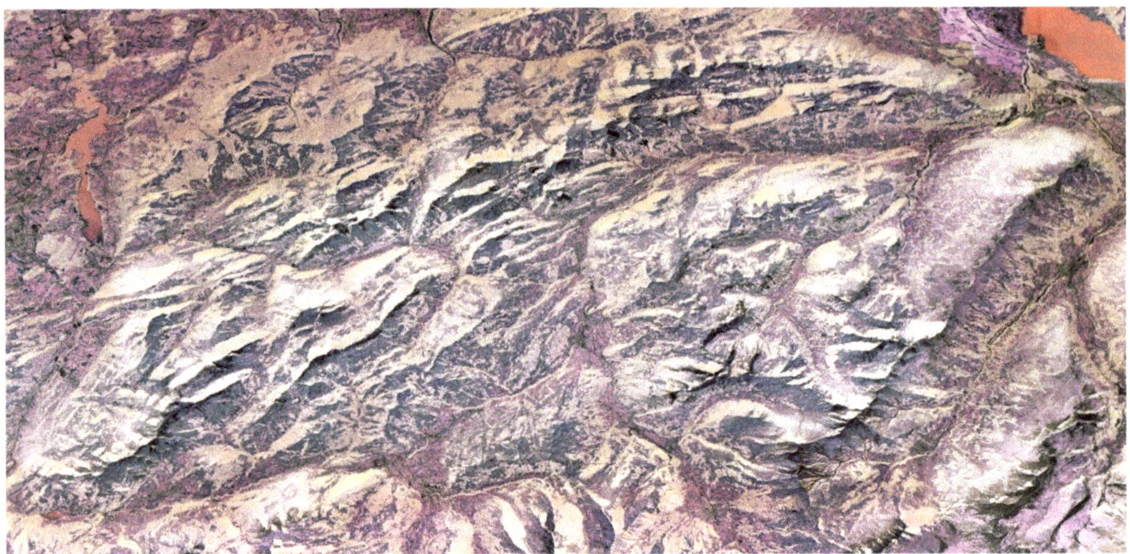

or you're experimenting, or because you've been praised for them in the past. You might consider letting them go, and concentrating on what means the most to you. If you feel this might be the case, then you could ask your instructors to help you choose which works seem to have more potential, and which might be put aside.

2. It may also be that you are divided, as a person, as a personality. You might find your art moves in several directions at once, and you can't see how they're connected. In that case you might want to continue to pursue several very different paths at once. If you feel this way about your art, it's a good idea to ask your instructors to judge you that way. That will save a lot of time, because otherwise your instructors will naturally try to find the common ground between your different practices. Your instructors will in effect be thinking like Romantics—just because that is the commonest way of thinking about the relation between art and an artist.

3. Or you might feel that the different kinds of work you make are all actually united. In this case it would be good to listen especially carefully in critiques, because if instructors and other students don't think your work is coherent, then that coherence might not be making it out of your head and onto the canvas, film, or screen. Listen, in your critiques, for moments when people say, "Oh, I could see that the painting and the film belong together, but only because you told me." That kind of judgment points to a disconnect between what you feel you're doing and what you're actually producing.

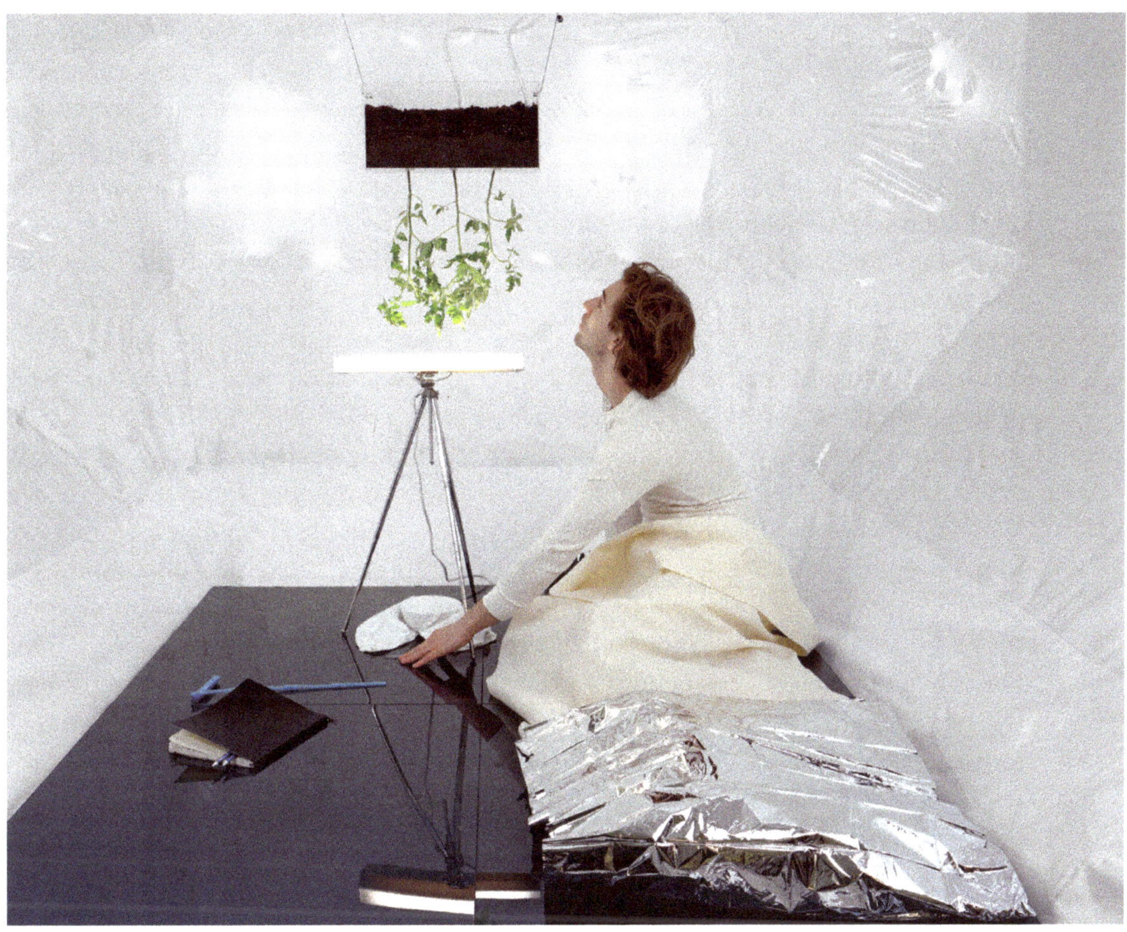

My sense of Chris's work is that it's more like the second or third option than the first one. Her challenge is to create work that will persuade viewers that every mode and style is *necessary* to convey the person she is.

Here is a second example, which belongs more to the first of these three modes. The student, Sean Lamoureux, showed five photographs, printed at least 20" wide.[2] The first showed the corner of a room, with a broken desk lamp, some photographs, and a book in a box. (See the photo a couple of pages back.) A second showed a brightly lit office space, with no one in it. A third, which was the biggest print in the room (it took up the entire back wall of the critique space) was a grainy satellite image of mountains, printed a garish magenta. Then there was a photograph of the student himself, lying under a space blanket, inside some kind of soft plastic structure, looking up at some hydroponically grown tomato plants that were hanging upside-down. And last there was a photograph of something resembling a Buckminster Fuller dome, in a dark landscape.

These five photographs baffled the teachers in the critique. One of us asked him what he was thinking of, and he said his themes included architecture, environments, and environmentalism. The pictures were all cleanly printed, and when we asked if they'd been digitally manipulated he said that he'd invented the dark shape in the landscape, but that he'd arranged and posed the self-portrait and the broken lamp.

Essentially, the panel gave up on thinking of Sean as an artist who had a single theme or idea. Despite the fact that the work was all photography, and most of it was printed in the large format that signals serious art photography (and hints at large-format cameras), it didn't hang together. The panel drifted into talking about one image after another, separately. Some teachers had ideas about the self-portrait; others liked the anonymous office space.

My own take on all this was that Sean was influenced by different streams of contemporary photography. The picture of the broken lamp reminded me of Jeff Wall's carefully posed and arranged photographs, where everything is supposed to look random. The office space reminded me of Thomas Demand's photographs of paper constructions that look like office space. The satellite image reminded me of Andreas Gursky's enormous prints of interiors. The posed picture reminded me of Wall's figural compositions that were inspired by academic paintings. And the polyhedral structure reminded me of any number of photographs of strange structures, starting with the Bechers' water towers. I said I thought that given the tightly contested field of contemporary fine art photography, Sean should give more thought to which of the various practices suited him best. Otherwise, I thought, critics would continue to say what I'd just said: that he hadn't made up his mind yet which mode of contemporary photography was best suited to him.

For me, this is an example of a student who hasn't quite decided how he is situated in relation to a smorgasbord of choices. It's a typical problem, which begins as soon as you become aware of the range of possibilities, and continues on through the MFA, and sometimes into the PhD and onward. Many artists never quite solve it. In theory, BFA programs are supposed to foster experimentation, and MFA programs are supposed to help students find their voice, their mode, manner, or style. But life doesn't always work out that way.

Note the difference between the two students. Chris chooses to work in several distinct modes; she may be a person who naturally thinks and works in different ways, as in the second or third of my three options. Sean hasn't so much chosen as been carried along into different practices, as in my first option; he may be an artist who has more of a single mode, but he hasn't found it yet.

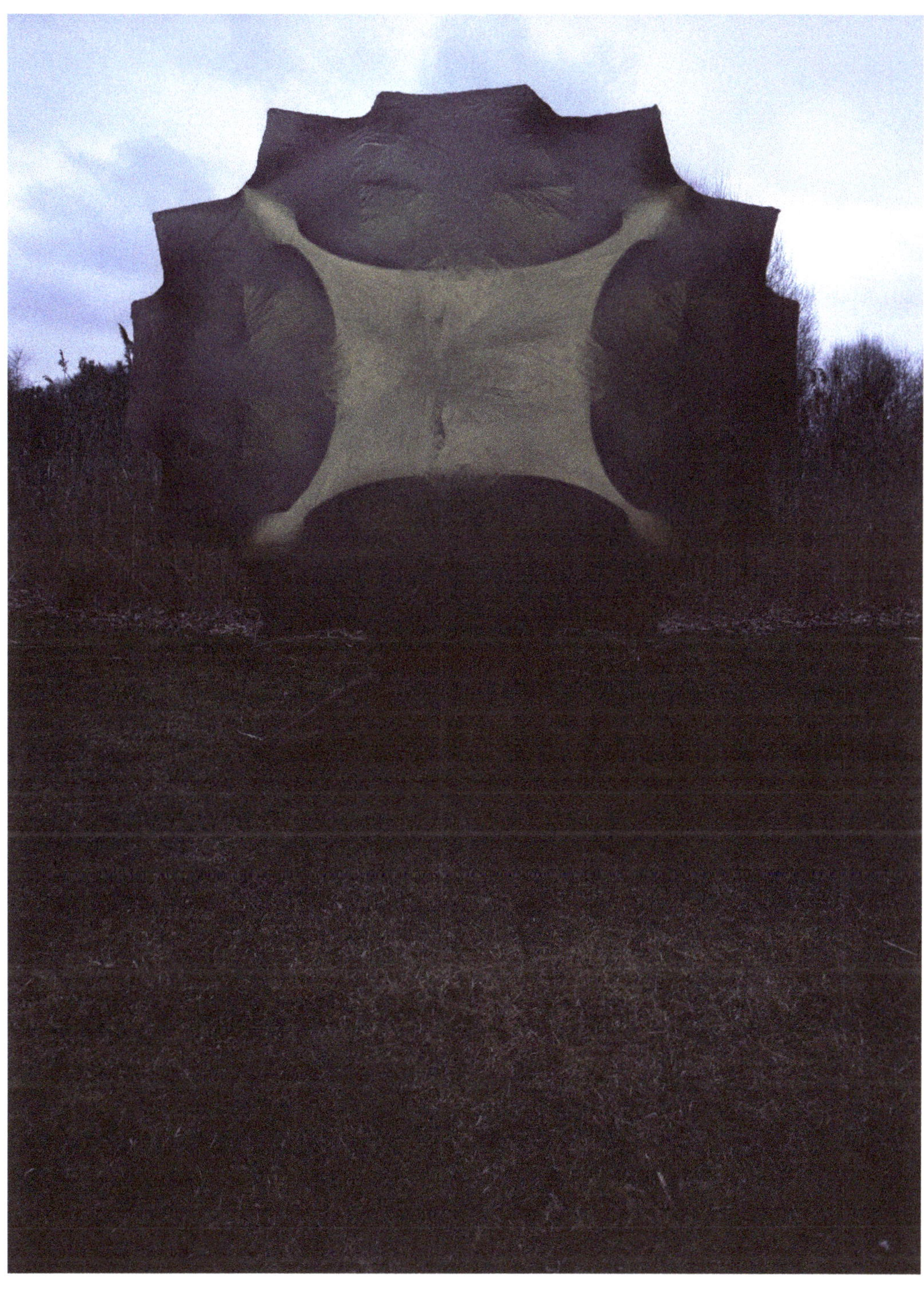

29

Managing Interdisciplinary Critiques

Some departments and some art schools and academies have *interdisciplinary critiques*, meaning that some of the faculty who respond to your work will be in other fields. If you're a sculptor, you may have a critique with an instructor who is a painter, or a composer; if you're a designer, you may have a critique with someone who is a filmmaker or a ceramist. That sort of critique requires flexibility and openness.

Here, for example, is an architecture project. The student was assigned the project of designing a community center. She produced plans, elevations, maps, and other graphics, which she tacked up on a wall, and she also made some small-scale models out of balsa. (That is a fairly standard kind of architecture presentation.)

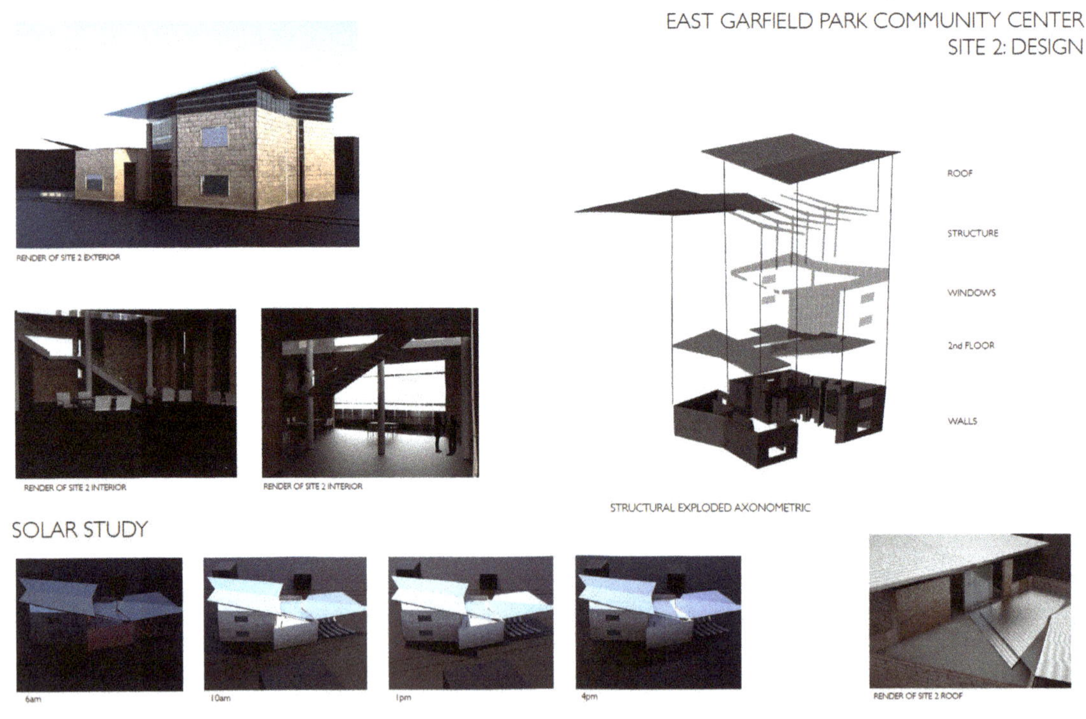

Alexandra Helene Copan, design for a community center near East Garfield Park, Chicago. 2011.

This is a very much reduced image of one of the sheets she printed out and put on the wall. It shows the building she designed, an exploded view, two interior views, a study of how the sunlight would look at four different times of day, and (at the bottom right) a close-up of part of the roof.

She also showed several plans, one of the ground floor, and one of the second floor (see opposite page).

If her critique had been in the architecture department, she would have been asked about all sorts of technical things. Her roof design, for example, is somewhat complicated. If you look on the exploded view, you can see it is in two parts. Between them is a rooftop garden. But on the second-floor plan, it is hard to picture how the roof attaches. An instructor might ask about that, and give the student advice about how to use the software more effectively. An architecture department critique might also point out that these images use very fine lines, and are hard to see at a distance. (When I was sitting in this critique, about ten feet away from the graphics, I could barely see some of the detail.) An architecture professor might say it would be good to light up those two somewhat small and dreary-looking interior views (in the first image, middle row, on the left), in order to make a greater impact on a potential client.

Those sorts of comments are based on professional experience: the architecture faculty will know the software, the engineering, and the politics of presentation. If it's an interdisciplinary critique, the entire conversation might be different. A photography professor might say the 3-D view (in the first image, at the top left) looks weirdly artificial, like a cheap video game. A painter might not want to try to decipher the plans and elevations at all. She might react to the printouts as if they were formal compositions. I had a different reaction: I noticed that the "amphitheater" is open to the public, even though this building was proposed for a poor part of the city, where there is no public outdoor seating, so that homeless people were fairly sure to colonize the seats.

An interdisciplinary critique has the virtue of changing the terms of the conversation. It has the drawback of sometimes producing incoherent conversations that are less than helpful from a student's point of view. If you're in an interdisciplinary critique, one of the best things to do is to imagine it as a test for a real-life opening, because in real life, outside the classroom, comments can reveal a far greater range of reactions than you may be used to in your own department or medium.

Here is that idea using the metaphor of a spectrum.

The full spectrum of interpretations includes stray comments on all sorts of subjects, made by people with varying degrees of interest and knowledge. (Top half of the diagram on the second page following.) Within the medium or department comments can be much more detailed (bottom). I have drawn two lines in the middle part of the spectrum to suggest that in this case, the comments in the field are highly focused.

This isn't a criticism of architecture critiques. Sometimes it makes excellent sense for a department or a medium to keep focused, especially if it's a highly technical field, and none of the comments I put in the top half of this chart would be unwelcome in an architecture critique. But it helps to be aware of the flavor of the department's preferred sorts of criticism. Listen for the kinds of questions your instructors tend to ask, and note which kinds of comments are generally absent.

An interdisciplinary critique can be very useful, because it can make you aware that your department or medium has a style, a set of habits, customs, or expectations,

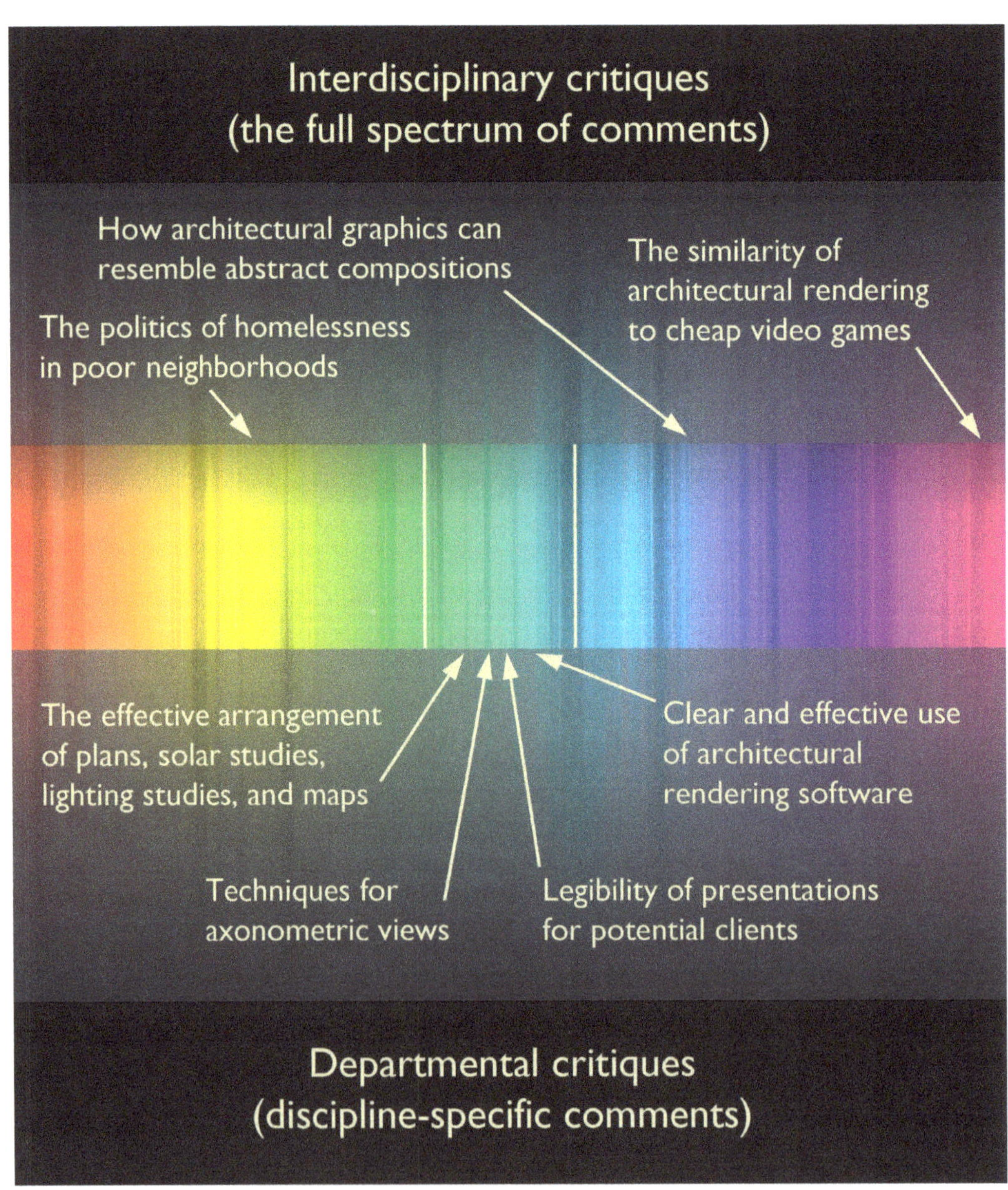

EAST GARFIELD PARK COMMUNITY CENTER
SITE 2: FIRST FLOOR

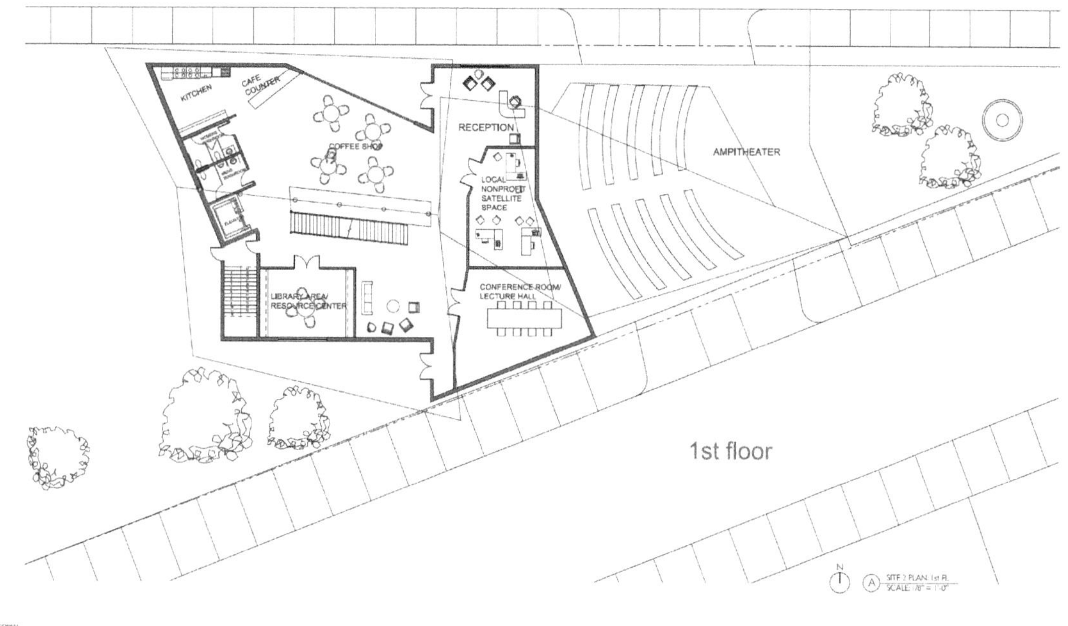

EAST GARFIELD PARK COMMUNITY CEN
SITE 2: SECOND FL

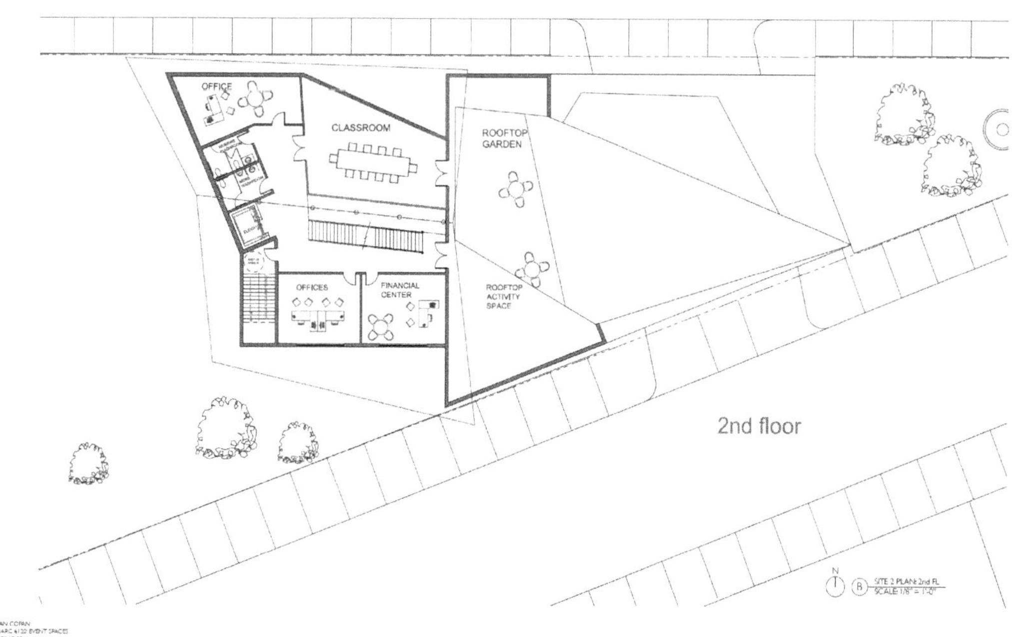

and they're different from other departments or media. In large art schools and academies, departments can grow apart from one another, until they have entirely distinct ways of speaking, like dialects or even different languages. For some years, the Photography Department where I teach was strongly psychoanalytic. Students were likely to be asked about their desires, their feelings for their family, and their hidden motivations. Meanwhile, the Ceramics Department was strongly formal: there was a lot of talk about what makes vessels different from art objects, and how to manage glazes. If you were a student in the Ceramics Department, you could make a clay object in the shape of a grotesque purple head, and your faculty might not mention how creepy it was. On the other hand, if you were a student in the Photography Department, you might take an abstract photo of a dark room and be asked why you felt such anxiety about the world. Things change, and both departments are very different now.

It's helpful to keep interdisciplinary critiques in mind, because otherwise the way of talking in your part of the art world may begin to seem like it's just the normal way of talking in the entire art world.

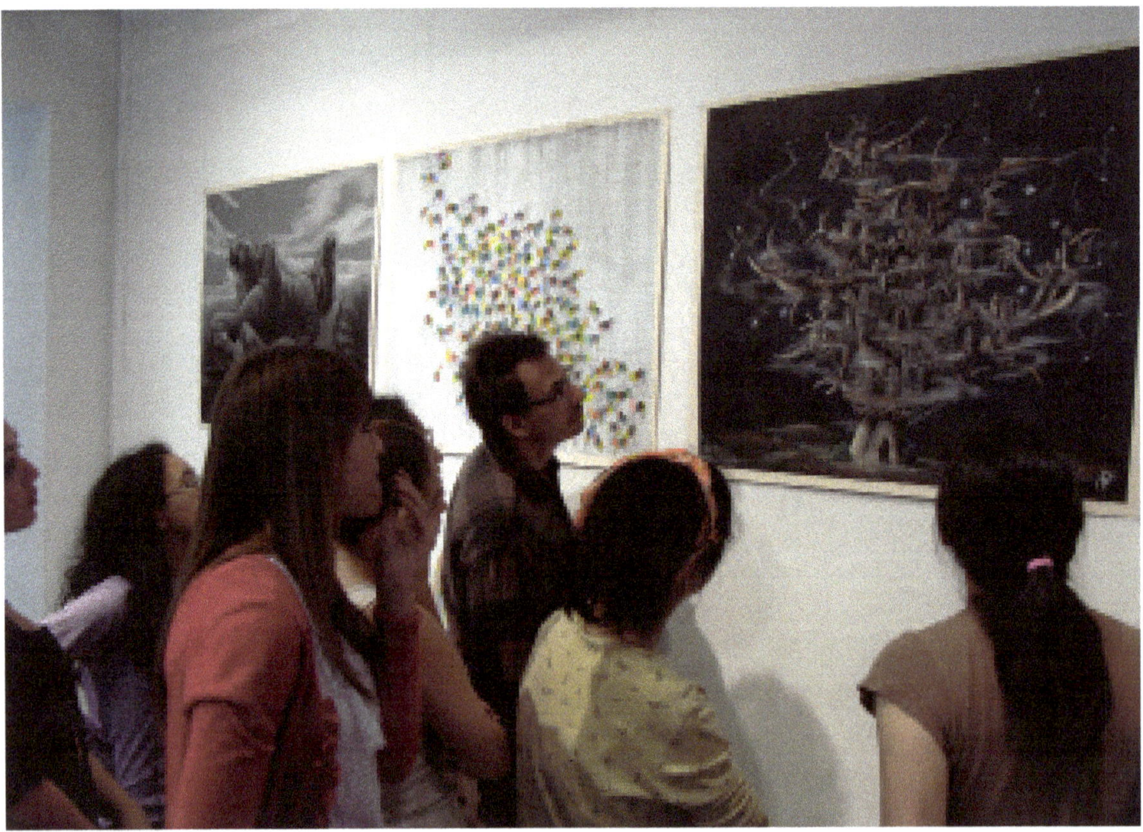

30

Being Behind the Times, Being Average

It is normal to be average: not everyone is astonishingly original. And it is common to be a little behind the times: not everyone is bleeding-edge avant-garde. It is also normal, and common, to be unhappy about being average and a little behind the times. Here are some ways to think about that.

A. *Most student work is a bit behind the times.* If you're an art student you're likely—but not definitely!—to be doing work that is unoriginal. In part that's just the way it should be, since you're a student. (No one expects undergraduate physics students to come out with major discoveries. The art world doesn't either, but people always sort of hope it will happen, and sometimes it does.) The bulk of art students practice older styles of art making. Those styles include old-fashioned naturalism, neo-expressionism, late Romantic landscape painting, collage forms derived from Rauschenberg or Bearden or Dada, fantasy art derived from *fin-de-siècle* Symbolism, types of Abstract Expressionism, post-minimalism, late 1970s-style conceptual art, 1990s style installation art, 1990s style institutional critique, and late-Surrealist figural abstractions. In the early 1920's it was the same: art students back then made nineteenth-century style academic figure studies, history paintings, imitations of Toulouse-Lautrec and illustrational art, and works in the style of Picasso's Pink and Blue Periods. Even further back in time, the 1850s, academy students produced works in the eighteenth-century academic style of David and his followers.

There have been time lags between students' works and avant-garde works ever since there were art academies. It's normal: the question is how your instructor handles it, because it isn't usually helpful simply to be told you're behind the times. What matters is how you encounter the earlier art practices, how you put them in new contexts, what you think of them, how you understand them, how you engage them, how you distort and adapt and critique and augment them. As a student, you can ask about those things, and defuse the simple assertion that you're following some older art practice.

B. *Art made in institutions outside major cities is likely to be slightly behind the times.* One thing I have learned from visiting so many art departments in state colleges, liberal arts colleges, and small regional colleges, is that institutions outside major cities are more likely to have students who are behind the times. Every art institution has some students who like traditional kinds of art, but regional and rural institutions are likely to have more of them.

It's all a matter of degrees, but there's also a tipping point: when most of the faculty is a little out of date—say they're in their thirties or forties, and so they're about ten or twenty years out of their MFAs, and working outside of major cities most of that time—then they are increasingly likely to accept students who are also a little out of date. Eventually a culture forms that is less than cutting edge. All this is relative, of course, and there are plenty of counterexamples. But if you're in a regional institution, measurably far from a major urban center, and if most of your faculty spend most of their time in town, then be aware of the possibility that you may be learning slightly out of date practices.

C. *Art made in smaller institutions might also be a little behind the times.* Even if your school, college, or academy is in a major city, if it's a small institution it may also have a preponderance of faculty and students who are not engaged with the most recent developments. In the age of the internet, this isn't a matter of *not knowing* what's being made in Tokyo, Berlin, London, and other places: it's a question of your institution's attitude toward the most recent art.

Every major city in Europe and North America has conservative art academies in it. The students and faculty of those academies and schools do not always mix with the wider art world, even though they may be only blocks from the city's main museum, university, or art school. I won't name names here, because conservative institutions like "studio schools," self-styled "academies" in North America, and ateliers naturally resist being described as conservative.

D. *Art made in smaller countries might also be a little behind the times.* So it's the distance between your institution and a major city, and the size of your department or institution: those two factors have a lot to do with how closely your teachers and fellow students follow what's happening in the international art world. A third factor is the country you're in. If you're in a first world country, then there's usually no issue; but art academies in developing countries can be starkly different from those in the first world. I have been to art schools and academies on four continents, from Paraguay to Kyrgyzstan, from Tibet to Estonia, from Iran to the Republic of Georgia, and even though there are many counterexamples, I am not surprised when I visit a school and find strongly regional styles that are only tenuously connected to the contemporary art world.

(Parenthetically: I don't mean that it's a bad thing to be out of touch, out of date, or to return to a style from the past. In art theory, no return is a pure return anyway; if you're interested in this, you might look at Hal Foster's *Return of the Real.* Returns and retrenchments are interesting and integral to modernism and postmodernism. I'm pursuing a different idea: practices that are echoes and instances of art from the 1990s or 2000s may need to be revalued in art teaching because they are part of average, non avant-garde art practice. But back to the argument.)

I know points B, C, and D are very contentious. There are some people who say that the world is effectively a single art market now, and that communication is effectively uniform. I don't think that is true.[1] Most countries I have visited have at least one principal art academy that is attuned to the global art world, but any number of countries have smaller academies and schools that are not. Even in the United States and western Europe, regional art academies, and smaller colleges and universities can show a time lag in relation to the larger centers. Just because you're in a first-world country doesn't mean you're current.[2]

Up to this point I've been saying "average" or "behind the times" because that is how things get talked about. I mean statistically average, in a neutral, statistician's way of thinking, but still the word "average" sounds negative. It sounds too much like "mediocre," which is clearly pejorative. I could have said "normal," but that raises all sorts of questions about standards and social ideals. Or I could have said ordinary," but even that sounds a little critical. What I am really getting at here is a kind of art that is *unremarkable:* it doesn't seem to call for any special attention, because it is something that your teachers will have seen before. It is not "marked" by properties that no other artwork has. (Thanks to Paul Gladston for suggesting "unremarkable.") Another way to describe this kind of art is that it is unoriginal, or ordinary, or that it is *apparently only moderately interesting.* It's not compelling, amazing, new, bewildering, never-before-seen, avant-garde. It's important to add the qualifier "apparently," because, as I'll argue on the next page, what appears uninteresting or unremarkable to one person might be quite remarkable to another.

E. *Most student work is unremarkable.* As an art student you're likely—but not definitely!—making work that is more or less unoriginal. We're not all Duchamp or Picasso, and that's absolutely normal. In the book *Why Art Cannot be Taught,* I spent several pages wondering about the problem of teaching *average* students. From a teacher's point of view, instruction is always geared to the high points of art: all the terms of criticism, all the points of comparison, are the Mt. Everests of art. As a student, you are continuously encouraged to look at famous artists, and you are given difficult texts by historians and philosophers.

But most of us, students and teachers, are unremarkable. It feels a little painful to say so, but it's true. We're under the main umbrella of the bell curve, not off in the genius range. It's also the case that most of us see average art all the time. In the words of the authors of *The Critique Handbook,* "we are continually being influenced not by creative interesting [art], but by provincial, second-tier, watered-down examples of art. The result is that we are not influenced to produce highly original inventive work, but rather to make work that resembles what we *think* art should look like" (p. 90).

So I wondered how art instruction might possibly be tuned so it is responsive to ordinary work by ordinarily skilled students, who have some energy but not a huge amount, who are sometimes inspired but more often not, who produce art that is within the ordinary range between utter failure and earth-shaking innovation. It is not an easy problem, and I did not solve it in that book. Our critical language is full of superlatives, and our history textbooks are full of exemplars: it's a serious issue, and I think no one quite knows how to address it.

This doesn't mean you should accept being unremarkable. Art is all about experimentation. But it means you should be aware that the languages of criticism, theory, and art history, and therefore the languages of teaching and the critique, are stocked with exceptional artists and practices, and have almost nothing to say about average art production. So you're surrounded by values and judgments that are based on the idea of endless astonishing innovation.

It's necessary to be careful and listen to the language that is used to critique your work. Almost always, the concepts and judgments are slanted away from the ordinary, the unremarkable, the moderately interesting, and toward the amazing, the unexpected, the exceptional, the unprecedented. Your work probably has a fair amount of energy, moments of inspiration, certain points of interest, and moderate successes. That's ordinary practice, in ordinary life. Your provisional achievements are not well described in the demanding, world-historical languages of art history, theory, and criticism.

When I posted a draft of this chapter online, I got an avalanche of comments. No one wants to be unremarkable! Jeremy Gilbert-Rolfe wrote: "A moderate amount of originality doesn't sound like very much originality, it's like a moderate sex drive. What is that and where does it leave people who are drawn to the immoderate, where are they in relation to an idea of what's average?" I am all for "bristling," as one person wrote, against whatever is ordinary or unremarkable. But I suppose I'd say there really shouldn't be anything wrong with a moderate sex drive. Lurid dreams are part of what we are (as Hollywood is continuously showing us), but I am concerned that the current languages of the art world are so laced with superlatives that as teachers we lack words to help us appreciate average art production, and as students we have no way to tell ourselves that our ordinary drives have their own virtues. And it's just a fact that most of us are unremarkable in the end. So I'm not advocating mediocrity here, and I'm not suggesting we teach mediocre or unambitious art: I'm proposing that we need to pay more attention to the virtues and qualities of ordinary unremarkable art, and to mismatches between the languages of art and what we are actually producing.

(I'm also not aligning myself with some critics, such as Dave Hickey, who say that art schools produce die-cut students, all from the same mold, and that artists are better advised to remain independent. It's not that the tens of thousands of MFAs all make similar work—that is a claim that could also have been made against the French Academy in the 18th c., or against any products of widely adopted educational models. The apparently uniform work produced by MFA programs has its own qualities, and they can be as variegated and diverse as the qualities that are valued in internationally successful or art historically significant work. We may miss those qualities because we lack the language, or the interest, to see them.)

In life, none of these things I have listed need to be problems: happily there are many kinds of art to make, many places to make art, many people to see it. But in an art school, it can be a problem when your teachers feel they've seen it all before.

Mira Schor, who has written one of the few essays on this subject, admits that she averts her eyes when it comes to seeing the outmoded styles that she's writing about. When jurors see art in styles they've seen a thousand times before, they put "a zero on their chart," indicating "their absolute lack of interest" in ever seeing work like that again. And yet derivative art, in warmed-over versions of older styles, is ubiquitous. It isn't documented, because art history isn't aimed at unremarkable, average art. But for experienced teachers, gallerists, jurors, and curators, it's everywhere. "These are the bad yet eerily familiar works that form the déjà-vu-all-over-again feeling of teaching," she writes. (Her excellent essay has a history of some of these styles, in case you'd like to try to avoid them: "Trite Tropes, Clichés, Or the Persistence of Styles," in her book *A Decade of Negative Thinking*, 2009.)

As an art student I never suspected that an instructor might be less than interested in what I was making, but as a teacher I am familiar with the feeling of walking into a studio and seeing something that reminds me of an endless series of similar works by other artists and by last year's students. I find I can usually become interested in the particularities of the work at hand, but it is not possible to entirely forget that initial judgment. When this happens in critiques the result can be disastrous. It is not uncommon for teachers to find ways to let students know they are being mediocre or unoriginal. I have heard instructors say so bluntly, I guess in hopes that they were doing the students some good. And if your teacher doesn't say anything, you may realize what's going on and wish she would speak. The problem is endemic simply because it is rare for a teacher to encounter something that seems entirely new. (And by the inexorable law of the avant-garde, if you really do make something genuinely new, your teachers won't recognize it and they'll usually dislike it.)

Students and teachers both remark on the low energy level of some critique panels. (Think of the long transcript in chapter 11.) That can happen because the teacher sees work she's seen a thousand times before, and she loses interest. She's been through it so many times that she has set speeches memorized. She has a speech on the problems of continuing to paint, a speech on the limitations of conceptual work, a speech on the problems of effective political critique.

But if your work seems unoriginal, ordinary, mediocre, average, slightly old-fashioned, or just plain familiar and uninspiring, your teacher may just fall silent. Silence can result from either boredom or annoyance, but either way, it usually means your teacher does not think your work is original. (It may also be that your work appears confusing, but in my experience confused teachers usually talk *more* than un-confused teachers.)

In this case you face a double challenge: to admit the possibility that your work might provoke such a reaction, and to find a way to jump-start the depressed or silent teacher. (As a teacher you can think along the same lines: you can ask yourself whether there is a way to talk about the work that can rekindle your interest.)

There is no easy solution to a critique stuck in the doldrums of boredom. It is good to keep in mind that this kind of dissatisfaction might be a hidden subtext throughout a critique. The underlying fact is that if your teacher liked your work without reservation, she would try to make it herself! There is always *some* disapproval—that's only natural. The challenge is to keep enough interest going, and enough honesty, so you can figure out three things:

1. Do I think my work might actually be average, normal, or ordinary?
2. If it might be, do I mind?
3. If I mind, how can I identify the things my teachers think are average, so I can rethink them?

It's always a good policy to be honest, and keep asking your teachers questions about their lack of energy, their silences, their reticence, their evasiveness, until you see exactly why they feel as they do.

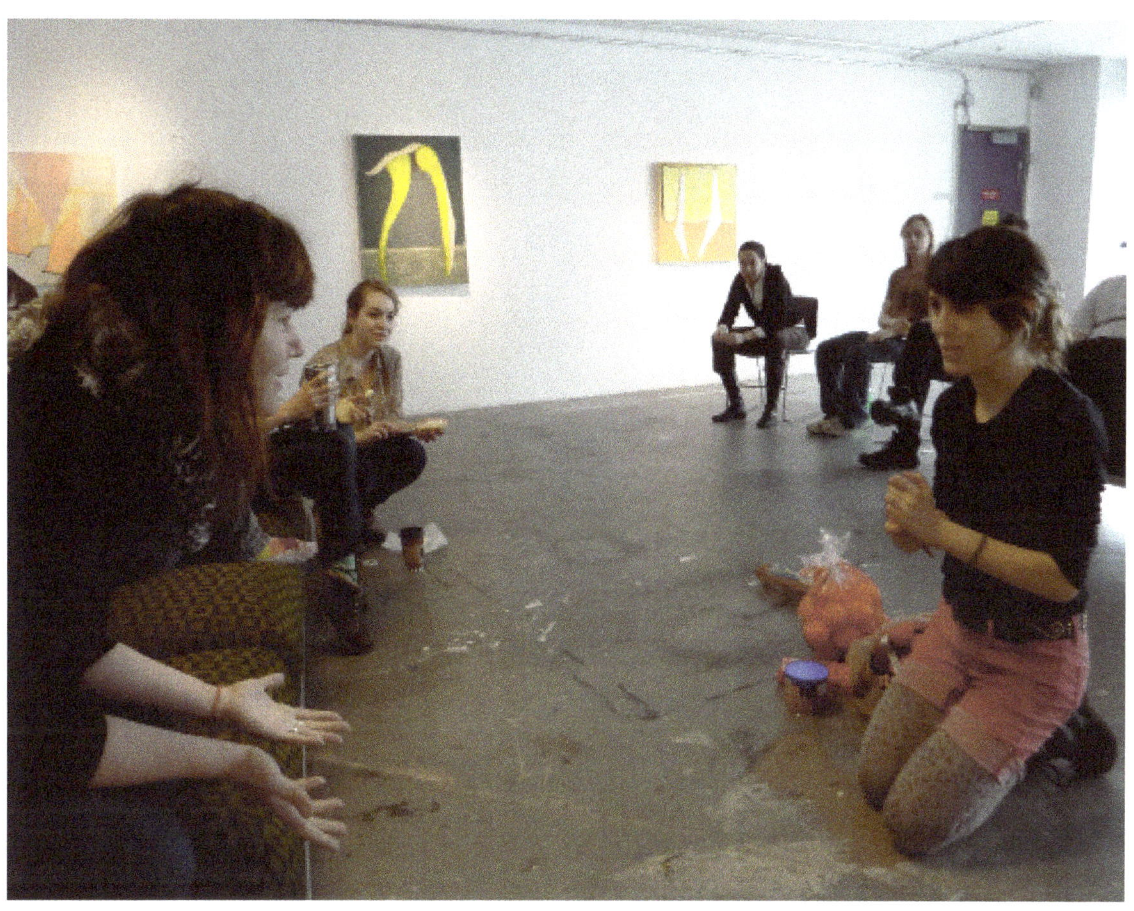

31

Some Teachers are Judicative,

and Others Descriptive

Judicative and descriptive are terms from ancient rhetoric, and they name two fundamentally different ways of talking about an object. Judicative statements pass judgment. They value or devalue the work, or some element of it, and they can either present themselves as subjective ("I don't like that green") or objective ("That green is no good"). Judicative commentary includes anything that urges, persuades, or cajoles. ("But why use so much green?") It wants to change something about the work. Most advisors will suggest possible avenues to explore, and some will prescribe certain ideas. ("Don't use green, use blue.") Thus judicative commentary can appear subjective, objective, prescriptive, or suggestive, and in various combinations of these modes it accounts for the majority of what is said in art schools. On the other side is descriptive commentary, which does not try to change the artwork itself, but rather to translate it into words. As in judicative criticism, some examples present themselves as objective ("That's a very bright green") and others as subjective ("To me that looks like a bright green."). Descriptive statements are also sometimes questions: "Is that a horse?"[1]

As Greek and Roman rhetoricians knew, there is no sure way to separate judicative and descriptive analysis.[2] Saying "I think your green is very bright" (a descriptive statement) is also saying "I think that green is too bright"—a judicative statement. In practice descriptive and judicative comments are always mixed. There is no such thing as a neutral observation or a neutral fact. Even naming something is valuing it. If a panelist asks, "Is that a horse?" the idea of "horse" and of the difficulty of identifying the horse are both planted in peoples' minds. They become terms in the ensuing exchange. When instructors claim they are "only describing what's there," or they "don't mean anything" by a remark, they are making inadequate excuses for judicative statements that failed to disguise themselves as descriptive statements. And this in turn indicates how often teachers make judgments that are couched as neutral description.

Despite all this, it is often very helpful to pay attention to the difference between statements that are intended to be judicative (pass judgment) and those that are meant to be descriptive (they're only attempts to understand).

There are two ways to deal with this distinction in conversations about art. When your teacher makes a statement, she can frame it so that it is clearly either descriptive or judicative; and when you hear a statement, you can categorize it as primarily descriptive or judicative. The question, "Is that a horse?" can be understood in two ways: either it is meant to gather information, or it means something more like "Is *that* a horse?" In the former case, you can take it as provisionally descriptive, and in the latter, as primarily judicative. A "rhetorical question" is an ironic or self-evident judicative statement: the person who asks a so-called rhetorical question has no doubt about the answer, so she is really just prodding you. If your work is a huge bronze horse, and someone asks, "Is that a *horse*?" they may mean it's too obviously a horse, that it suffers because it is too horsey. Even instructors who are genuinely interested in gathering information or in learning more about the work have judgments that they hold in abeyance. But that doesn't mean it is necessarily good to search for the hidden judgment behind the ostensibly neutral description. The fiction of purely descriptive statements also provides the possibility of more equitable exchanges between students and teachers, where the main purpose is just to learn about the artwork. Whenever mutual learning and discovery are goals, it is best to assume that the primary force of a statement is descriptive rather than judicative.

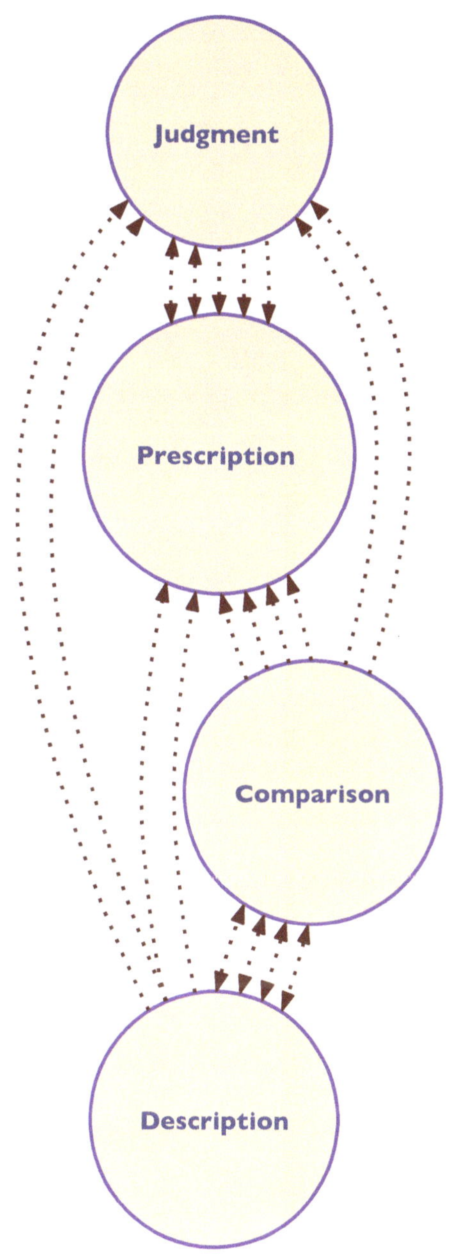

When I am in critiques, I try to keep a clear distinction between statements that are primarily descriptive and those that are primarily judicative. I try to imagine myself either as judging, or else as just looking for information.

I am aware that my more-or-less disinterested search for the truth does not extend very far, and that I am really just gathering information to enable be to judge more effectively. But often I am just trying to understand what I see. In other cases, I

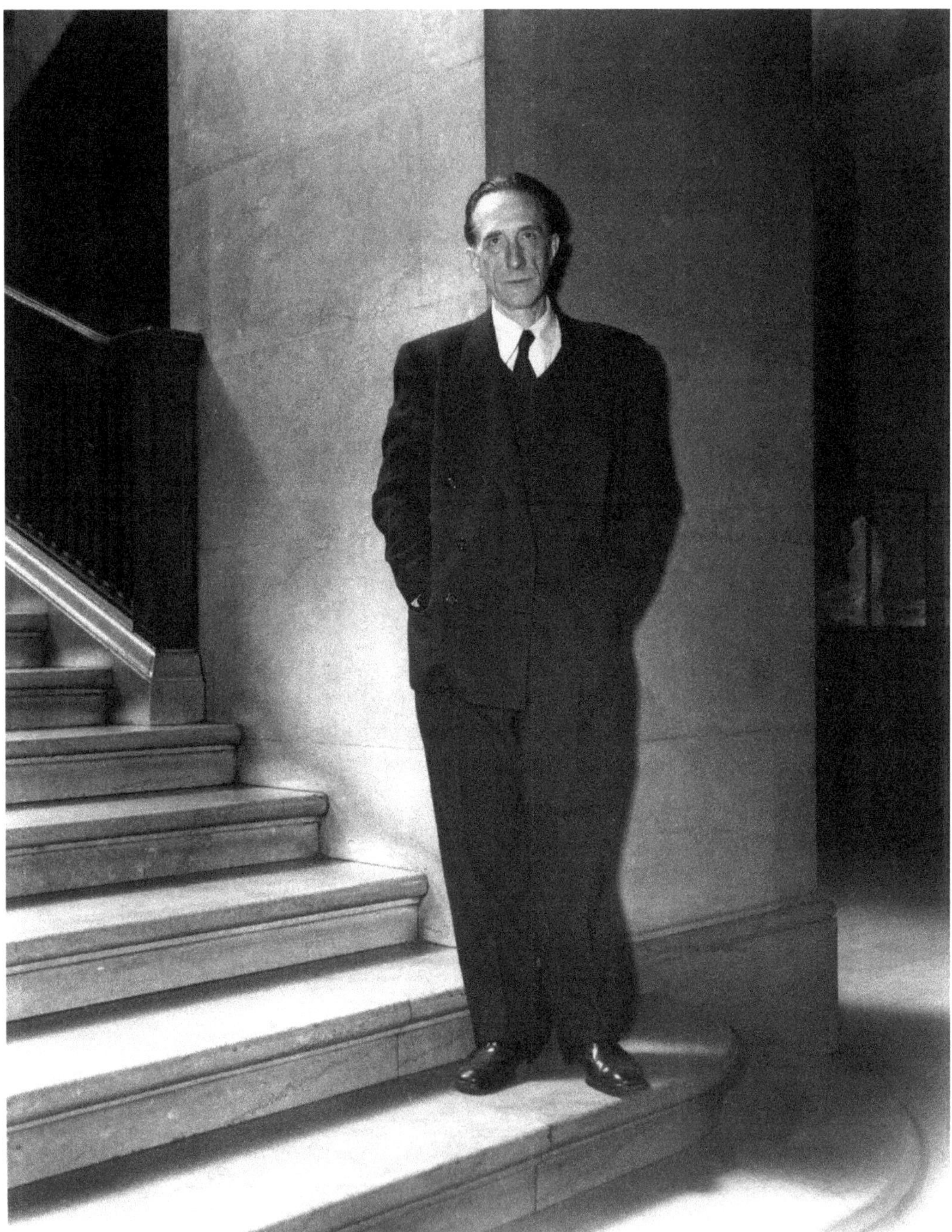

am immediately critical and judgmental. In either case I try to make the distinction clear to the student.

It is rare for teachers to intend to be purely descriptive. Art teachers are supposed to point out possibilities, and encourage change and experimentation. Teaching and critiquing are often equated. Often enough judicative criticism is thought to be the only mode of criticism, and it comes to seem as if the instructor's job is to inspire change. Here is an imaginary critique of a well-known artist, in which every comment is judicative:

— Well Rembrandt, these are really wonderful paintings. But you know, I like the backgrounds as much as I like the faces. What would happen if you just left out the faces?

— I'm interested in faces.

— But I think you say a tremendous amount in those backgrounds. In a way, they express the faces. I think you could do without the faces. Those backgrounds are very, very powerful.

— I like faces.

— I think you should try more things. Get away from that gluey paint. Use more turpentine. Use color. I want to see bright colors. And bigger paintings. And smaller paintings. And sculptures. Why don't you do sculptures? You know, it won't hurt to experiment. That's why you're in school.

— Okay.

— You know, in five years you won't be doing this same stuff, nobody works the same after they get out of school. So you might as well change now.

In such a case descriptive criticism might be more sensible, because as we know, there is a great deal in Rembrandt's work that is worth learning about. Judicative criticism can be naïve, since it is aware of what the work is not, rather than what it is. The imaginary teacher speaking to Rembrandt is not thinking of the virtues and expressive power of Rembrandt's chiaroscuro, his amazing muddy paint, or his investigation of psychological portraiture. Judicative criticism can be an inventory of the things that are not seen in a work. Judicative critics are like reluctant explorers who map the boundaries of a country and never explore its interior. Often the boundaries are placed incorrectly, and the student needs to think about expanding or adjusting them. But the territory itself is usually just as interesting.

On the other hand, there are several problems with descriptive criticism that do not often apply to judicative criticism. To most teachers, what counts is the work: what they can get from it, how it affects them. (I will call that *primary analysis*.) To someone bent on describing and understanding the critique format, rather than bent on understanding the art, what counts is *anything* that happens in the critique. To some extent this always happens, but when a person interesed in descriptive criticism is in the room, the artwork is only one fact in a larger situation. Instead of analyzing the work, such a person might turn her attention to her own reactions to the work (what I will call a *secondary analysis*), so that she will end up commenting on a whole series of her own previous comments. Sometimes the comments are directed at what the other speakers say, in an attempt to construct a theory of all responses (*tertiary analysis*). The game of descriptive analysis can get entirely out of hand when it is not reined in by the underlying purpose of helping the student.

As a student, you can recognize runaway descriptive criticism and learn what you can from it. Descriptive criticism may be disruptive, but in my experience it is not a source of confusion. The difficulty can be trying to get firmly descriptive instructors to provide judgments. To a confirmed descriptive theorist, personal judgments are irrelevant. I have seen students become enraged when such instructors refused to say whether or not they liked a work. "Just tell me if it's good!" one student screamed, and his advisor replied, "Well, that's just not my place."

Here is an excerpt from a critique where the speaker A is practicing descriptive criticism. (He was a philosopher, visiting the studio department.) The panel of teachers has just seen a film containing some funny social satire along with some experimental camera technique. In this dialogue, B is the student. This is only a small sample of a long discussion in which speaker A went on, at great length, analyzing the other instructors' reactions to the student's film. The student, and her film, were nearly forgotten. No judgments about the film itself were ever made.

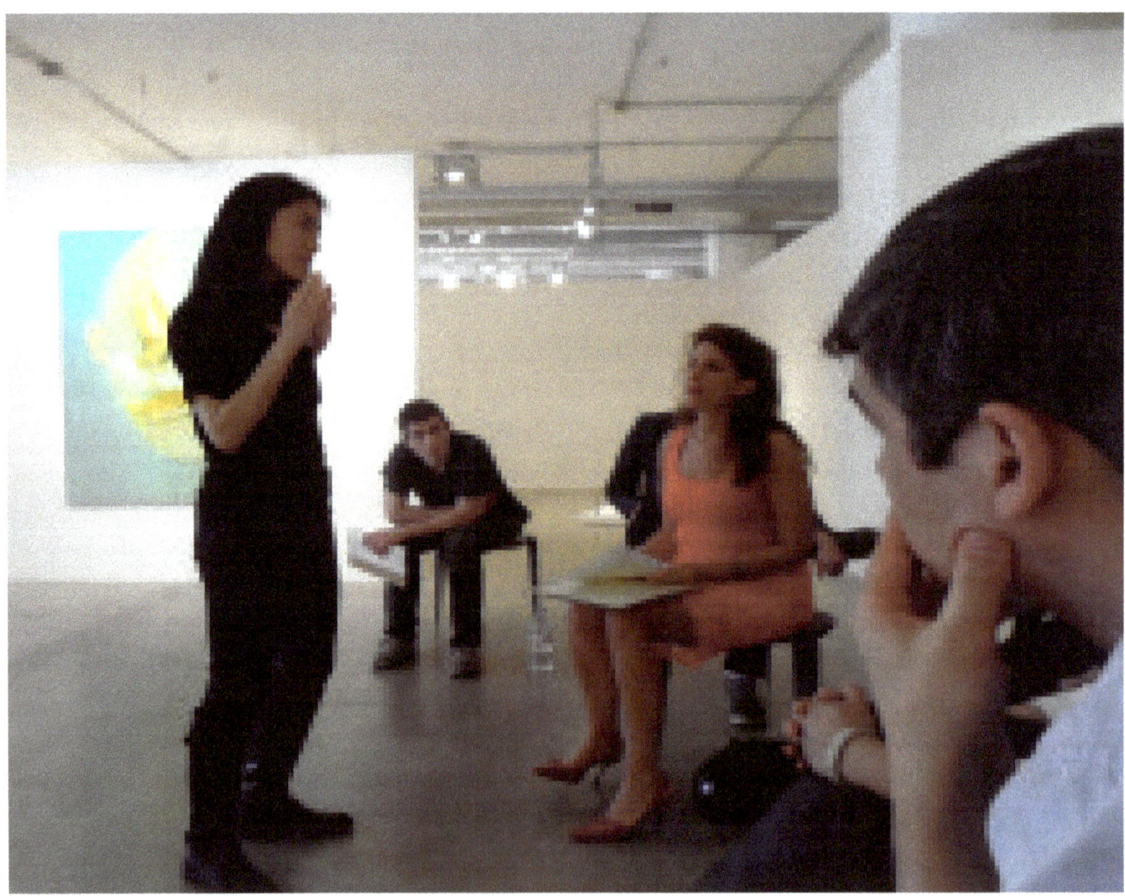

A	What seems interesting here is that when the film ended, we all laughed—and it was a very funny film.	*This is a secondary analysis: an account of the panelist's own reaction. He is interested in the fact that he laughed—and now he's done laughing.*
B	Thank you, I meant it to be.	
A	But I think that is absolutely unimportant, it is absolutely not the point of the film. I don't think anyone here would argue with the idea that the film is purely formal, that none of that [our laughter] makes any difference.	*This secondary analysis is made possible by the time that has elapsed since the panelist had watched the film. He is now attempting to describe the way his thoughts have changed since the film ended. He cares more about the transition between laughter and sober commentary than about what was funny in the film.*
C	What? No… to me, this was a comic film, and it had some very funny moments, little epiphanies.	*Like the other panelists, this speaker is still trying to understand the film itself, and especially the reasons it made her laugh.*
A	Surely you don't believe that the [comedy] makes any difference? It's just a vehicle, so he can give his… so he can make formal points. The very idea of an "epiphany" is that it is transitory, it leaves, and it leaves you… and it makes you think of other things, your shopping, your errands, what you're going to have for dinner. You resent [that], maybe, but that's life.	*This is a tertiary analysis: the speaker is now trying to account for the other speaker's reaction. As he does this, he moves further from anything that might be helpful to the student.*

In the following example a critique panel has been considering paintings that depict mythological scenes. The painter, Catherine Arnold,[3] showed several dozen works, some of them large figural compositions.

Near the beginning of the critique, after a short silence, one teacher asked these questions:

A What year is it?
B What?
A What year?
B You mean now?

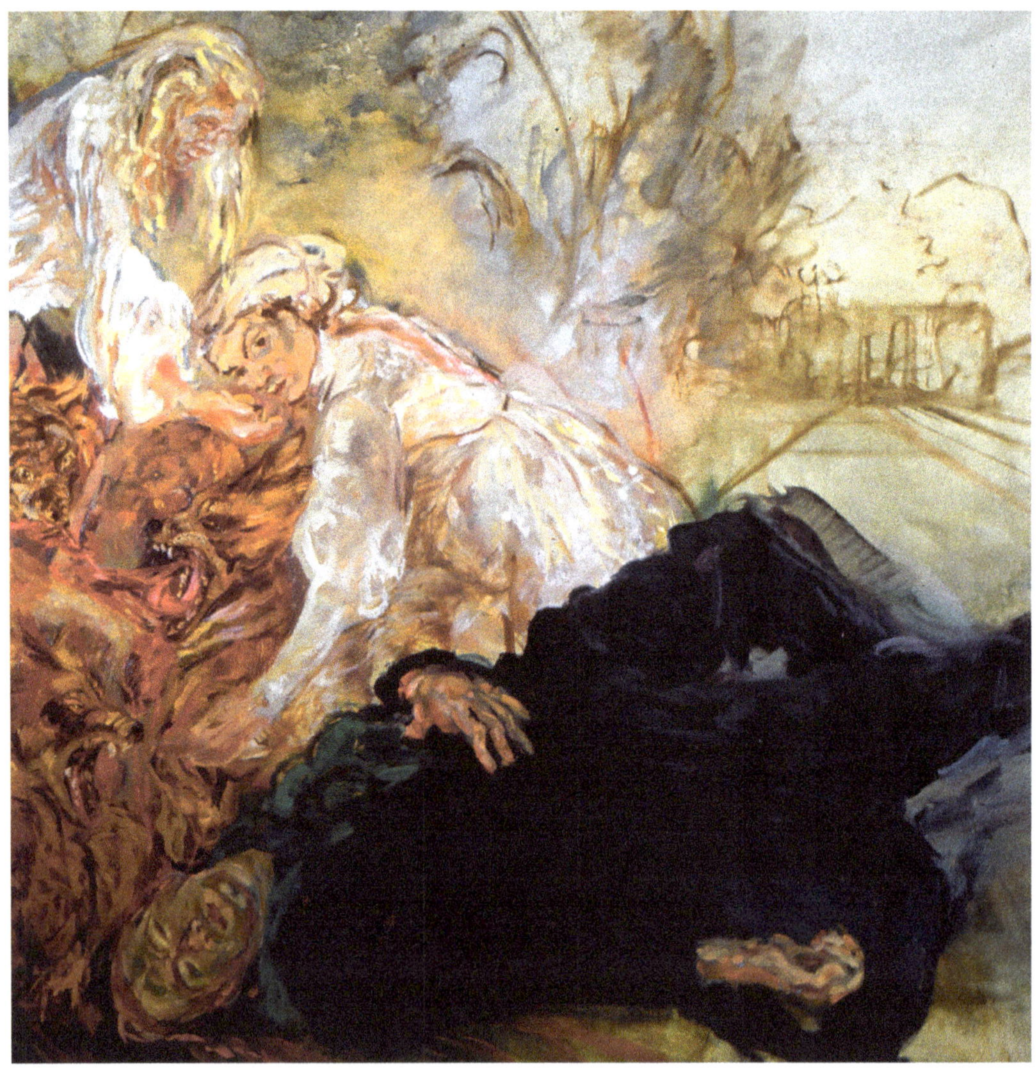

A   Yes.

B   1990.

A   What year is it in your paintings?

B   It's the years that my mind inhabits, and that seem most important and relevant to me.

A   Because to me, that's the problem with your painting. It's that you are… the paintings are such a fantasy about the nineteenth century that you scramble into the paintings to get emotionally connected to them.

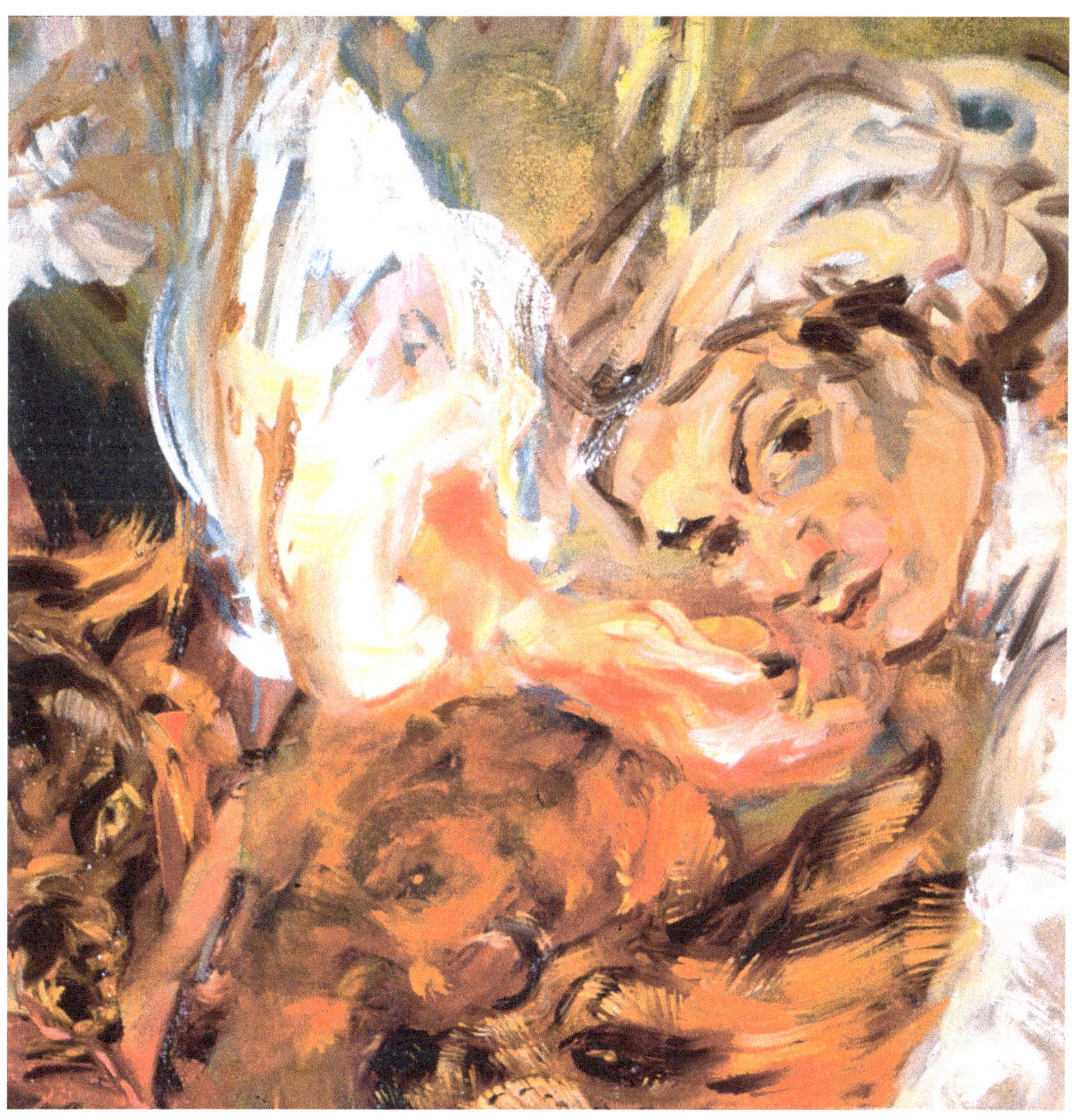

B   Well, I don't think it's quite accurate to say that they are fantasies about the nineteenth century, it's more the Renaissance and Baroque [...]

This sets the terms for a debate about the possibility of retrieving the past. If this conversation had been continued, it could have developed the concepts of "fantasy," "relevance," and how the mind "inhabits" periods. But instead the panelists made those concepts dependent on the metaphor of *space*:

C   But if you were to describe the imaginary space of your paintings, how would you do it? I know it sounds sort of corny to ask you this, because everybody, in talking about the space in paintings, including yourself, has been using this notion of the nature of the space. And in some ways, that is the question. What is the nature of the space you use?

B   Well, it varies from painting to painting, and in some paintings I'm really not particularly interested in space… because space didn't seem very important for what I wanted to say, but—

D   How can you make a painting without being interested in space?

C   But she has a very particular space.

B   No—not *very* interested in space, it's not the *highest* thing on the hierarchy—

D   No, but no matter what you do, you're going to have some kind of space. I mean, you can paint—

B   Yes, you are.

D   —I mean it's unavoidable.

And at last the critique veers off in another direction:

A   Well, before when I talked about the sense of time, I thought it connected to the sense of space. That's the reason I brought it up. To me, these paintings have a real *strong* urge to be incredibly corny.

This dialogue is fundamentally judicative, because the panelists are trying to impress the student that it's futile to paint in the style of a past century. The vehicle for that is the term "space," which means something quite different to the student and to the panelists. To the student, it is partly an irrelevancy, since she also wants to talk about "fantasy" and narrative. To the panelists, it is the key, the way to drive home the concept of anachronism. It is typical of judicative exchanges that a single overdetermined concept serves as a fulcrum, tilting the critique one way or another.

Late in the critique this largely descriptive dialogue took place between Catherine and an art historian:

E   Catherine, as long as I've known your work, it seems that the crux of one of your processes is that when you deal with landscape you are able to be generous with the space. You use the space in a different way: in fact you use panoramic views. But your basic method has always been to be very much a literary painter, in the sense that your figurative elements are very important.

B   Yes.

E   And once that happens, you lose the space. And a part of that (and I remember we said this one time, in the distant past) is that you come out of the British tradition of literary painting, where the theme and the story is very important, where those things are very relevant.

Yet you also come out of the other British tradition, the landscape tradition, and [they are merged in your work]….

That again, if you think about Baroque painting, which has always been important to you, that the dialogue in Baroque painting is a dialogue of dualities, which is what you're really trying to bring about here, with the contrasts between the foreground and background. So that's certainly one thing which is a parallel.

The other thing is, that remember, in the Baroque, the narrative picture, with few exceptions, used the horizontal. That was considered to be the narrative mode.

The art historian's comments also revolve around fictive space, but his intentions were to describe and to provide new meanings and terms that Catherine might use. He sees no problem in making "Baroque" paintings in the year 1990, and so his comments about space aren't judicative—they are not used to support judgments. The sense of space in the earlier passages is confrontational and polemic. This panelist's use of the word "space" is classificatory: to him, every mention of space is an opportunity to expand upon the possibilities of the painting. To the other panelists, the concept of space is an opportunity to demonstrate that the artist paints anachronistically. The historian and the other panelists did not talk together in this critique, and it is difficult to see how they could have done so. The different senses of space are also incommensurate from the artist's viewpoint. Different purposes—descriptive and judicative—may have prevented a higher-level synthesis of opinions.

These are only brief excerpts from a more involved conversation. In the full text, there is a sense of hopelessness as the teachers continue to veer off in different directions. It is conceivable that a secondary analysis—such as the comments I have been making—might have been helpful. At least that would have given everyone the opportunity to think about why their conversation was so much at loggerheads.

Teachers Make Idiosyncratic Pronouncements

Timothy van Laar and Leonard Diepeveen's book, *Active Sights: Art as Social Interaction* has a description of a studio critique with four teachers.[1] One is a "picture doctor," who talks only about formal elements in the student's painting (its color, its composition);[2] the second is a "passionate guru," who is interested in the student's emotional relation to their work (what is now called affect); the third is a "social construction" theorist interested in ideology and political critique; and the fourth is an "introspective mystic," for whom art is so deeply subjective that it can hardly be communicated. These are all very familiar types in art critiques.[3]

A group of people who think along the same lines form a stable interpretive community, meaning they will be likely to agree among themselves.[4] Today we have evanescent interpretive communities, and no one kind of art is valued for very long.[5] It may seem as if van Laar and Diepeveen's four types have become forty, or four hundred. But we need to be careful in assuming that there is more disagreement

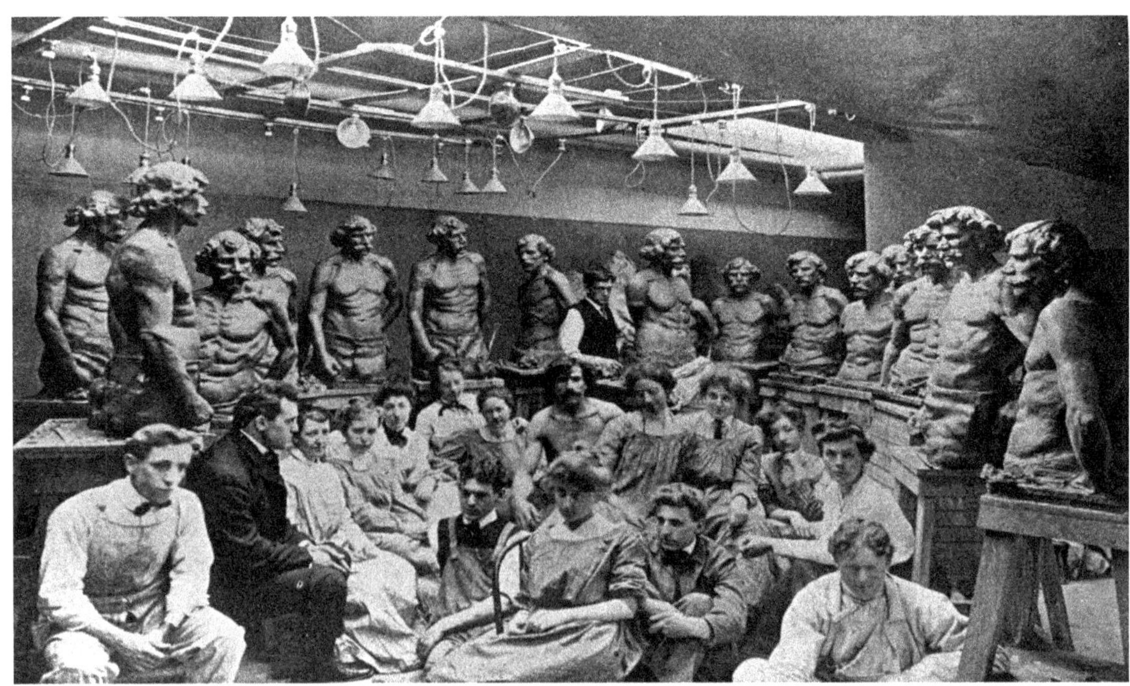

today than there was in the days of the academies, or even that standards of judgment change more rapidly now than in the past. It is not true that more people in the eighteenth century agreed more of the time than we do. (The bizarre photograph here is meant to suggest just how much people used to agree.) Then as now, the judgment of artworks depends on a consensus of like-minded people—the question is how many "communities" there are in any given critique.

Let's take the simplest case first. In a critique it sometimes happens that all the panelists agree. In that case, the critique panel comprises a stable interpretive community—stable, at least, for the duration of the critique. Standards of taste or quality will remain reasonably constant. This does happen, but it's rare, and people tend to be surprised when they agree too much.

When two teachers do not agree, you could say they are representing two disparate interpretive communities. To take an artificial example: one of your teachers might like Andrew Wyeth, and another Joseph Beuys. You can expect them to disagree in some predictable ways. In such a case the teachers are like ambassadors for absent interpretive communities.

One difference between older art academies, before modernism, and contemporary art schools is that today there are many more points of view. There are more movements, more "isms," more styles, schools, modes, media, "positions," and "projects," than there were in eighteenth- or nineteenth-century France. The art world appears to change rapidly and contemporary artists can be pluralistic and work in a variety of media; but as a matter of practice, it is often fairly easy to decide what affiliations a faculty member has.

The "picture doctor," the "passionate guru," the "social construction" theorist, and the "introspective mystic" are representatives of four very widespread interpretive communities. There are dozens more: the Committed Ab-Ex Believer, the Determined Regionalist, the Second-Wave Feminist, the Eighties Comic Artist, the Urban Sociologist, the Transcultural Ethnographer, the Humble Practitioner, the Radical Anti-Artist, the Transgressive Videographer, the Rational Social Critic… that's just off the top of my head, thinking of faculty I've met recently in critiques. van Laar and Diepeveen's four types can be assigned places in history: the "picture doctor," for example, is a formalist academic; the "introspective mystic" is a late Romantic. (These are named in chapter 37.)

It is generally a good idea to identify your teacher's interpretive community, within limits: most people are mixtures and don't belong unequivocally to any one community. The tool for understanding your teacher's interpretive communities is art history: the more you study the history of the last hundred years of art, the more you'll recognize your teacher's orientations.

This idea of categorizing a faculty member according to her "community" may sound coarse. But the idea that a person can represent an interpretive community is indispensable to critiques and studio teaching in general. To see why this is so, imagine a version of postmodernism in which there were as many schools as there were artists. Everyone's opinion would be theirs alone, and no one would stand for a community of any size. Each person would have only her own standards to rely on, and she could change them at will, perhaps every day, without anyone being able to follow the changes. In such a world there would be no purpose to art criticism: meaningful criticism demands a set of standards that can be comprehended as instances of standards held by other people. A teacher who is absolutely unique would also be absolutely useless: a student might want to imitate such a person, but it would not be possible since the teacher's judgments would be incomprehensible.

In the real world some people approach that condition. In effect, they are evanescent interpretive communities comprised of one person. Here is a speech that is, I think, nearly incomprehensibly idiosyncratic:

A   They don't look like Baroque paintings. They look like nineteenth century versions of Baroque paintings. And you believing that you are somehow more connected to that space is where you're meeting your invisible barrier. You're not really connected to that space, you're doing something about that space, and that's why, as you try and move toward that space, you constantly have to repaint the painting, because *there is no such space, really.* You're trying to paint something very representational, and it's meeting up against the fact that fantasies don't have substance.

It may be that this is hard to understand because it expresses the panelist's personal thoughts about space and history. Certainly it would take time to untangle the various judgments, and it is not normally possible to take that time in the middle of a critique.

This kind of idiosyncratic commentary can also be a problem for critiques because it is not easy to interpret the *cause* of an idiosyncratic remark. An incomparably odd statement might proceed from at least five causes: (1) When a teacher disagrees with something she herself said a few minutes before, sometimes she is in the process of switching interpretive communities. The result is self-contradictory advice. (2) Judgments can also be self-contradictory because the teacher habitually works in several partly incompatible styles. In that case, "self-contradiction" may not have a negative value: it may be a quality the teacher is praising. (3) It may also be that the teacher is day-dreaming or free-associating, and the comments do not owe allegiance to any particular set of values. (4) It also happens that teachers can be ironic or just perverse, and say the opposite of what they might ordinarily say. Sometimes this is done in order to play Devil's advocate, and other times it is destructive in intention. (5) And finally, it is not uncommon that panelists confuse themselves as they try to articulate a difficult idea (*discovering* thoughts rather than *reporting* them, as I said in chapter 26). A comment that seems "strange" may also signify a state of confusion, either conceptual (an error in thinking) or grammatical (an error in speaking).

Truly idiosyncratic commentary is a special problem because it leads to radical interpretive quandaries. Why is the statement self-contradictory? Why does it sound odd? Is the speaker contradicting herself out of perversity, confusion, or absent-mindedness? Idiosyncratic speakers just make things that much more difficult: their comments are like static in a radio signal. The usual case is that all of us—students, teachers—actually belong to one or more interpretive communities. Our judgments aren't just our own. We're all more or less clichés! I'll have more to say to this in the closing chapters of the book.

A last thought on this topic: sometimes the most idiosyncratic teachers are the best, simply because they are inspiring. There are many stories about teachers who excel in critiques. I never heard Clement Greenberg, but he was memorable for many people. Among our contemporaries or near-contemporaries, I have heard great things about a number of critics.

Here's an honor roll, just to give some excellent teachers their due:

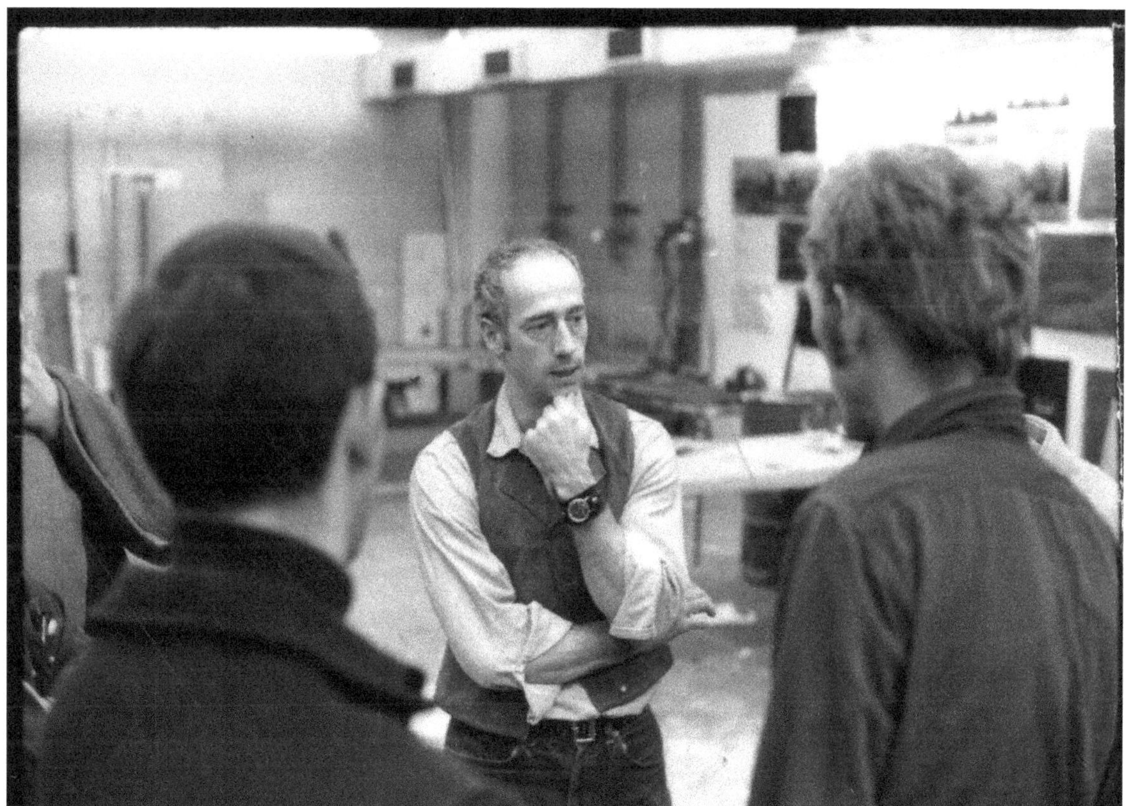

Alan Kaprow
Robert Morris
Buzz Spector
Michael Asher
Larry Sultan
Mary Kelly
Italo Scanga
Bob Irwin
Chawky Frenn
Sam Messer
Pablo Helguera
Larry Bakke
Daniel Bozhkov
Michael St. John
Domingo Barreres
Joe Zucker
Philip Lorca Dicorcia
Richard Benson
Roni Horn
Chuck Close
Cheryl Donegan
Collier Schorr
Dana Schutz
Deborah Kass

Lisa Wainwright
 (photo, p. 120)
Eric Fischl
Suzanne Doremus
Gary Stephan
Dave Hickey
Joan Kelly
 (photo, p. 196)
Julian Lethbridge
Jacqueline Humphries
Ken Johnson
Sean Landers
Kate Gilmore
Laurie Simmons
Linda Norden
Hamza Walker
Nancy Spector
Lynn Cooke
Lari Pittmann
RoseLee Goldberg
Richard Phillips
Vince Aletti
Lim Lee
Jill Dawsey

Gerry Immonen
Jeremy Gilbert-Roth
Scott Grieger
Katy Siegel
John Baldessari
Bob Irwin
Peter Plagens
Michael Craig Martin
Les Levine
Vernon Fisher
Jessica Jackson Hutchins
George Pappas
Kurt Kauper
Rochelle Feinstein
Marie Thibeault
Linda Day
Nancy Baker
Jerry Saltz
Roberta Smith
Lisa Davis
Molly Zuckerman-
 Hartung (photo, p. 115)
Sam Tchakalian

There's no rhyme or reason in this list, because it's all about inspiration. Infectious enthusiasm and inspiration don't solve the problem of critiques, but it's great when they happen.

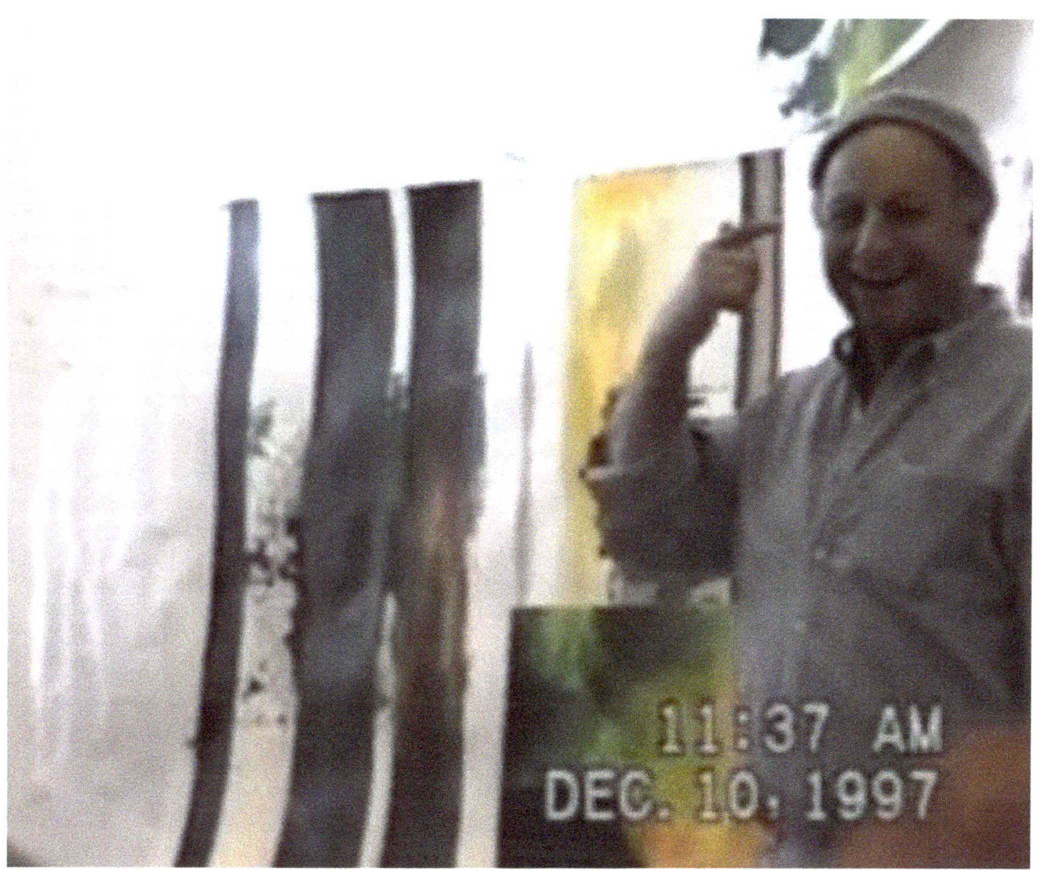
11:37 AM
DEC. 10, 1997

Music Critiques, Dance Critiques,

Theater Critiques

It's always a good idea to compare critiques in your medium with critiques in different media, or different departments. Sculpture critiques are generally different from painting critiques, which are different from photography critiques, and so on. More on this in chapter 43.

If you're in a college or university, you also have the luxury of comparing critiques in different fields.[1] An especially interesting kind of critique, largely unknown to people in the visual arts, is the music critique, and especially the "master class."[2] (Even if you don't have music classes in your institution, you can arrange to sit in on music master classes. Just call the department or institution in advance: music master classes are usually open to the public. There are also some very good music master classes, including some by András Schiff, on the internet.) In master classes the students, faculty, and a visiting "master" performer listen while a student performs a piece in part or in whole, and then the master critiques the performance. (I love the "master" part. Wouldn't it be great if visiting artists were called "masters"?) Often enough the master will sing or play an instrument to give her own version of what the student had done.

Criticism-by-doing is widespread in music and rare in the visual arts. In a visual art studio class, a teacher might take up a brush to change a portion of a painting, but that does not happen in critiques. Another difference between music master classes and art critiques is the relative unimportance of verbal criticism in music. Music teachers and conductors sometimes hum or beat out the passages they are critiquing instead of playing them properly. A master class instructor may say something like this:

> — I like the part where you go "dum, dum, dum, *dee*, dum, da, dumdum," but I would put more bite into that last beat, like "dum, dum, dum, *dee*, dum, daaah, dum *dum*!"

I have heard "master" performers and music teachers do this sort of thing completely out of tune and off pitch: it doesn't matter, because the point is timbre,

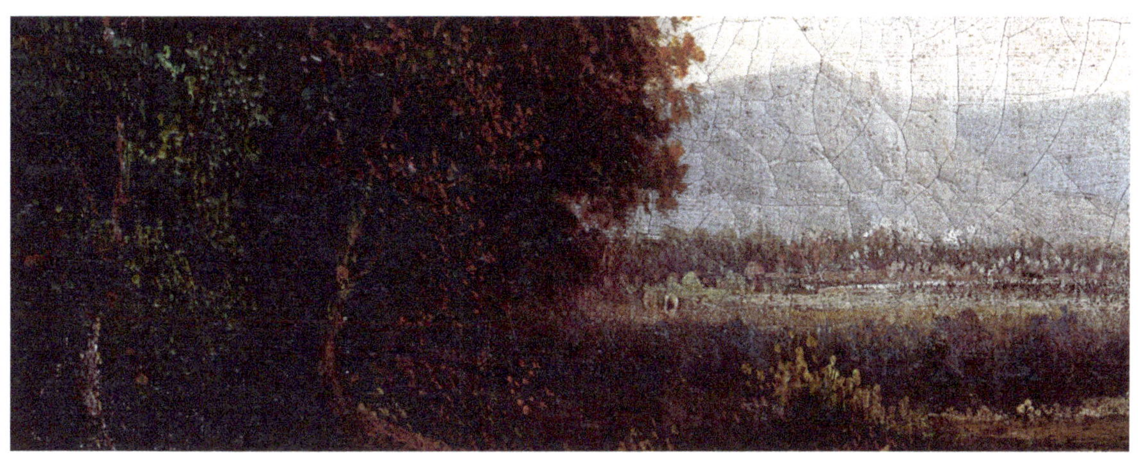

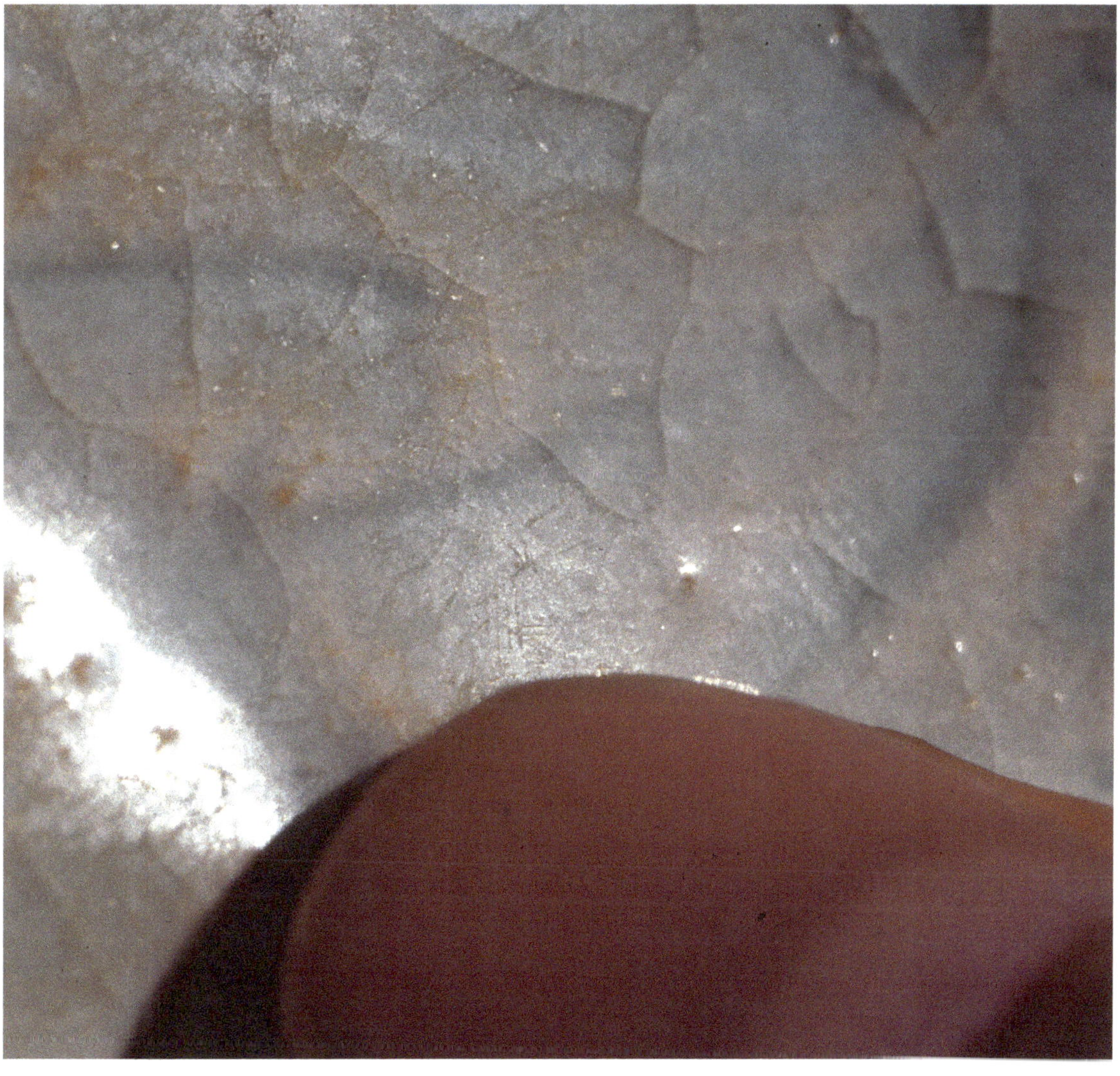

rhythm, or some other nuance.[3] Notice how *specific*, how *exact* this sort of criticism is. It can't be captured in print. It specifies a particular way of understanding that passage. It seems abstract, but it is actually precise. Even the master's and performer's gestures are significant.[4]

Sometimes the master will sit at the piano, or take the student's instrument, and play a little, to show how a passage should sound. In that case the only words you'll hear will be something like this:

> — You have [*playing music*] but you could have [*playing music*]

Or:

> — So here's a way of doing that [*playing music*] or [*playing music*] or [*playing music*]

Sometimes the master goes on and on about just a couple of bars of music. The equivalent level of specificity in painting would be a description of a square inch of canvas:

> — I like the way the little blotchy leaves keep going into the distance, so that in the background each little white blob is basically a whole tree…

Close looking also happens with media like ceramics, where surface really matters:

> — It's nice that when you look really, really close, there's the surface, and it's translucent, with little reddish and blue veins…

I'm using old artworks as examples, because they tend to get looked at more closely than contemporary art. I couldn't find examples from recent art critiques where objects were looked at this closely. Art critiques rarely get this specific, because past a certain level of detail things aren't easy to put into words. Because music critiques involve performance, the student can be asked to play a passage repeatedly. The subtlety of it can be amazing. If you sit in on one of these classes, you'll see: even if you play an instrument, you may not be able to follow the fine differences between incrementally different performances. A tiny difference in how the hands are held can have an effect on the music, just as a tiny difference in grip can alter a painted mark.

It would be interesting to try a critique in which the instructor makes her own version of a small part of an art student's work. That would be the analogue of the master performer humming or playing her own version of what the music student had just played. Alternately, an art student could be asked to repaint or redraw some potion of her own work. That would lead to the same kind of close attention to nuances of gesture.

There are many other parallels between studio critiques and master classes. For example, I attended a master class in which the student was playing a piano sonata by Beethoven. In that sonata, called "Les Adieux," there are moments when the pianist's fingers just run up and down the keyboard. There is no melody. In classical music, those moments are called "passagework," to contrast them against the places where there is melody or counterpoint. Sometimes those other kinds of passages are called "detail work." The master thought the student played the passagework unreflectively, as if it were busywork—as if it were just something Beethoven did to introduce the more interesting parts of his music. She said, "There is no such thing as passagework." She was trying to get the student to make her passagework as interesting as possible. Of course for Beethoven there was such a thing as passagework, so in a literal sense what she said wasn't true. It occurred to me that the analogue of passage work and detail work in visual art is ground and figure. I remember being told by an instructor in my MFA program that I had to stop painting my figures against gray backgrounds. "There is no such thing as background," he said, meaning that the figure and its ground have to be integrally related: ground and figure are inseparable, and the same quality of attention has to be paid to ground as to figure. I now realize my instructor had a modernist attitude: a lot of modernism has to do with rethinking the relation between figure and ground, and rejecting an old academic way of thinking in which the figure just sits against a relatively uninteresting background. So when the master pianist said, "There is no such thing as passagework," I saw that she was drawing on a modernist idea. For me, there was a lot to think about in the surprising analogy between ground, figure, passagework, and detail work.

Whether it's music, dance, theater, or just an unfamiliar medium, the principal thing to be gained by sitting in on other people's critiques is a sense of the conventions of your own department, medium, or institution. What seems natural to you might begin to appear like a restrictive ritual; and then you'll be free to ask whether or not other rituals might be better.

Part Four

Theories

34

Criticism, Critique, Crit, Criticality, *Kritik*

We come now to the theory section of the book. That will raise red flags for some readers, I know. Just consider two things as you read these chapters: first, nothing isn't theory (see chapter 5); and second, this theory isn't somehow more distant from critiques than other things in this book.

The most fundamental of the theories that can help illuminate critiques is about the word "critique" itself. If you stick around long enough in the art world, you will start hearing the word "criticality." It can be a kind of mantra for what art should accomplish or embody. You may also hear the German word *Kritik*, and you'll definitely hear "crit" (shorthand for "art critique") and the expression "art criticism," as opposed to simple "criticism." These all have different meanings.

A. *Criticism*. First there is plain ordinary criticism, as it is used in everyday conversation: it means judgment—often personal, often negative. Criticism in this sense is the activity of finding fault and giving praise. This narrow but common sense of the word inflects the other five.

B. *Art criticism* is the subject of a mountain of books. If you take a class in the history of criticism, you will probably read a Greek text (Pliny), a Renaissance text (Vasari), Enlightenment texts (Winckelmann, Diderot), a Romantic text (Baudelaire), and a modern text (Greenberg). It is not clear that these authors comprise a single tradition. Today no one writes like any of them, so art criticism is not a subject with a normal history: it seems to reinvent itself every couple of decades. There is also no agreement about whether an art critic should judge art or not, and if she should judge, what kind of judgment is best. There is also no agreement about whether the texts written for commercial galleries or newspapers should count as criticism. The whole subject is in massive disarray, and for me that makes it as fascinating as critiques themselves.[1]

C. *Critique, and "crits."* They're the subject of this book, but "critique" also means an activity that is more rigorous than simple everyday criticism, but less constrained than *Kritik*. People in art schools say "crits" as much as they say "critiques," and

I could have titled this book *Art Crits*. But I have never liked the term: it's like a nickname, but nicknames should be for things and people we know. I don't think anyone understands critiques very well. Also, "crit" sounds a bit rude, and that implies that it's making fun of the institution, or having fun with it. But how can you know how to make fun of something you don't understand?

D. *Kritik*. An art critique is very different from a philosophic critique, which is—to put it succinctly—an analytic inquiry that attempts to find the rational conditions under which something might be known. Immanuel Kant's critiques were meant to discover the "categories of thought," the ways that we can perceive and understand the world.[2] It is helpful that there is a proper term for that kind of critique: Kant's own term, *Kritik*. Very rarely, an art instructor will mean *Kritik* and not just critique. In an art critique setting, *Kritik* means the attempt to see what makes a given practice possible, or what can and can't be known about the practice. It is therefore rigorously non-judgmental: it's not about evaluation, but understanding.

E. *Critical theory*. Here is another expression you will run into, especially in upper-level and graduate classes. The expression has a range of meanings in academic life, including social theory that draw on Freud, and theories of literature. In the art world, it is usually applied to the work of the Frankfurt School of philosophers, especially Theodor Adorno. In that context it implies a concerted, philosophically informed inquiry into the social conditions that give artworks their meaning and value, with a special interest in the avant-garde. In art schools and departments, there are instructors who specialize in Frankfurt School theory, and who seek to apply it to art in preference to other kinds of critique and criticism.[3]

F. *Criticality*. This generally means artwork that is reflective and oppositional with respect to constructions of power. Art that does not possess criticality may be considered to be recherché, conservative, rote, uninventive, conventional, or disengaged from questions of institutions, identities, and historical contexts. An uncritical artwork might be a flower painting or a landscape. Projects that engage criticality include the Yes Men, the Critical Art Ensemble, and the many extra-academic collectives studied by Greg Sholette.[4] The theorist Irit Rogoff proposes criticality as the third stage of critique, after criticism (her name for what I have labeled as *A, B,* and *C*) and philosophic critique (which would include what I have labeled *D* and *E*).[5] The art historian Hal Foster proposes criticality as a third stage after modernist judgments such a Greenberg's and minimalist positions such as Donald Judd's (which are about interest, not quality), and before the current fourth stage, which might be about *beauty*.[6]

This is one way of putting some order to the different meanings of "critique." Here is a diagram with some of those meanings, together with some other words: *reflectivity*, *reflexivity*, and *intuition*. They are related to criticism, criticality, and the rest:

A. *Reflexivity* is when you're thinking of yourself, and what you're doing and thinking. If you're aware that you're reading a book, that's self-reflexive. It's common, at least in humans. A good synonym is *self-aware*. If you're aware that you're thinking about awareness, that's reflexivity.

B. A more interesting state is *reflectivity*, or *self-reflection*. It is the capacity to think about the assumptions that are driving you. If you're aware of the fact that you have an ambition to be an artist, and that's why you're reading this book, that is self-reflection. It's not very profound self-reflection, but it's more than simple self-awareness. There are lots of layers to self-reflection: you might realize your ambition is empty, that you don't have anything much to say as an artist; or you might realize you're ambitious because you're trying to be different from your mother, who isn't ambitious. Wherever it leads, *self-reflection* is about the conditions of understanding, so it is like *Kritik* and criticality. *Self-reflexion* is more a kind of built-in consciousness, or self-consciousness, so I haven't linked it to criticism.

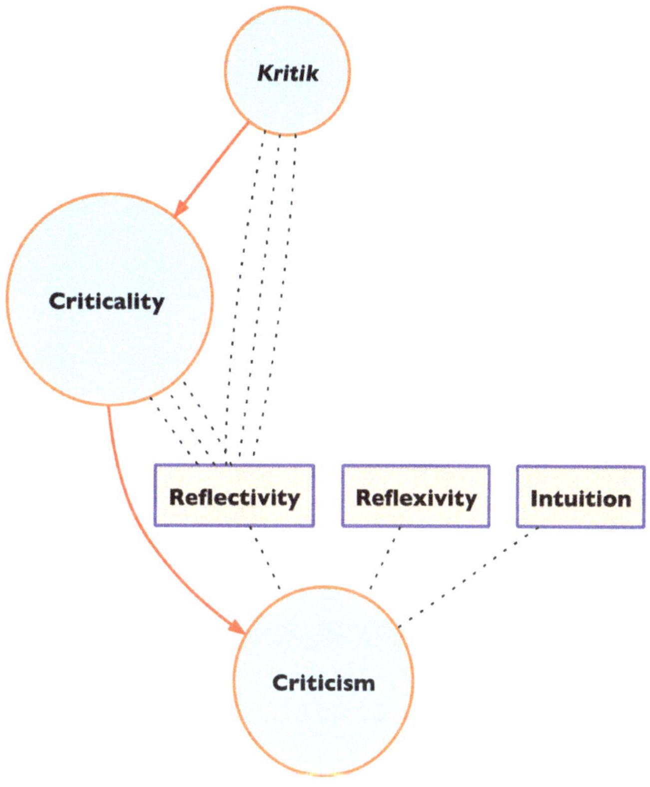

C. *Intuition* is the furthest from criticism and criticality. In this context, it means any hunch, feeling, mood, or other sort of direct, often inarticulate reaction. It is what people who run Conceptual Critiques dislike, and what people who are interested in beauty and the visceral appeal of art often cherish. Of course philosophers make much more of these terms! But for this purpose, this is how I arrange them.

Five Purposes of Criticism

Here's another way to classify critiques. It's possible to say that critiques have several purposes, what one author calls *meta-normative* goals.[1] Some critiques are *ethical, theological,* or *metaphysical,* while others are *scientific* or *teleological.* Again I'll consider these one by one.

A. *Ethical critiques.* Teachers in the military, law, and political science sometimes organize their material along *ethical* lines. Their purpose is to teach responsible social action. When a military instructor criticizes a soldier's performance, she may be thinking of that soldier in relation to her squadron, her unit, her social stratum, or even their shared society as a whole. That kind of criticism is *ethical* because it is intended to establish the relation between the soldier's performance and some

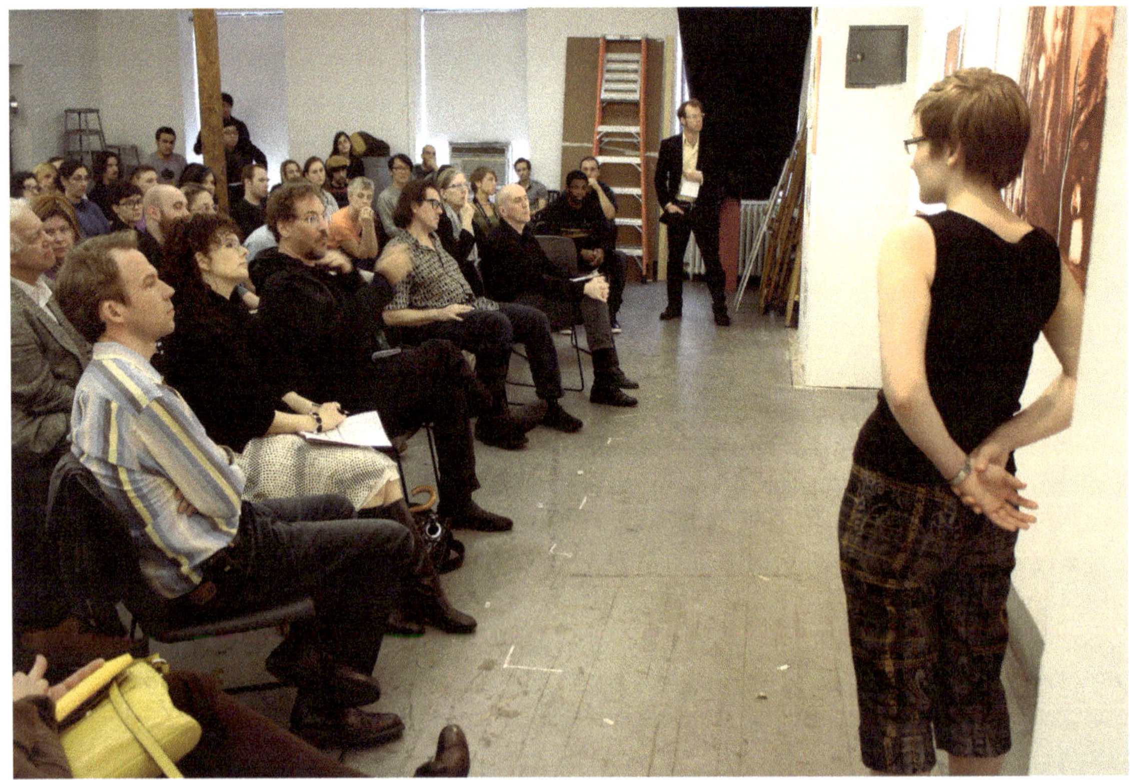

larger social context. It may be that the soldier has slept late, or said something insubordinate. The *goal* of the criticism, the instructor might say, is to get the soldier to stop sleeping late, or speaking out of place. But there is a goal beyond that goal, the *meta-normative* goal, and that is the ethical ideal of producing a soldier who is an exemplary part of the social fabric.

Ethical criticism is fairly common in art critiques. Some more conservative art academies are explicitly founded on ethical criteria. The Angel Academy of Art, the Academy of Art Canada, the Atelier Studio Program of Fine Art, and the Web Art Academy are examples; each presents itself as a counterbalance to the unappealing, unskilled, or misguided art of the present.[2] A teacher in such a setting might say a painting has too much sky in it, but her meta-normative goal will actually be to encourage the creation of beauty. Ethical criticism also exists in more central art schools and academies, where the purpose of art education is sometimes said to be the formation of citizens, not just the guidance of artists. From this perspective, teachers are "ethically and morally obliged" to give students an "adequate general education."[3]

If a teacher says your work is "honest," that might be an example of ethical criticism. But in critiques, it usually means something more like "straightforward," and it isn't always a compliment. It's also sneaky, because it implies that other work is dishonest—maybe even your own work! And it's coy, because it is rarely clear what dishonest work might be.[4]

B. *Theological critiques.* Teachers in divinity schools teach with a *theological* purpose in mind. Ideas are judged according to their relation to the possibilities of pastoral care, divine laws, or personal belief, rather than simply their logical sturdiness or their historical origins. I have participated in theological critiques at art departments in Christian universities such as Westmont College in Santa Barbara, Lipscomb University in Nashville, and BIOLA (The Bible Institute of Los Angeles). In one first-year drawing class in Westmont College, the students had been asked to make a drawing representing a hand or hands holding an object or objects. I looked at several drawings of the students' own hands, holding things like feathers and rocks. One student explained, "This is my hand, reaching up, and that's Jesus's hand at the top. I can't reach it because Satan's hand is coming across the picture holding a rock." I could have asked the student if the drawing might not be just as good without the symbolism, but I knew the answer would be no. Theology, or religious belief more generally, was the point of art for those students.

C. Overtly *metaphysical* principles guide some philosophic and literary-critical studies. A philosophic critique, like Kant's, may be concerned with the laws of logic and sense, the conditions of the apprehension of space and time, the limits of what can be seen or pictures—that is, by metaphysical criteria. I have been in many architecture and interior architecture critiques in which the theme is *space*, in its Kantian form: infinite, Euclidean, and three-dimensional. Any number of critiques in photography, painting, video, film, and other fields are concerned with the limits of what can be represented. Blurred photographs, smeared paintings like Richter's, dark videos: they can all be presented as inquiries into the ends of representation, which is a genuinely metaphysical interest.

D. By *scientific* criteria I mean experiment, hypothesis, and falsification, which are commonly taught at the PhD level, and less commonly at the BFA and MFA levels. In PhD programs such as those in Reading, Dundee, and Goldsmiths (in the U.K.), students are critiqued according to the cogency and practicality of their research programs. They are expected to develop goals at each stage, and to propose hypotheses, which the work is expected to answer. Art becomes a form of research. The function of critiques is to assess whether the artist's program can be achieved, or has been achieved, and to locate plausible goals for the next stage of the investigation. Teachers in these programs probably wouldn't say that they follow scientific models, but there is a large literature on research, outcomes, hypotheses, assessments, and other criteria borrowed, ultimately, from the sciences. All this is discussed in Part Six of this book.

E. When teachers develop courses aimed at imparting experience, skills, or information, they are thinking first and foremost of *teleological* criteria: that is, they are asking how to put the material to use, whether it is important that it be useful.[5] The Pennsylvania Academy of Fine Arts runs an annual event called the Wall Panel Review, where three professionals sit with their backs to the audience, and review slides, as if they were reviewing them for residencies, teaching positions, or juried exhibitions. They say just what they would if no one was sitting behind them.[6] I attended a critique once in the Center for Creative Studies in Detroit, where the student was showing small metal sculptures. One faculty member said that he thought the zinc sheets in her work could be sourced more inexpensively from a supplier on the far side of town, which would potentially give her a higher profit when she sold the work. That entire critique was about materials and profit margins, which I suppose was appropriate for a city where design is still closely allied to the automobile industry. Still, it surprised me to hear such a consistently teleological— in this case market-driven—critique.

36

A Sixth Purpose of Criticism,

and Words for Success

Meta-normative goals is a mouthful, but it is useful. The five purposes of criticism I mentioned in the previous chapter are common, but there's a sixth, meta-normative criticism, that is more common than any of them.

If you were to ask your teachers what their underlying goal was in art critiques, they might say they are trying to help students make better art, or richer art, or have a fuller and more rewarding art practice. Some might say they would like to inspire students to make more compelling work, or more powerful work. Words like those are the meta-normative goals, the ideals, the ultimate terms of praise. There are a number of such words for success:

Interesting	A knockout
Powerful	Just don't know what to say
Fierce	Gorgeous
Strong	Beautiful
Nice	Sublime
Really nice	Cool
So nice	Stimulating
Nicely done	Quite stimulating
Moving	Innovative
Kind of moving	New
Original	Really new
Really sort of original	Something new
Inventive	Excellent
Fascinating	It works[1]
Compelling	Wonderful
Difficult	Pretty good
Challenging	Your best yet
Amazing	Okay

I mentioned "interesting" earlier, as a word for failure. It's an especially slippery word, sometimes nothing more than what linguists call a *placeholder*, the way that in the U.S., "John Doe" stands for anyone's name.

Note that these terms are neither ethical, theological, metaphysical, scientific, nor teleological: they don't fit any of the kinds of critiques I have just named. They are *rhetorical* criteria. If an artwork possesses one of these, people will pay attention. An artist whose work has some of these criteria may be more likely to get a show, or get a good review, or sell her work. Rhetorical criteria do not say anything about what the work looks like, how true it is, what it's about, or what it says. Rhetorical criteria are practical, and they may crop up in any sort of critique, whether it is ethical, theological, metaphysical, scientific, teleological, or something else. (By the way, if you've decided to listen for these nice words in your critiques, remember that they can be just as misguided, just as irrelevant to your work as the words for failure.[2])

This list of words for success is the complement of my long list of failure words in chapter 21. The list of words for failure is completely disordered, and it seems like it could go on forever. That's more evidence that the criteria in art critiques are mainly rhetorical, because otherwise you would be able to see some ordering to the list, some sense of what guides it. The words for praise seem to fall into three groups: aesthetic terms (beauty, the sublime), expressions of engagement (compelling, interesting), and terms for the avant-garde (new, innovative). But I'm not sure how far that would get you, because something can be compelling because it's sublime, or sublimely compelling. I think both the failure words and the success words are fundamentally rhetorical: they are about pointing to, or away, from the work in question. The work might also be sublime or beautiful in the proper sense of those words, but that isn't usually what is meant when someone says "beautiful!" in a critique.[3]

The success words are very common, and you hear them over and over. I can think of a few others, but not many. Looking at the short list of success words and the enormous list of failure words, I wondered: why are there so few words for successful art? Here are a couple of guesses:

1. It's true that you hear "I love that!" or "That's amazing!" or "That's beautiful!" a lot, but that is because teachers like to encourage students. But on the other hand, this can't be the main reason why there are more failure words, because it doesn't explain why teachers don't use lots of words to praise students' work.

2. Words like "great" and "wonderful" are necessarily vague, because new work is hard to understand. It is easier for a teacher to say exactly what is wrong with your work than it is to say what makes genuinely new work successful.

3. "Wonderful" and the other main success words are sometimes euphemisms. I've seen artwork that is very old-fashioned, romantic, or sentimental, and I have wanted to praise it: but I couldn't say what I liked, because that might sound like an insult. So instead I've said "That's wonderful!"

When I posted the failure and success words on Facebook in 2011, I got lots more failure words, but only a few more success words. And then, after a week or two, my colleague Frances Whitehead emailed me with an enormous spreadsheet: she had tried to write the opposite of every failure word. She wanted to show me that there are just as many "complimentary" words as there are "pejorative" ones. Here is the beginning of her list. I have made some small changes, so this isn't verbatim, but virtually all of it is hers. It follows the list in chapter 21:

Pejorative	Complimentary
Didactic	informative
Anachronistic	current
Fancy	sophisticated
Pretty	stunning
Merely pretty	elegant
Vague	paradoxical
Just fun	Fun
Easy	easily understood
Almost insulting	confrontational
Boring	intriguing
Bland	spicy
Dull	sharp
Painfully dull	satisfyingly insightful
Unintelligent	intelligent
Stupid	smart
Trite	fresh
Doesn't make sense	coherent
Has useless additions	well constructed
Uninvolved	involved
Dishonest	honest
Immoral	moral
Stupidly, gratuitously immoral	revealingly immoral
Unreflective	reflective
Over-controlled	disciplined
Uncontrolled	wild

Weak	denies heroics
Thin	light
Odd	idiosyncratic
Not odd enough	nicely odd
Too much	just right
Self-serving	outreaching
Too amiable	amiable
Simple	clear
Simplistic	straightforward
Literal-minded	legible
Corny	populist
Ridiculous	slapstick
Awful ("bloomin' awful," etc.)	nicely done
No motivation	highly motivated
Impersonal	personal
Careless	careful
Makeshift	improvisational
Thoughtless	thoughtful
Been there, done that	classic
Poor composition	well composed
Maudlin	dark
Melodramatic	dramatic
Too sci-fi	sci-fi
Schlocky	well done
Garish	bright
Kitsch	familiar
Not close enough to kitsch	everyday
Its only thrill is	
how close it can get to kitsch	hard to pin down
Not kitschy enough	high-minded
Unaware it's humorous	sly
Distracting use of medium	materially focused
Obvious	direct
Blunt	blunt
In your face	in your face
Gratuitous appropriations	historicized
Obscure	mysterious
Obscure, bordering on obtuse	intriguing
Condescending	erudite
Heartless	reserved

Repetitive	serial
Incoherent	coherent
Too satisfying	addictive
Plays to the audience	seductive
Manipulative	manipulative
Looks lousy	visual
Commercial	appealing
Overly commercial	convenient
Subject matter and idea are disconnected	integrated
Form and content are disconnected	unified
Too serious	serious
Too corporate	authentic
Too manly	strong
Sexist	ungendered
Silly	delightful
Too light	light touch
Too dark	brooding
Finicky	quirky
Unstable	irreverent
Neither accessible to all, nor accessible to none	multivalent
Colors dissonant	courageous
Colors too harmonious	harmonious
No congruence between artist, aim, and result	consistent
Cute	approachable
Too cute	charming
Cutesy	bawdy or erotic
Sweet	empathetic
Campy	campy
Stale	traditional
Mismatched styles	postmodern
Half-hearted	affective
Disengaged	engaged
Less than overwhelming	overwhelming
Too overwhelming	wonderfully overwhelming
Cultish about the avant-garde	new
Looks like art	artistic

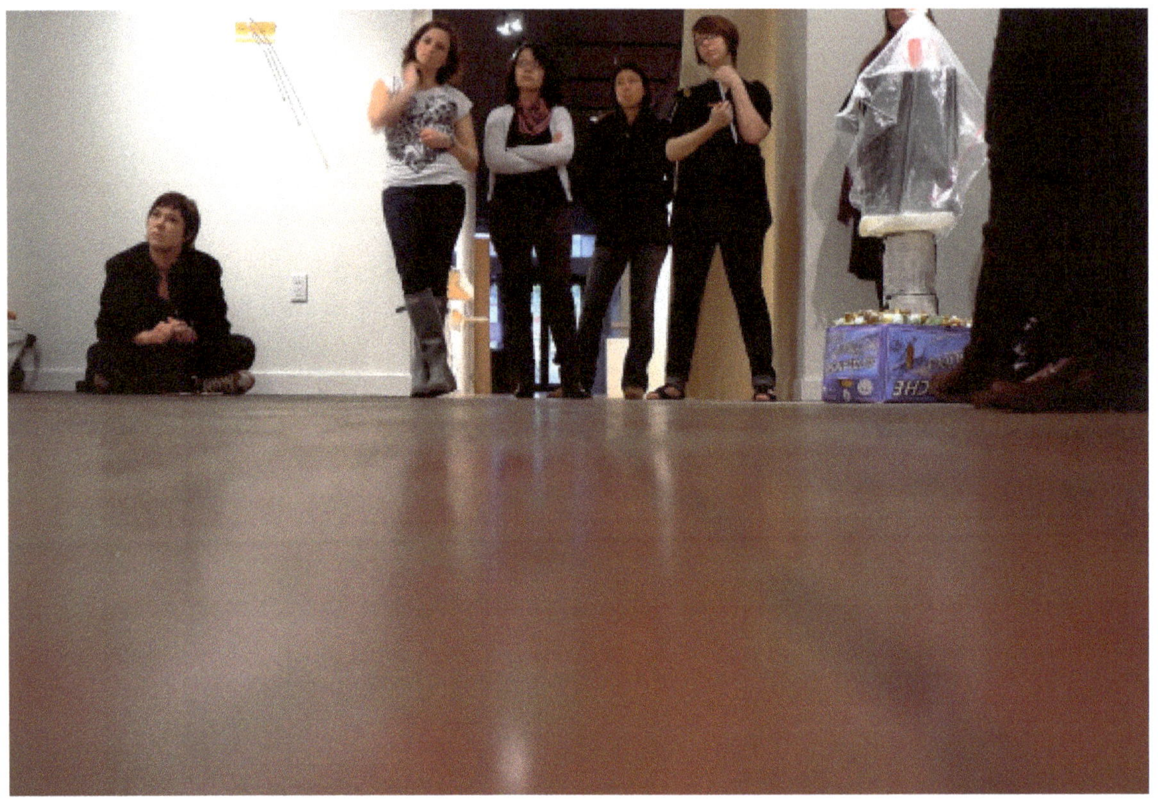

Too trendy	current
Wrong medium	well wrought
Propaganda	expressive
Illustrates a theory	metaphoric
Too systematic	conceptual
Formulaic	genre aware
Makes no sense,	
but seems like it should	clear
Just tossed off	studied
Badly done	well crafted
Mystical	mystical
Spiritual	spiritual
Not spiritual	earthy
Intentions unclear	intentional
Intentions too clear	rational
Meaningless	meaningful
Empty	rich
Bullshit	brilliant

It's an interesting list, and it goes on: the original is twice this long. I notice a couple of things. Most of Frances's "complimentary" words are good, strong words. But some are just as ambiguous as the failure words: "manipulative" could be a word for failure, and so could "brooding," "overwhelming," "hard to pin down," "slapstick," and "easily understood." In fact it's not entirely clear that the right-hand column has more success words than the left-hand column. The words seem to shift back and forth. Only a few words are relatively stable: "wonderful" is pretty much a good thing, and "awful" is generally bad. Most words change meaning in different contexts: they work rhetorically.

Take one word on the list as an example: kitsch.

This was originally applied to mass-produced emulations of handmade furniture in the late 19th c.: in that context, kitsch meant the sorts of things bourgeois consumers could afford. As late as the early 1990s in art schools, kitsch was one of the worst things a student could hear. I remember students being apoplectic with despair when their teachers told them their work was kitsch. That was an inheritance of Greenberg, Adorno, and avant-garde modernism, which reviled kitsch. Sometime in the mid 1990s, kitsch turned into a good thing, but it can still paralyze critiques.

An effective strategy here is to change the terms. "Kitsch" may function as a log jam in a critique, stopping the flow of thought. "Sexism," "commercialism," and "decoration" are other words that can work this way. They are like the legend "THE END" that used to appear in movies: words like "kitsch" give the teacher permission to stop looking. Critique panels can get stuck on those words, like a phonograph record stuck in a groove. When a word like "kitsch" is ruling the discussion, the conversation will not build and progress, but hammer on the same point again and again. What is needed is a way around the word, a way to associate the work with some other, more flexible term. It can help to break the word apart into its component concepts. For "kitsch" you can substitute words like "sentimentality" or "mere beauty," or you can use Hermann Broch's useful distinction between "sweet" and "sour" kitsch.[3] You might ask something like this: "Let's leave 'kitsch' aside for a moment. I think it's too general a term, and I'd like to talk about a certain *quality* of kitsch that applies here: I know my work is sentimental, and I'd like to know what you think of that." In general failure words are entirely relative to their cultural contexts, but because those contexts are not often known, they can jam up the conversation. A long list like this one can help divert the conversation around the obstacle word.

Rhetoric is a miscellaneous category, the "category" of whatever works best. Rhetoric is also the name of a field of study, a discipline that goes back to the Greeks: it is the study of persuasion, of public speaking, of multi-voiced argument: a teacher of classical rhetoric finds advantages wherever possible, and she may shift her strategies and even her beliefs in order to persuade her audience.[4] (Think of lawyers;

in ancient Rome, lawyers were trained in rhetoric.) Ultimately, rhetoric is in danger of becoming *sophistry*, the art of persuading an audience regardless of whether or not the argument is true or false, good or evil. (Again, think of lawyers, who have to defend their clients no matter what they think they've done.)

I would almost call art teaching sophistic, except that I don't want to imply that art instruction is just clever, devious, or dishonest. It is rhetorical, however, because it is not concerned with consistency or even content as much as the art of persuasion. Art critiques are less dependent than other kinds of critique on guiding principles.

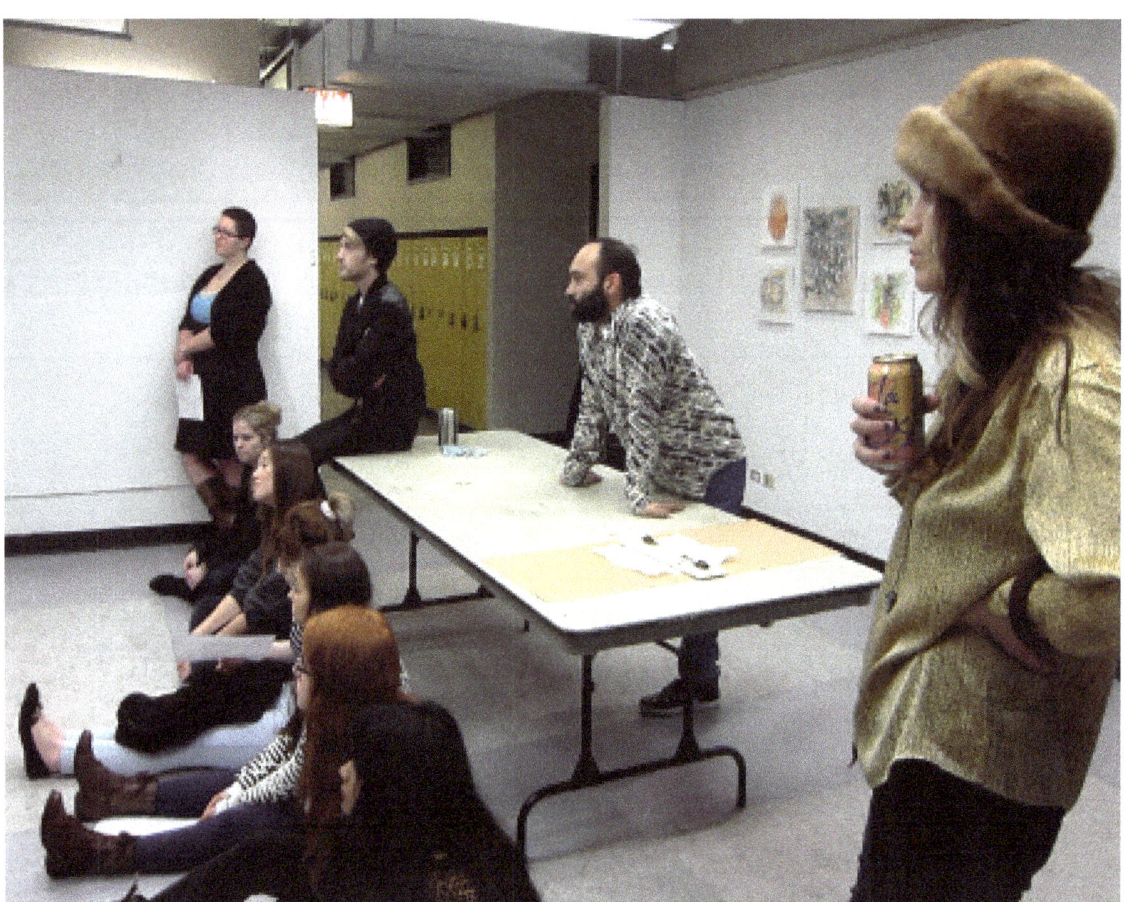

M. H. Abrams's Theory

So far, I have suggested two ways of classifying critiques: by looking at who speaks and who remains silent, and by looking at the critiques' ultimate goals. Here is a third way, which I will call "critical orientations," following an account by the literary critic M. H. Abrams.[1]

A. The first orientation is *mimetic*, meaning that your work is judged according to how well it matches the world. These days mimetic criticism seems narrow because it sounds like the kind of instruction that nineteenth-century academics gave to their painting students. But it is still common in undergraduate drawing and painting classes, where you'll be working to draw heads, models, and still lifes, and you'll hear comments such as, "The hand bothers me. I think you should spend some time looking at hands."

But mimesis is a wider category than that. It has been said to be the sole principle for all of criticism,[2] and it can be applied to any case where art recreates something in the world—whether it's a model, an apple, a concept, gesture, or a mood.[3] To Aristotle, Socrates, and Plato, all arts were imitations, even flute-playing, poetry and dancing.[4] (*Mimesis* seems to have been originally connected to dancing, before it became a general critical term.[5]) As Abrams says, imitation "is a relational term, signifying two items and some correspondence between them."

In this general sense, mimetic criticism is very much relevant to contemporary art critiques. After the first year or two in the BFA, skill is no longer the main issue, but recreating concepts, moods, and other non-visual things definitely is at issue. It is mimetic criticism to say to a performance artist, "That gesture doesn't look like something I would do if I were *really* exhausted," or to say to an abstract painter, "This really has the quality of evening light in Atlanta."

What counts as the visual equivalent of the concept of empowerment or marginality? How can a work of visual art communicate the mood of diaspora or neoliberalism? Those questions are mimetic, and they go back to Plato and Aristotle.

B. Abrams calls the second orientation *pragmatic*, meaning that it is intended to help the student move, please, delight, or instruct her viewers. Horace's *Art of*

Criticism, the key classical text for this approach, tells poets how to keep their audience "in their seats until the end, how to induce cheers and applause."[6] Horace says the poet's aim is either to profit or to please, or to blend the delightful and the useful into one. These days I do not think many teachers would say that "delighting" or "pleasing" the viewer is a good idea, and only a few teachers would say that artists should "instruct" or "profit" the public. The words sound old-fashioned. But like mimetic criticism, pragmatic criticism is very much with us. Try substituting some other terms: instead of "instructing," say "interrogating" or "revealing"; instead of "delighting," "compelling" instead of "instructing," "convincing." If a teacher says, "I think that would be compelling if only you had used aluminum," that's a pragmatic criticism: your teacher wants your work to have a certain effect, but she has nothing to say about *content*. (What does your compelling artwork compel you to think or feel? That's not at issue in pragmatic criticism.)

Sometimes you may think of your work as something you do just for yourself. It doesn't need to please anyone, or be compelling for anyone. But that is often more a stance you take than a reality. It is hard to make an artwork without introducing some element designed to convince some specific viewer. When you work only for yourself, without thinking at all about other people, you rely on an inner "viewer" to assess the work and act as a spectator as it is being made. That inner division between the self that is making the work, and the self that is viewing it, is all that is needed for pragmatic criticism to gain a foothold. If part of you is standing off to one side, viewing the work you are making, then there is already an audience, and the artist-audience dynamic is already in place. Even the most private art is made according to criteria of pragmatic criticism.[7]

C. With the end of the eighteenth century and the beginning of Romanticism came a third orientation, which Abrams calls *expressive*. It shifted attention to the artist, and art was seen as "the overflow, utterance, or projection of the thought and feeling of the poet." A work of art was "essentially the internal made external, resulting from a creative process operating under the impulse of feeling."[8] Here we are closer to home. The audience is no longer as important (as in pragmatic criticism) and neither is the external world (as in mimetic criticism). Spontaneity arises as a new criterion of excellence, since it is important that the artist is communicating inner feelings without the imposition of some conventional rule.[9]

The expressive orientation is fundamentally romantic (as in early nineteenth-century Romanticism). van Laar and Diepeveen's "introspective mystic," who thinks all art is so deeply personal it can hardly be put into words, is a late Romantic, a follower of the expressive orientation.[10] The one-on-one critique, and idea of having just one principal advisor in an MFA program, are ideas that came out of Romanticism. These days the Romantic orientation goes under other names, like "mentoring" or "advising."[11]

Art instructors don't undertake expressive critiques with much consistency. Teachers don't usually try to interpret an artwork exclusively as the product of the artist's sensibility or psyche. Pragmatic and mimetic concerns usually intrude. But contemporary art is fundamentally late Romantic in this sense: art is understood basically as an expression of something inner. I think of this as a deep secret of the art world: most of what happens in any given school, department, or academy is grounded in the expressive orientation. We're more late Romantics, on the whole, than we are modernists or postmodernists. But that's a subject for another book.[12]

D. Abrams's last "orientation" is *objective*, meaning that the teacher concentrates on the object itself, and tries not to mention the external world, the audience, or the artist's inner world. The objectivist orientation shows up whenever your teacher tries to talk only about what happens in the work, without mentioning you as a person, or other viewers, or the mimetic correspondences with the world.[13] This is van Laar and Diepeveen's formalist "picture doctor" from chapter 32. The two most common kinds of objectivist criticism are formal analysis, which restricts itself to colors and shapes, and iconography, which is the study of symbols and signs in artworks.[14]

Logically speaking, objectivist criticism does not exist, because it is impossible to speak about shapes, colors, or symbols without referring to things outside the artwork. Everything that can be said about an artwork is also a statement about the world, the viewer, or the artist. If I say, "That blue is beautiful," I'm evoking the feeling of melancholy (drawing on the Romantic sense of the artist's mind), and the blue of the sky (recalling Ancient mimetic critiques), and I am also pronouncing a judgment (introducing pragmatic concerns). What Abrams calls objective criticism can only be a fiction, but it is important and widespread. Sometimes it is helpful to listen to a formal analysis as if it were only referring to the artwork, and other times it is best to listen more skeptically, in order to hear how the analysis avoids references to the world, the audience, and the artist.

Abrams's schema is over fifty years old, but I think it is one of the strongest conceptualizations of the basic orientations of criticism, and it's as true for visual art now as it was for literature back when he wrote it.

Five Allegories for Critiques:

1. Critiques are Like Seductions, Full of Emotion

This chapter and following ones propose five allegories for critiques: they are like seductions (they're amorous); they are like different languages all spoken at once (theoretical "discourses," studio talk); they are collections of stories (they are narratological); they are like battles (they're warlike, people fight); and they are like court cases (people argue, judgments are expected).

It is a dogma of art criticism that a critique should not be taken personally. I regard that as an "enabling fiction": a lie that lets us get on with what we want to do. Critiques are supposed to be focused on the work, rather than the artist, and to that end they usually proceed as if the artwork is separable from the student who made it. Poststructural theory lends support, by claiming that artworks are effectively autonomous objects, detached for purposes of interpretation from their makers. I do not need to disagree with the poststructural stance to say that at root any criticism of an artwork is also a criticism of the artist. That is so because the very terms and notions of criticism are themselves rooted in "agency"—in latent connections to the maker. Even when critiques stick to talk about form, color, media, or software, the teachers' judgments are connected to issues such as extroversion and introversion, emotional control, stability, and exhibitionism. It's hard to imagine how a work could be decisively disconnected from the artist's personality, and typically the connections run deeper than the artist or the teachers know. Even so, most critiques maintain the strange fiction that the work can be considered entirely apart from the person who made it. There are exceptions: in performance art, for example, the emotional content of the work cannot always be distinguished from the emotional state of the artist, even if the "character" can be distinguished from the actor, and the actor from the student. Perhaps the most extreme exclusion of psychological criticism occurs in architecture critiques, where it is not usual to speak of the student's emotional investment in the work except as a matter of assessing their commitment. Since most critiques are somewhere between those two extremes, it is usually possible to proceed as if the critique is not personal, though I would say that it is not a bad idea to keep in mind just how artificial that enabling fiction really is.

When personal elements rise to the surface, they can become a *dis*abling fiction. For that reason it is good to have a theory about emotion in critiques that get out of control or are psychologically destructive. I especially like the idea of understanding critiques as enactments or metaphors of seduction.[66] There are some obvious signs that seduction is a pertinent model. Instructors declare "I love that!" or "That's wonderful!" or "I'm very taken by that!" And beyond those sorts of exclamations, seduction works in more abstract and intricate ways.

At the very least, an artist wants attention. The teachers in the critique should be engrossed, interested, intrigued, responsive, excited. The work is meant to draw them in, to invite them, to provoke them. Sometimes, to be sure, the artist wants something more like friendship, a lasting and renewable dialogue of equals. But often, given the briefness of the encounter and the difference in rank and age between the teachers and the students, the aim is more immediate and also more intimate than friendship. I want to distinguish this from what happens between

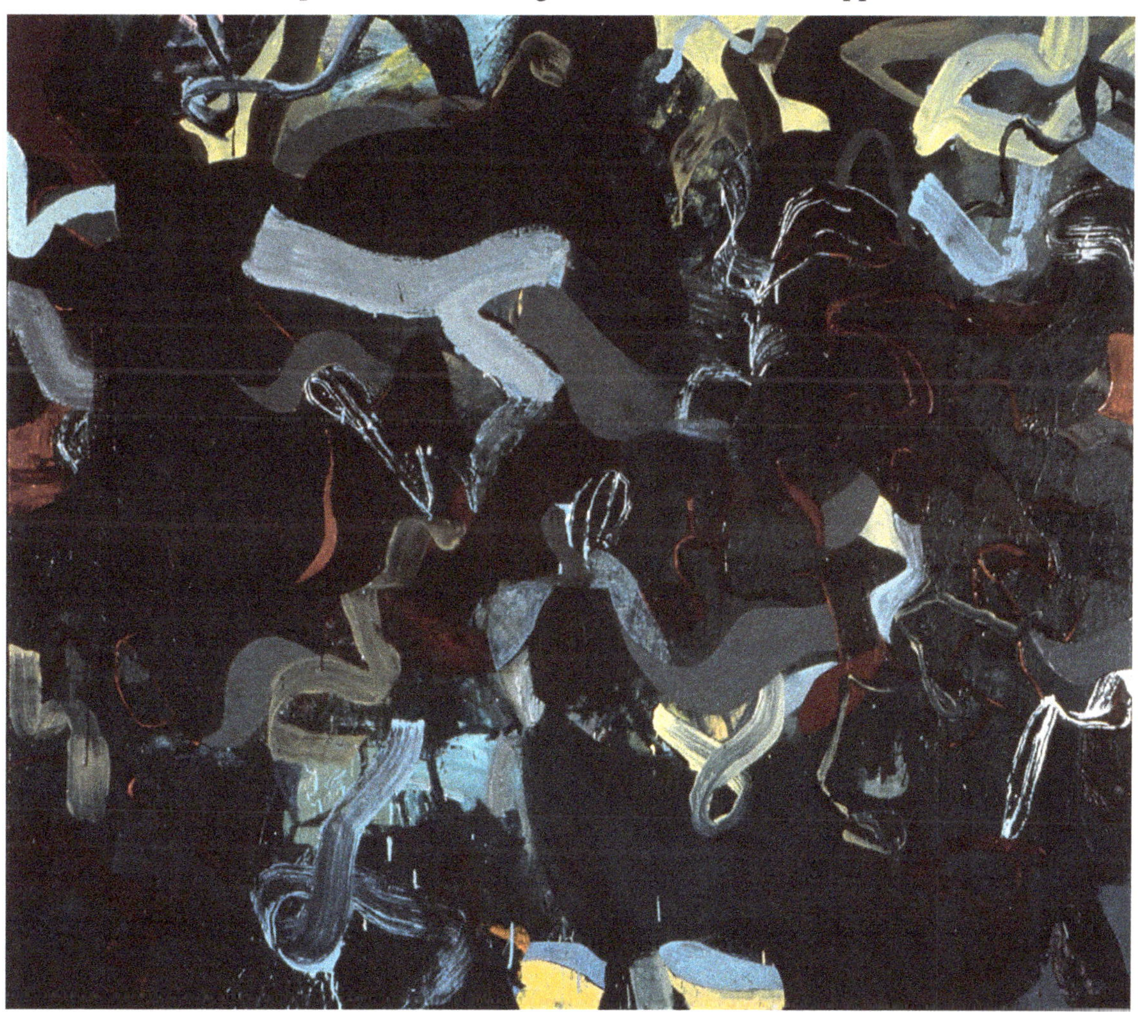

teachers and students; what I think is worth modeling is the indirect relation between teachers and artworks, where the students themselves play variable and sometimes unimportant roles. The artwork "presents itself," or is introduced, and *it*, not the student, is to be the object of the teacher's attention. At it best, the artwork can incite a range of responses within the compass of a critique: a teacher might be repelled, then attracted; there might be the promise of "depth" or lasting interest; the work may seem "coy" or overly aggressive; it may appear as an "other" or as an acquaintance, as a relative or as a stranger.

This way of thinking about critiques helps explain the sources of strong emotion that sometimes ruin critiques. Note that even a successful critique ends with the teacher being unfaithful. If there are teachers in the critique who are not the student's usual teachers, they will leave the work at the end of the session, and most will not return. Even the student's own teachers will eventually be unfaithful, when the student passes their class or graduates from their institution.

Teachers who are themselves artists know what it feels like to be alone with the work for days or months, preparing the work to be seen. The classical metaphor for this is childbirth, since the work is like someone's offspring; but in this context, I think that the solitary time spent creating is more like time spent in front of a mirror, "fixing" or primping your ideal image, and it is that image that is displayed for the teachers. Given the importance of this time spent in preparation, it follows that the brevity of the critique and the inevitable dispersion of the critique panel correspond to rejection or unfaithfulness. Often enough the teachers will continue to discuss the work, and it will remain in their minds for some time, but eventually will come the moment when each teacher will forget the student's work. This is a principal source of emotional difficulty for students and for teachers. Showing work is like an invitation, and so there is a potential for injury. Everyone involved knows that spurning and unfaithfulness, in so many words, are commonplace consequences of showing art work.

I am not suggesting you should imagine each critique as a bedroom scene. Seduction is a model, a way of understanding the curious emotional charge that often accumulates and discharges during critiques. In this sense critiques are veiled psychodramas, as the visitor to my own MFA program called them, and they involve the entire spectrum of "unnatural" as well as natural responses to seduction, including voyeurism, lechery, perversion, and bad faith. In ordinary critiques the fundamental sequence of display, appreciation, and unfaithfulness runs its course like a familiar story, and is not obtrusive. Typically there is a fair amount of praise in critiques, and if you listen carefully it is apparent that the praise is sometimes inserted into places in the dialogue where it does not logically belong. In such cases its function is to reassure. An incongruous, sudden or irrelevant statement of praise says, in effect, that the seduction is going well, and there is no cause for alarm.

Sometimes it can be useful to actually talk like this, and to say, for example, that a certain work "is seductive" or appears "friendly." But it is rarely useful to mention that a student is behaving as if he or she wanted to seduce the panel. Doing that would ruin the real seduction that is going on between the work and the panelists. In an emotional critique, this is exactly what goes wrong: the seduction is not succeeding, and both parties know it. Discomfort and suspicion build on both sides, until they find expression in remarks overloaded with emotional freight. Ultimately pretenses are cast aside, people become openly rude, and the dialogue breaks down. If you spend enough time in art schools and departments you will witness critiques like that, where people not only cry (as they did in my MFA program), but run out, hit each other, scream, and lose control.

The example I choose here is from the earlier stages in this process, when the critique can still be salvaged. The panelists have just come from a frustrating critique in which they saw work that most of them thought was misguided. They had been unable to persuade with the artist to change. That was on their minds when they came into the new studio, and even though that emotional charge had no relation to the work at hand, it carried over—much as a lover's quarrel will cast a shadow on the rest of the day—into the new critique.

The work they discuss here is gestural abstract painting, done by a student named Chris Fennell. I reproduced one in chapter 26. The one reproduced in this chapter shows the metallic paint he used.

S	Anytime you're ready, or anytime anyone else is ready.	
F	We just realized how incredibly bad the light is in this room. Looking at the [previous student's] paintings in the hallway, they actually looked better than in the studio.	*By starting out saying how "bad" the light is, this panelist is also insinuating—but not yet implying—that the paintings themselves are bad. It is a troublesome opening comment.* *Speaking about the quality of light is also insidious, because it obliquely declares that the paintings are invisible. What can be said, after all, when the paintings "themselves" cannot be seen?*
C	Yes, ideally would like to have had them in my studio [at home], because I have the combination of fluorescence and incandescence. You know, these are actually brighter than they look.	*Chris agrees that the paintings cannot be seen, but he suggests that the defect can be compensated for, since it is only a matter of brightness and not something less tangible.*
F	What kind of paint is this?	
C	Oil; the silver is enamel, oil-based enamel.	

S	Do you mind that they're going to fall apart?	*A deliberately provocative way of putting it. The question implies that the panelist does not care about the paintings, that the seduction may have already failed. The first words, "do you mind," belong in a more courteous sentence, so in this context they are ironic, as if to say, "Can we be friends if we agree that these paintings are not important?" The proffered intimacy of the initial phrase turns into a challenge.*
C	I don't think they're going to fall apart.	*Chris does not respond to the ironic politeness of the panelist's challenge.*
S	I can guarantee you they are.	*And so the panelist responds in kind, with unalloyed aggression.*
C	Ah—	*It's a skeptical "ah—" but no argument is offered.*
S	What are the ingredients?	*The question is a declaration that the seduction is still on, since if it had failed entirely, the panelist would have been silent. It is still possible for the student to win her affections.*
C	It's mostly oil, and there's some enamel. The silver is enamel.	

R	The silver is the only enamel?	
C	Yes. I think what's going to happen is that at some point the silver is going to start to deteriorate, but because it doesn't leave a thick, gestural brushstroke, the—	*A moment ago, Chris didn't think the paintings were going to deteriorate. Here he accommodates to the teacher's belligerent claim, improvising an explanation.*
R	If we stay here long enough, we may be able to witness the event. It's fugitive paint.	*The second teacher puts it in dramatic terms. The imaginary drama—of everyone standing around, watching paint fall—makes it more explicit that what has just been happening is a drama, and it opens the way for less decorous, more directly destructive comments.*
C	Yeah. I mean, but I can—	
S	It'll sit there in puddles. If you don't care, I don't care either.	*She repeats the ironic bid for friendship: "We can be friends if you'll agree the paintings are going to be puddles." At this point, the seduction (or proffered friendship) can only proceed with the sacrifice of the object of attention itself—which both parties know is not possible.*
F	So these [paintings] don't matter.	*Another teacher joins in. When this happens, the critique can become a one-on-one dialogue: one student and a combined panel that is against him.*

C	Yes, I think eventually, if something starts to happen—I mean I don't mind a certain level of deterioration; I can just go back in with the silver, because it's flat, it's not like a thick gestural work, I could touch it up if I had to.	
F	Trying to put conservators out of business?	*The first conciliatory comment comes without any reason—and it's still fairly belligerent.*
C	Yes.	
F	These are the sort of paintings they live for.	
C	Yeah.	
F	So next time, answer, "Yes, I want them to deteriorate."	
C	Yeah. "Rapidly."	*The intimacy is partly restored by this joke, which is still at the expense of the paintings.*
S	No, it's a little embarrassing to have somebody call you after they've owned a painting for four or five years, and say, "The God damn thing is falling off the wall."	

C	Yeah.	*Chris is joking along, taking punishment.*
S	Especially if they've given you twenty-five, thirty or forty thousand dollars for it.	*This is the second conciliatory remark, since it implies the work may have value—and again there is no rational connection to what had been said before.*
C	Well, I'm not in that position yet, so... If they're willing to pay that, I'd be glad to come back and touch them up.	

That ended the confrontational portion of the critique. As in a seduction, it isn't always rationality that rules the day. Chris's willingness to make jokes at his own expense, and to stop arguing back, might have saved the day. But these things are ineffable, as they are in relationships. The impending argument did poison the well, and the remainder of the critique was conducted under a double shadow: on the one hand, once this level of antagonism surfaced it remained possible that it could resurface, and possibly more quickly and violently than before; and on the other hand, all succeeding positive comments were tainted by the panel's tacit agreement that the paintings were going to fall apart anyway.

I have suggested a sexual metaphor in order to help explain the violence that sometimes accompanies critiques. In particular I would say that when untoward emotion rises to the surface, it can sometimes be assigned to some problem in the half-hidden script of wooing and refusal. When things go well and the critique is productive and inspiring, that means script is running smoothly. The seduction theory has pragmatic consequences, because students and panelists can repair some nasty or problematic comments by distinguishing their emotional elements from their analytic content.

Thinking of panelists and students as jilted lovers can explain highly emotional, provocative responses, but it is not necessary when the critique is running smoothly, at a lower emotional level. It would take a separate book—or better, a novel—to rehearse all the emotions that can take place during critiques. The passage I have just quoted contains betrayal, coyness, insinuation, and slander—four elements of the classical repertoire of love.[2] And I would also say that there is nothing demeaning or irrelevant about seduction as a model for critiques: after all, sexuality is a central fact of life, and it is always possible that critiques may be at their best or purest when they are most like successful seductions.

When the work itself has sexual content, these themes are likely to be more explicit, and the critique is more likely to go out of control. In my experience, people have a great deal of difficulty looking at sexually charged work and not using sexual metaphors, and when those metaphors are repressed, the sexual content may rise to

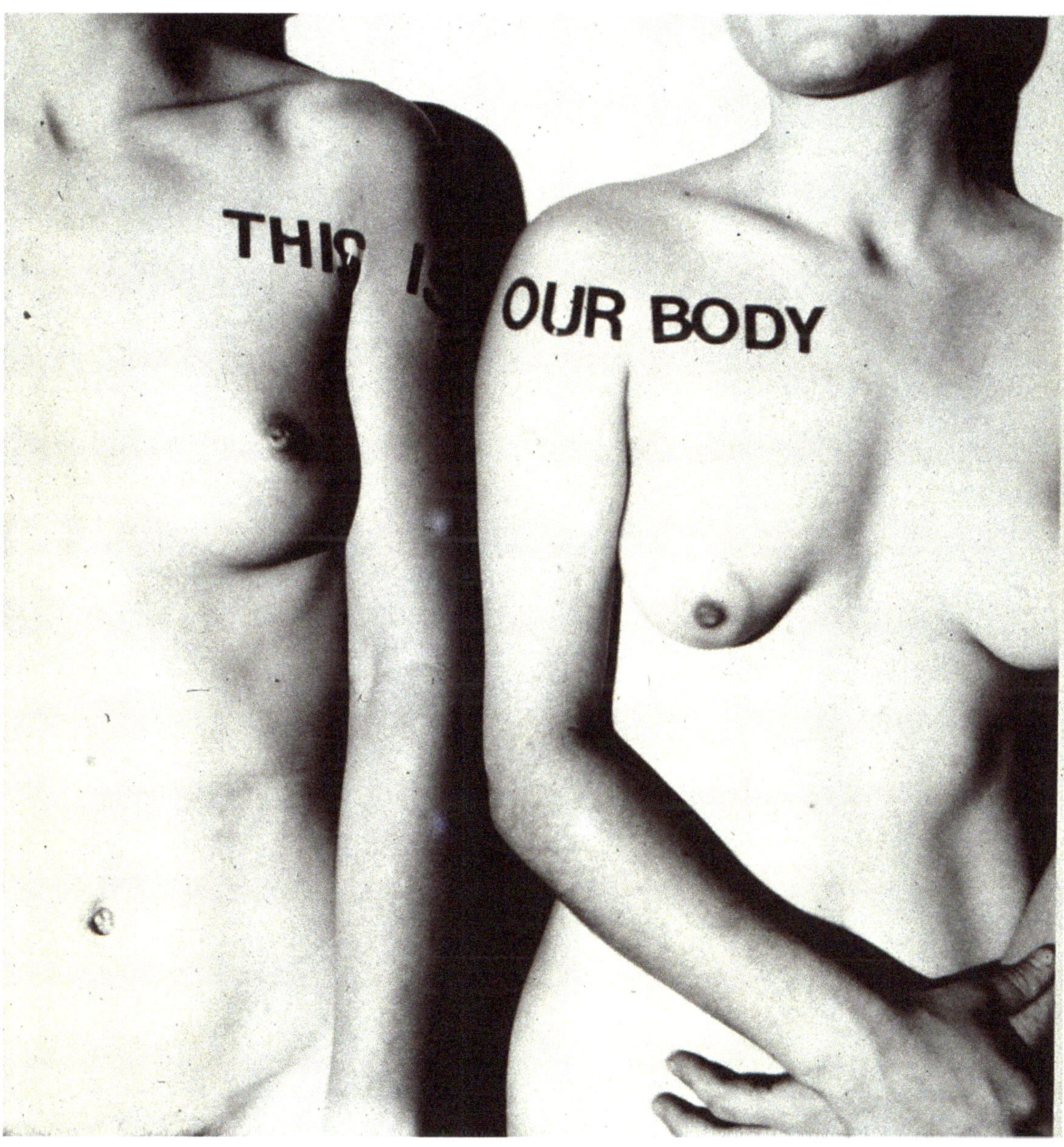

the surface in the form of bizarre verbal images, disconnected statements, and non sequiturs. The student in the following dialogue, elin o'Hara slavick, showed life-size photographs of women's bodies and photographs of close ups of women's crotches and other body parts. (Elin is a successful artist and teacher now, working at Chapel Hill, North Carolina.[3]) Here is one of the large photographs she showed:

And below are two of smaller photographs, which were parts of a wall hanging arranged in an ellipse.

My transcription of this critique is full of verbal images that were not in the photographs: panelists talk about things like pulling up a little girl's skirt (proposed

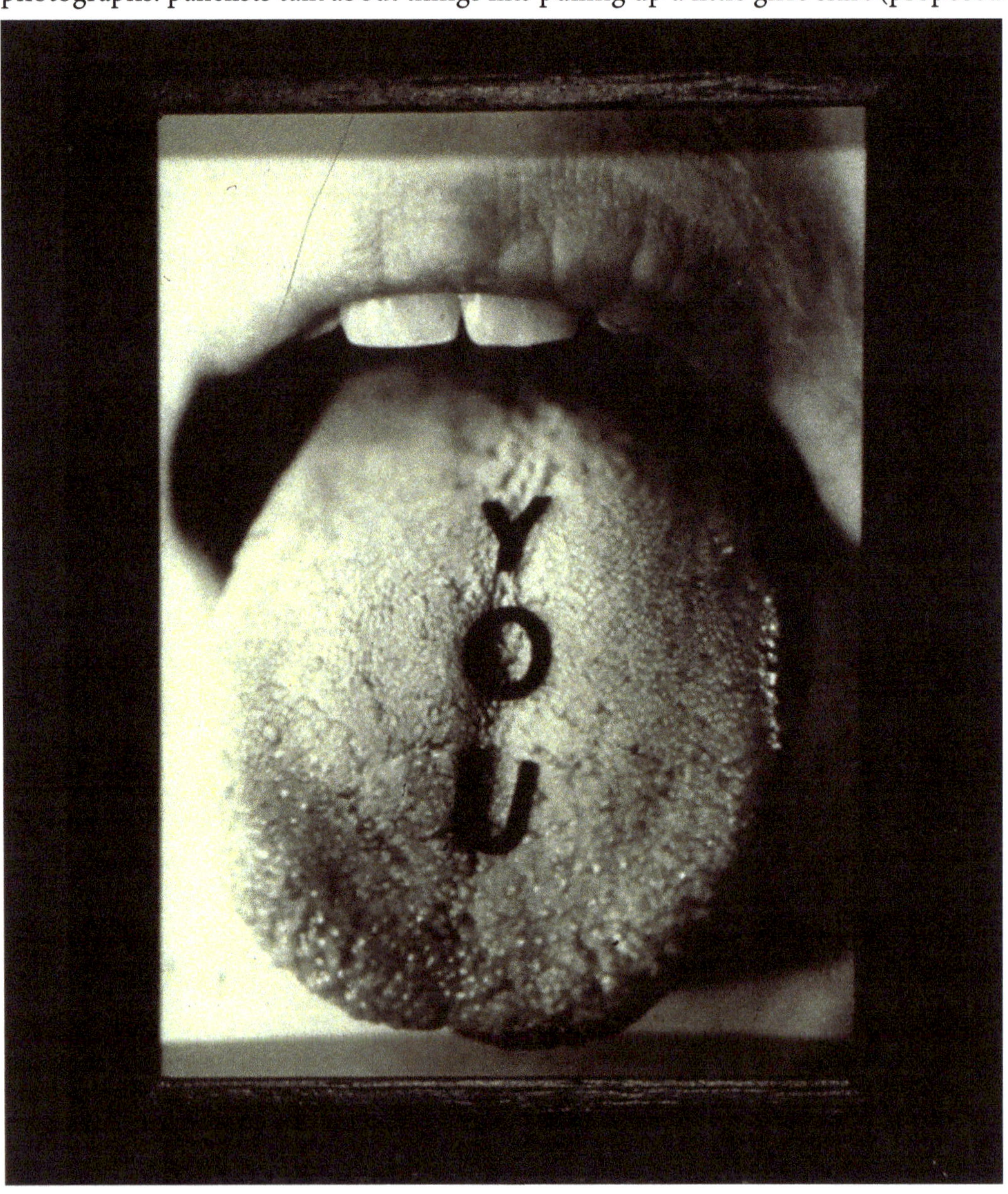

by one panelist as an example of what men "naturally" want to do), and they use words like sticky, glossy, cheesy, dirty, "big, white, and clean," and other fleshy metaphors. One panelist expresses his ambivalence about the images by saying that he wants to be "slapped and patted at the same time." The conversation is ribald and very entertaining, and to some degree sensual metaphors are both inevitable and expressive of the work. The difficulty, I think, comes from the fact that ordinary judgments get put in such strange ways that their meaning is skewed or they become unintelligible, as in this excerpt:

C	What begins to operate for me in these [larger pieces], is that there is a bombastic quality, like you don't earn the bombast. But what I find myself going to, which is sort of interesting, is like the crinkle in the nipple… the sort of detail… which I'm not supposed to be… but which I find myself thinking about.	*She means something like, "Smaller artworks are more interesting," or "All pictures need a certain amount of detail," but the example of the crinkled nipple is so bizarre (even by the standards of the works themselves) that it distracts from that idea.* *When she says she knows she's not supposed to be thinking about things like that, she almost chastises herself for her original judgment, nearly contradicting the initial idea.*
W	That's what it does…	
X	They don't have red in them and I wonder if—	*This is another strange—and sexually charged—image, since the photographs were monochrome, and no one had mentioned color. Like the crinkled nipple, it may be hiding a perfectly ordinary judgment.*

E	Well, I wanted to have just… a way that you could just enjoy the image, without texture, so there's space.	*The artist would rather not talk about her images that way. She mentions space, cleanliness, coolness, and similar metaphors.*
C	Well, to go back to the notion of private parts, because [in the smaller photos] there's a sense of privacy. The peep show thing is interesting for me to think about, because there, there's attention to private parts that I love in that piece.	*Speaker C tries again, finding a way to admit she likes "private parts." The problem is that her taste leads her to accept the idea that the works are like a peep show, which the panel had earlier decided was a device that serves prurient male interests.*
X	I hate the word "affirmation," but there's something about these that says "Oh, yes." Whereas, I was thinking about the way people were talking about these pieces, and you're talking about the female body, you're talking about my body. And the fact that these pieces spark this kind of discussion…	*This is a nearly incomprehensible thing to say. "Affirmation" by itself has the connotation of naïveté or sentimentality, but the phrase "Oh, yes" makes it sexual. Why should the two be related?* *She feels a personal relation to the images, as if they are representatives of her body. That makes the issue even more difficult to resolve, since she has to talk about the work and her body at the same time.*

These teachers' tribulations are typical of the critique of sexual work in general, which throws people off, peppering conversation with sexual innuendo and sexual tropes. It seems to me that behind the speakers' tangled thoughts are some relatively straightforward ideas: for example, that large works are difficult to control, and that to some degree a spectator will always identify herself with a depicted body. The pressure of sexual thoughts renders the dialogue somewhat opaque. I think there may be a larger lesson here as well, since we routinely borrow our verbal images from what we're seeing. In front of a landscape painting, we talk about airiness, brightness, and depth, and in front of an iron sculpture we talk about hardness and durability. We let images suggest their argumentative strategies and judgments. So it stands to reason that even outside the sexual arena, where things are less emotionally charged, our conversation is slurred or skewed by the metaphors that the works seem to provide us. In the presence of sexually charged work, even simple judgments become inscrutable because they are overburdened or tossed around by whatever metaphors happen to be at hand.

This is another effect that can be modeled by thinking of critiques as theaters of seduction.

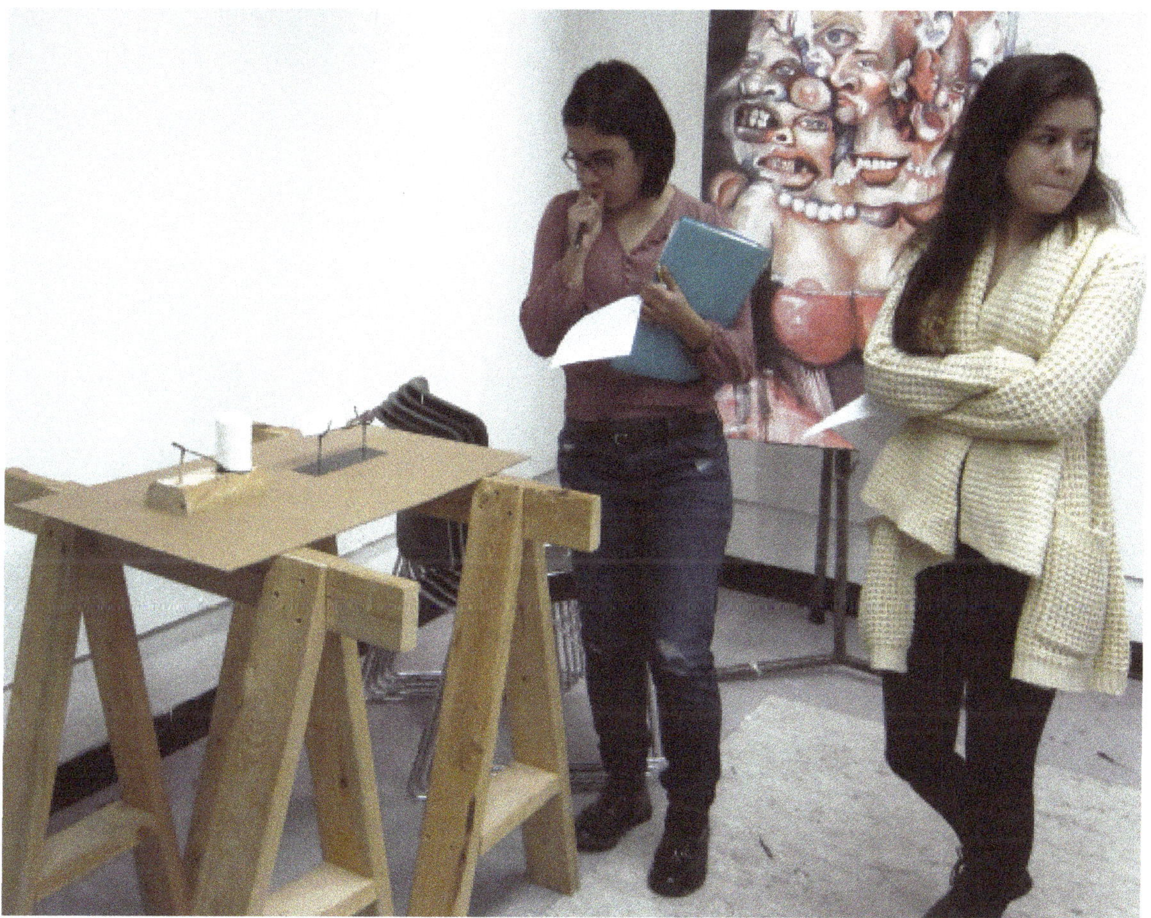

Five Allegories for Critiques:

2. Critiques are Like Different Languages

All Spoken at Once

Seductions are only one allegory for critiques. Here is another: a critique can be imagined as a problem in translation, because for practical purposes the teacher may be speaking a different language from the student. Say a Netherlander speaks to a German, and they each know only their own language. Each will understand a fair amount of what the other says, but neither will be quite sure they have been understood. Within the art world, there are different "languages": several dialects of philosophy, some distinctly different languages of literary criticism, art speak, journalism, and so on. The philosopher Nelson Goodman called differences like those "languages of art."[1] This is "language" in scare quotes because it is not the usual usage of that word. I once heard the philosopher Jacques Derrida say he spoke nine languages: French, German, Italian, English, Latin, Greek, ontology, epistemology, and phenomenology. He was only half-joking: those last languages (fields of philosophy) are very different from one another. They might even be mutually unintelligible.

Some theoretical art terms can be especially effective in establishing the dominance of one or another critical language: once a teacher mentions the "parasite," the "supplement," or the "abject," it is likely that the remainder of the conversation will be infected even if the other teachers or the student don't recognize the "languages" those terms come from. Some critiques can be read as being more dependent on theoretical terminology than others—critiques of architecture, film, and painting come to mind. There are also fields where a *lack* of critical terminology can result in improvisatory critiques that wander among many "languages." Performance art is an example, as in my opening story about the student with hairy legs. (That was a multilingual critique.)

A few kinds of art have their own languages. Painting has formal analysis, and film has film theory. It's also possible that a few metaphors can dominate discourse, without being part of any particular critical "language." In fiber art metaphors of skin, of the inside and outside, and of softness or pliability can dominate discussions without tying them to any specific theoretical platform.[2]

Sometimes the "languages" spoken in critiques can be easily identified. Some teachers of architecture, for example, use varieties of poststructuralism, and some filmmakers use a kind of criticism derived from writers including Jacques Lacan, Barbara Rose, Jonathan Crary, and Kaja Silverman. From a student's point of view, such critiques require specialized learning that is not always available, but at least it's clear that the teacher is speaking a specific "language," and that language can be learned. Critiques can become places where a student scrambles to translate a teacher's language into her own:

— Rebecca, I think that the question of projection is entirely open here. Instead of the external subject, you have an unmediated co-presence in the work, and instead of the mediating plane, you have—what do they call it?—the screen, the Lacanian screen.

— Lacanian screen?

— That's the place where the subject is inverted, its normal relation to the world is inverted, so that the subject—you—are caught there, "like a stain," like this portion here, or those marks in the center. It is a kind of anti-projection, a "chiasmatic inversion" is what it's called in film theory.

— Wait, let me write that down.

— These marks subvert the innocuousness of the projective gesture, the gesture of pure projection, like in the Renaissance. They are all about the failure of the unified field of objectivity, a kind of late-capitalist sense of attention or perception.

Of course, this dialogue is a parody—it's a collage of different critiques—not because conversations like this do not take place, but because teachers are usually a little more careful to explain whatever theory they are bringing to bear on the work. Unfortunately not all teachers also function as their own interpreters. The usual situation is that the instructor doesn't use any particular jargon, and may not even realize that she is speaking in a way that is dependent on some theory. After a few years' exposure to postmodern discourse, people begin to speak in ways that seem habitual but are really only fully comprehensible for other people with analogous exposure to the theory. Then the problem is compounded: first the student has to realize that something is in need of explanation, and then decide if it is a good idea to try to read the theory first, or ask for a direct translation.

I am using theoretical and philosophical "languages" as examples because they can sound like real foreign languages, but the analogy of translation fits more day-to-day art "languages" as well. There's a "language" of realist painting, another of abstract expressionism (as in the previous chapter), another of body-centered performance art, another of figurative ceramics, and so on, and so on. As a student, you'll learn a number of these, more or less fluently, and as you go on, you'll get more adept at translating from one to another.

I suppose this is the place to put in a note about Theory, with a capital T. For some students, the discovery of Art Theory is like a brick wall: it seems incomprehensible, overbearing, condescending, and useless. Art Theory gets demonized, and contrasted against the "real," "ordinary" language of the studio. I don't agree with this kind of assessment: I study theory myself, and I think it has many good uses. I am not allergic to complicated theoretical explanations of things, even if they are very abstract. And I don't oppose anything called "theory" to anything called "ordinary talking."

The problem arises when theory is badly explained, and badly used. There's a good parody of this on the internet, a website that generates sentences for use in art critiques.[3] Type in five numbers, and you get a sentence:

10432 = "With regard to the issue of content, the internal dynamic of the *facture* endangers the devious simplicity of the eloquence of these pieces."

Change the numbers, and the sentence changes:

10433 = "With regard to the issue of content, the internal dynamic of the *facture* endangers the devious simplicity of the remarkable handling of light."

88888 = "It's difficult to enter into this work because of how the mechanical mark-making of the figurative-narrative line-space matrix spatially undermines the substructure of critical thinking."

70188 = "I'm surprised that no one's mentioned yet that the internal dynamic of the sexual signifier spatially undermines the substructure of critical thinking."

The author of the Critique Phrase Generator, Petra Häschen, has absorbed a large number of critical clichés from the 1990s. (A Critique Phrase Generator for this decade would sound different.) It's funny for people who have heard this sort of thing in critiques, but not as funny if you care, as I do, about the ways theory is used. The Generator mixes and matches critical "languages," making a mess. In critiques, messes like this happen either because the teacher is confused about her theory, or because she is discovering rather than reporting her thoughts, or both.

(And last, a note mainly for PhD students: It's one thing to translate from some theoretical "language" into another way of talking, and it's another to translate the teacher's particular kind of theory-speak back into its original versions in philosophy. The versions of deconstruction and other poststructuralist "languages" that are found in the art world can be significantly different from those in the originating texts. The same is true of the relation of film criticism to its original models in feminism and post-Freudian psychoanalysis. The way that Lacanian terms are used in film theory is sometimes unrecognizably different from the ways it is used in Lacan's texts. There is no easy way to describe these differences. They are problematic but productive adaptations or applications—very free translations—of primary texts. Or they are like provincial dialects: from the point of view of readers of the original philosophers, film theory and architectural theory, among others, can appear misguided or just incomprehensible. That means that as a student, if you take the trouble to study Lacan or Derrida, you may not be able to understand your advisor; and conversely, if you understand you advisor, you may not be completely prepared to read the secondary literature on those same philosophers produced in university philosophy departments. Art language is often distinct from the languages out of which it has grown.[4])

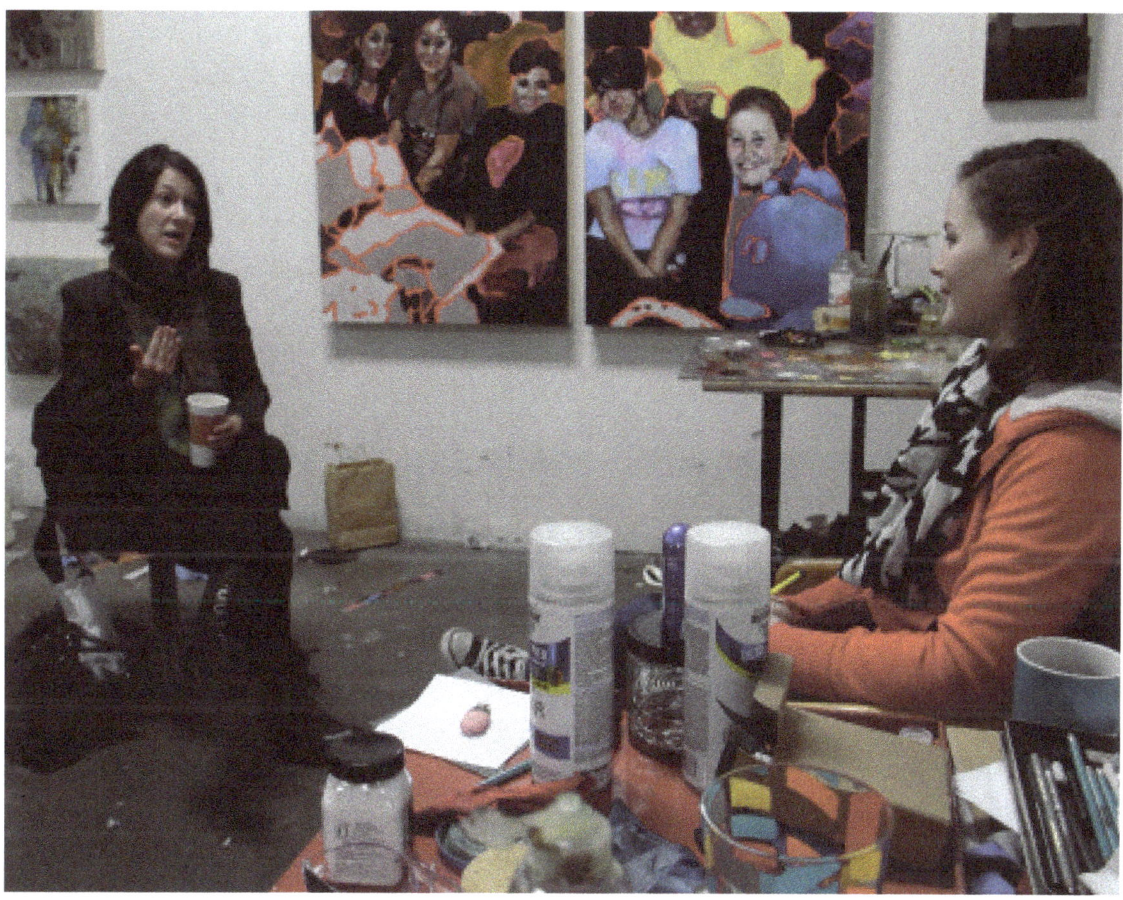

40

Five Allegories for Critiques:

3. Critiques Are Like Storytelling

Critiques can also be seen as *exchanges of stories*, or collaborative storytelling. If you set out to tell a story about your work, you may find it becomes a collaborate venture, because your teacher or teachers will pipe in, changing your story so it becomes a group effort. Critiques are a place where different stories about art flow together.

A story about yourself and your work is a kind of artwork in its own right: it is *performative*, as people like to say. The stories students tell in critiques are called "spiels" and "performances." Good stories weave the artworks, the studio itself, and the panelists together into one narrative. In that sense a story is also a work of performance art, or even of installation art. Sometimes panelists interrupt the critique to tell stories about their own lives, sometimes in belated response to stories proffered by the student. If you open your critique with a narrative about how difficult life has been for you in the last semester, the panelists may respond by being kinder about their criticism. Panelists also initiate stories, though they are more likely to be reminiscent of scientific or scholarly texts than short stories: panelists provide analyses, discussions, evaluations, "anatomies," "dissections," and other kinds of drier, less voiced narratives.

One student's story might be confessional, and another student's lyric, comic, tragic or epic. When all goes well, a sob story may become a comedy, or an epic may be shortened to a poem. There are different *genres*—epic, confessional, scientific— and within each genre are various *conventions*. In the Homeric epic the *Iliad*, there are catalogues of ships and warriors, and in the Artistic epic, there are catalogues of works:

— First I did that large piece, the one with the red, and that was the beginning of the semester. Then the two smaller pieces came, one after another, and then I was stuck. Bill helped me a lot then, and I did that large yellow one in one day, and the three little purple things, and that little "hairy ball" over there. That was very quick, about a week.

Notice how close the parallel is between the *Iliad*, with its catalogues of ships and people, and this student's catalogue of works and days. In the *Iliad*, the Homeric catalogues of ships and warriors help the reader believe the story, and it gives the poem a certain measured pace. The lists also seem to reflect Homer's desire to anticipate the issue at hand—in this case, warfare. The student's catalogue of works has analogous functions. Listening to it as a narrative helps us to understand its place in the larger succession of topics of conversation, and to get a sense of its limitations and potential. A student who is cataloguing her works is also in control of the pace of the critique, and so the catalogue is a way of saying that she will not let the critique get out of hand. The catalogue also bolsters the panelists' sense of the student's veracity and her control of her work.

Some philosophers think of narrative as a kind of fundamental condition for human experience. The idea is roughly that unless you can form a rudimentary narrative about an experience, you cannot understand it at all. Every thought, in this way of looking at things, is a story.[1] A story is not only something that a student or panelist might identify as such, but it is *any sentence* or sequence of sentences. People are sometimes aware of telling stories, and the catalogue is an example of something that might be recognized as part of a story. But in this view there are many other stories running throughout a critique: stories that people construct to help them understand themselves, stories that panelists tell themselves about how they usually go about explaining artworks, stories that students use to help understand their relation with faculty. The narrative model of critiques is potentially deeper than a list of specific stories. If the narrative model has a limitation, it is that there is not always much that can be said once the deeper narratives are uncovered. If you give a speech in your critique and then say it was "performative," all you're really doing is calling attention to the fact that you knew it was something—a story—that you had constructed. After that, it may not be clear what else can be said about it.

From a teacher's point of view, if a student tells a story about how she will be misunderstood, but also identifies it *as* a story (I mean, she might say "I know this is only something I tell myself, maybe to guard against failure"), it may not help to talk directly about that story in the context of the critique. It may be unproductive to say, "I think you should think about this story you tell yourself: if you think the story is only a story, why tell it?" In my experience people tend to become less interesting when I can understand their stories. I loved my grandmother's stories about growing up, but I didn't particularly want to hear them once I realized they were her way of rehearsing her unhappiness—of saying, in effect, "I was unhappy." But maybe this is too narrow a point: the narrative model is very versatile, and covers a lot of what happens in critiques.

41

Five Allegories for Critiques:

4. Critiques Are Like Battles

After the Homeric catalogue of ships in the *Iliad*, the battle itself gets underway, and a battle is a particularly tempting metaphor for a critique. The hatred, the fear, and the confusion of a real battle are sometimes parallel to what happens in critiques, even though critiques don't usually have real violence, and are usually much more controlled and low-key. But figuratively speaking, students and teachers can become determined adversaries, out to get each other, "sparring" and "fighting."

Most people who have spent time around critiques have anecdotes about aggressive teachers. Here are a couple of my favorites, which I found on Facebook:

- "Someone once told me, 'Well, you're obviously a very angry person' while she nibbled a stash of breakfast sausage from her pocket."
- "In grad school, we had a visiting critic come to our thesis shows. My visit was scheduled for the following day, but he got a head start by taking out a laser pointer and highlighting all the problems he saw in my exhibition with a glowing red dot, *at my opening*."

Later in the book, I'll be talking about teachers who pretend to be simply describing but are actually getting ready to judge the work. You could say that a negative judgment masquerading as a descriptive statement is "evil," because it is deceptive. Ulterior purposes, rhetorical questions, and dishonest judgments are not uncommon in critiques. Critiques are *agathokakological*—that is, they mix good with evil, deception with sincerity, the destructive with the constructive. A critique can become an *agon* (a battle) between good and evil, and at times it is not at all unhelpful to think of it that way.

All this seems promising, but I am not going to expand on the battle metaphor, because I am not sure how it sheds light on critiques. Does it help to notice that the aggression of a teacher is like the aggression of a soldier?

42

Five Allegories for Critiques:

5. Critiques Are Like Trials

There is another analogy for critiques that I like much more, and that is the legal proceeding. Of course there are big differences between a critique and a trial. A serious trial, like a murder trial, is final (it can't be repeated), and that has no parallel in the art world. Even a moot court, a hearing, or a deposition, are built around the idea that final decisions *are* reached, even if they may take years. Art critiques end with many opinions, so they are more like hung juries or mistrials than ordinary court cases. We do say "the jury is out" on an artist—thereby implying that artists do eventually get a final judgment—but teachers don't say that to students during critiques. (In art history, artists are effectively judged for the last and definitive time after their own lifetimes. A few artists—Giorgione, Vermeer, Piero della Francesca— have been revived after having been largely forgotten, but the majority are judged irrevocably. Art classes aren't like that.)

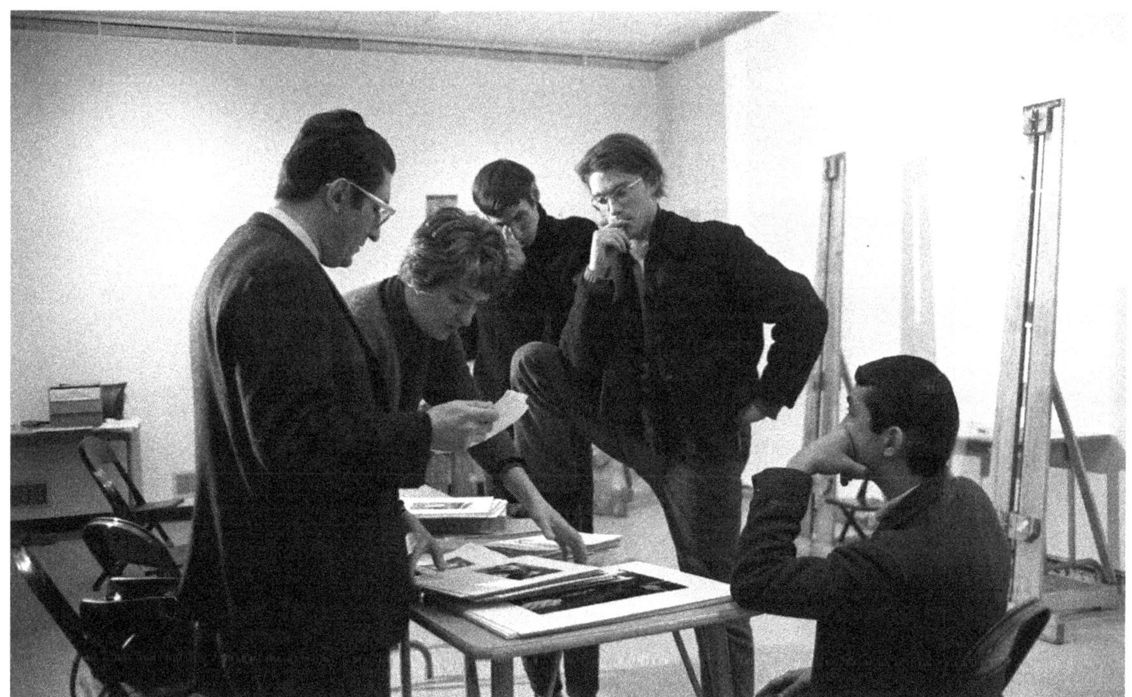

Despite these differences, the legal proceeding is a very good way of thinking about the exercise of power in art critiques. A critique can be like the trials in Kafka's novel of that name: the defendant's attorney is either incompetent or absent, and either the jury is absent or the judges do double duty as jurors. (In *The Trial*, the character Joseph never quite knows what he is accused of, and he can never find the proper courtroom, judges, or lawyers.) As in Kafka's novel, a student has to decide whether it is wise to speak in her own defense. Throughout the novel *The Trial*, Joseph knows that judgment is in the air, but the judges' knowledge is mostly secret, and their methods and rules are difficult to discern. In *The Trial*, the principal differences between Joseph and the world of the Law are power and control: Joseph loses a bit more freedom each time he enters a courtroom or lawyer's office. Like an art student in the middle of a critique, Joseph never knows quite what is happening.

Art critiques can have a heavy courtroom atmosphere. Imagine this dialogue between advisors, with the student keeping quiet like a defendant:

— Well, Jane, I just don't know.
— Hmm.
— Okay, well, I'll say this, that your work is very intriguing.
— Mm.
— Yes, that idea about the witches is very nice.
— Yes, I like that too.
[*Silence.*]
— But there's a great deal going on here, you know.
— Oh, yes.
[*Silence.*]
— There are things that can be controlled, and other things that can't be.
— Yes. An artwork is not something that just "goes right," all at once.
— Sometimes it takes years.

There is much to be said for the legal model, especially when it is modeled on Kafka's sense of justice, but I choose to leave it here, because it is also rather seriously misleading (students do not have their throats cut at graduation, like Joseph's is cut at the end of *The Trial*). Critiques are like courtrooms in that they are formal meetings bent on judgment, and they borrow some of their sense of control and power from the law, but they aim *away* from clear, unambiguous judgments and from punishment itself. In their place they put ongoing conversations, shifting and heavily qualified verdicts, and a queasy sense of imminent judgment—all as in *The Trial*. Perhaps critiques are more civilized versions of trials.

The parallel with the law brings the total of allegories for critiques to five: amorous, linguistic, narratological, warlike, and legal. It would be a nice project to expand this list. *The Critique Handbook,* which I mentioned on p. xi, also proposes critiques are like theater: they are certainly performative, and students are often like actors on stage. I think the only model I'd object to would be the idea that critiques are merely, or basically, just conversations (see chapter 3).

Critiques can be understood as allegories of many things—which is another way of saying their confusions are multiple. No one model will do. As I said in considering the model of seduction, these allegories do not become explicit unless the critique develops problems. Allegories like the five I have named are the substructure of the critique: they give it direction and shape, but normally remain out of sight—and conversely, when they are on everyone's mind, it is a sign that something may be going wrong.

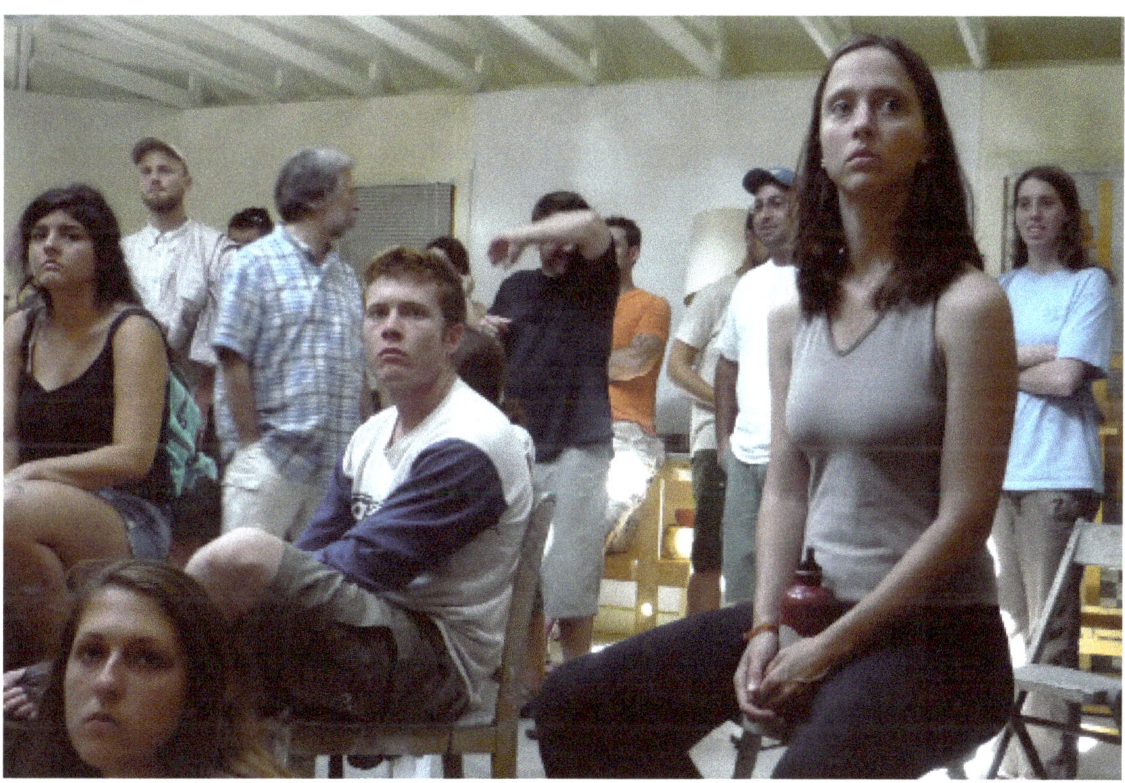

43

Critiques are Polyglot

Critiques speak different languages. That's literally true in different countries. It's also the case that ceramics critiques often sound different from photo critiques, which sound different from printmaking critiques, and so on. Where I work, there are about 15 studio departments, and each one speaks a different language: Photography is very psychoanalytic, and Ceramics is all about medium and material. These things change—I remember when our Photography Department critiques were mainly about point-and-shoot photography, and they wouldn't have gone anywhere near psychoanalytic issues. Our Architecture Department is very concerned with costing, presentation, and feasibility; our Sculpture Department is often interested in forms, space, and interactions with the public. There's no way to predict the "language" of the critique conversation, but in larger institutions the differences can be marked, and it helps to learn them. If you're in a smaller institution or art department, this doesn't apply, but each one of your teachers will have been educated in particular critique environments, and it can help if you have a sense of them.

All that has to do with languages of critique that depend on the particular faculty, the history of the department, and the medium. In this chapter I want to consider different way to think about the languages of critique.

A language depends on its words, and a specialized language, like visual art, depends very much on a relatively small number of words. Just as geometry can't be spoken about with using words like "line," "plane," "postulate," "axiom," and "proof," so art can't be talked about without certain key concepts.

Some of those concepts come from philosophy, some from art history, some from daily life, some from particular media. The problem is how to organize them. The book *The Critique Handbook* lists concepts like "line," "color," "modeling," "casting," "medium," "transparency," "originality," and "authorship"—in other words a mix of first-year studio terms and words from art theory. In the end, there simply isn't any way to gather all the important words, or put them in any order: and yet the subject is so important that I have decided to try.

Here is a very, very, very tentative listing of some languages that go into critiques. I'm not defining words here: for that there's the internet, thousands of books, and a lifetime of experience. I'm only trying to indicate that the languages that are all mixed together in critiques also sometimes exist separately.

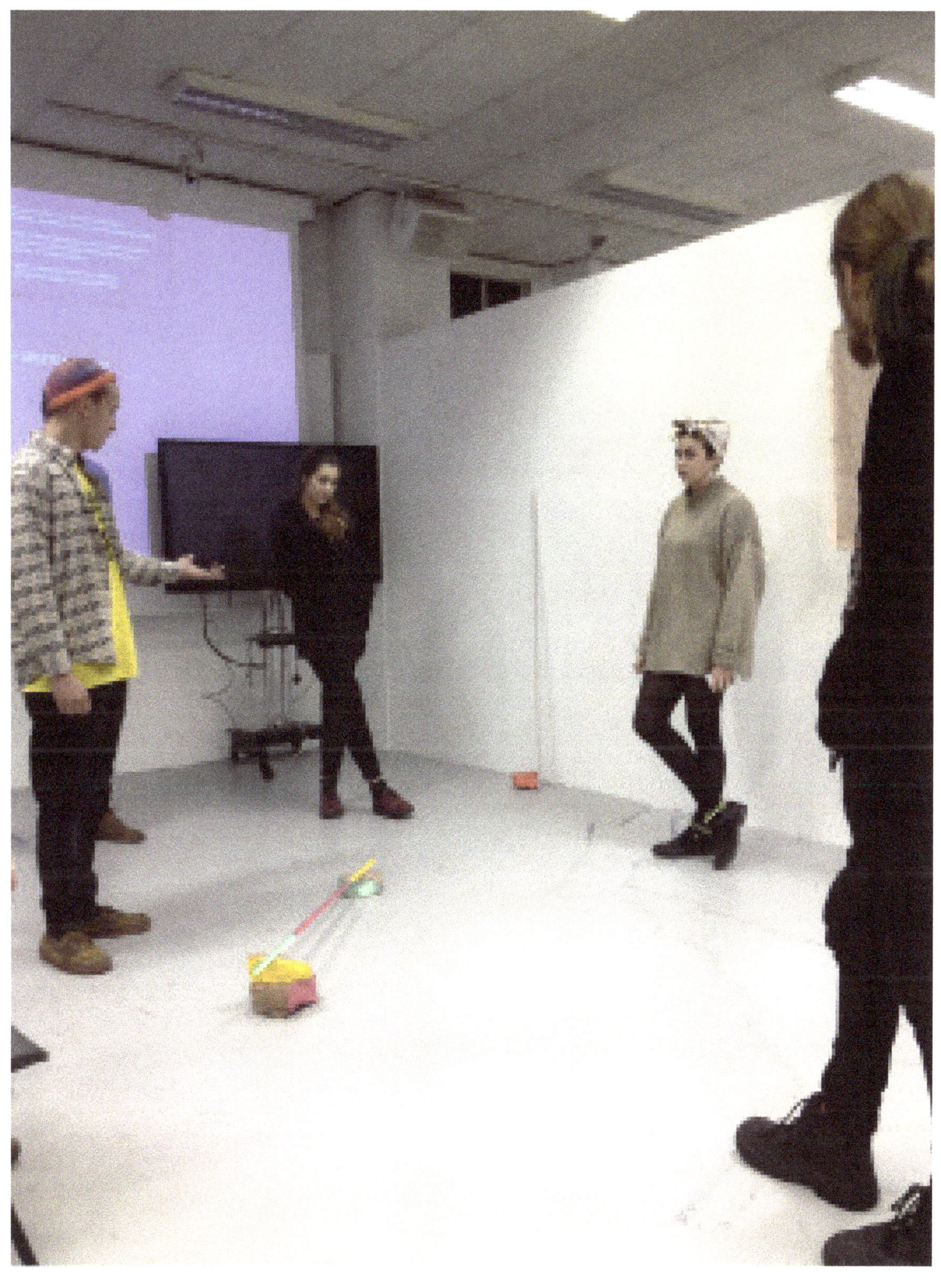

1. Everyday ordinary language

The list of words for failure (see chapter 21) has a number of words that are just borrowed, on the fly, from ordinary talk. Here are some, copied from that list:

> Weak, Thin, Odd, Self-serving, Amiable, Simple, Ridiculous, Awful, Finicky, Heartless, Repetitive, Corporate, Manly, Aimless, Mindless, Apathetic, Happy, Amiable.

This list is potentially endless, because people in critiques grab words from all over in order to make their points. Critiques are like magpies' nests: all sorts of junk may appear in them.

2. First-year art school words

You'll also hear words you learned in first-year classes and in the BFA. These are words like:

> Abstraction, Formalism, Realism, Composition, Format, Color, Line, Edge, Surface, Gesture, Texture, Space, Gravity, Room, Form, Mass, Process.

Some of these words have occupied teachers, critics, theorists, and historians for their entire careers. They can be rich and difficult, but they are also part of the first-year pedagogy in most art institutions.

3. Art theory words

By this I mean mainly poststructural, postmodern theory, including postcolonial theory and psychoanalysis, words like:

> Deconstruction, Liminal, Criticality, Reference, Presence, Binary Opposition, *Jouissance*, Simulacrum, Supplement, Trace, Rhizome, Hybrid, Transnational, Criticality.

People won't agree about what belongs on such a list, but anyone who claims not to recognize this as a group isn't being entirely honest. These words, too, demand special study.

4. Assessment words

I'm guessing this one might be a surprise to teachers reading this chapter. Assessment is something that chairs, deans, and committees worry about: it's the way your institution gets its accreditation, and it's also often the way you are evaluated at the end of the critique, the semester, or the entire MFA. Here are some words that are prominent in that language:

> Synthesize, Cohere, Integrate, Unify, Self-Reflexive, Visual Competence, Field, Capstone, Precedent, Influence, Reference, Innovative, Creative, New, Assess, Evaluate, Grade, Benchmark.

The assessment literature includes guidelines for your teachers to evaluate your work. Here are some examples, with the assessments words in italics:

- Does the student exhibit a *novel* idea?
- Does she *transform* ideas into entirely new forms?
- Is there a *clear* concept or *focus* in the portfolio?
- Does the student demonstrate evidence of *content development*?
- Can the student *articulately* explain her work?
- Has the student adequately *integrated* the influences on her work?
- Does the work demonstrate a good understanding of its *context*?
- Does the student explain her projects *clearly* and *eloquently*?
- Does the student exhibit a *creative* approach to problem solving?
- Is the student's work appropriate to our *capstone* requirements?

It's often helpful to know that words like these are circulating in your teacher's mind. They aren't the usual words of the studio: they are the technical vocabulary of grade reports, departmental self-study documents, and formal reports given by your entire institution to renew its accreditation. So they're never that far from your teacher's thoughts. In *Art Crits: 20 Questions,* Richard Bell says "Studio crits are an opportunity for students to develop skills in articulating through language, the concerns in their practice" (p. 21). This is a good example of assessment language coming into the studio: that same goal can be found in the official literature of a number of institutions, in the accreditation requirements for art programs, and in the institutions' criteria for graduation and progression. (I don't mean articulateness is necessarily bad: it's problematic, because it doesn't fit all art practices, and because it's so close to what teachers and administrators use to decide who passes, who fails, and what programs and institutions are accredited and funded.)

Your teacher may not be thinking, "That student needs to become more articulate in order to pass," or "I have to look for evidence the student has integrated her work into a clear whole," but the ideas of articulation, focus, coherence, integration, and synthesis will be on the table when it comes to evaluating and assessing your work.

Part Five

Projects

Tinkering with the Critique Format

If you've been having trouble in critiques, and you think that the faculty doesn't understand you, then the best thing is to talk to everyone, students and faculty, after the critique, and try to puzzle it out. Sometimes that doesn't help, and you may still feel like something's wrong. In that case, you might consider some of these ideas. They are interventions into the critique format:

• Take an artwork done by someone else, and place it among your own. See what kind of stories the critique panelists come up with in order to explain how that work is one of your own.

• Have a friend stand next to you in a critique. Don't tell the panelists which of you is the artist—tell them that at the end of the critique, you'd like them to guess.

• Have someone play your part at the critique, and listen in the background without identifying yourself. Note how the teachers react differently to the actor. If you're a man, ask a woman to play your part; if you're white, ask someone of color.

• Play a part in your critique. One student told me about how he showed up to his critique dressed in a transparent Alexander McQueen outfit with a red thong. His paintings were three-inch square portraits of male porn stars. (Note: this doesn't guarantee a good critique!)

• Present someone else's work. Choose someone whom you don't know. Do your best to represent that person's work as your own.

• Present work that you dislike (old work, for example) as if it was your newest. See if you can convince the panel that you think it's good work.

• Present the chronology of your works in reverse order. See if you can convince yourself, and your teachers, that you're going forward with your work.

• Borrow your opening speech from someone else. Present that person's concerns to your teachers, as his or her interests were your own interests.

I have seen some unusual critique formats. Not all of them work well, but in the right circumstances they can be very illuminating. For example:

• A critique in which the teacher doesn't see the work until it has been discussed for ten minutes.

• A critique in which the teacher has to look at the work for ten minutes without speaking.

• A critique in which panelists are not allowed to see the work until the student decides they are ready for it.

• A critique in which students write down questions they'd like to ask teachers about their work, and then put the questions in a hat. That way students get a mix of expected and unexpected questions.[1] (This is a variant of the very common critique practice of having everyone write opinions before anyone speaks.)

• A critique in which students make a circle around the art work, and each one has to say something about it. No repetitions are allowed. (The person who told me about this said they only went once around the circle: I think it would be interesting to go around twenty or thirty times.)

• If the energy level drops, or if people complain, take five and everyone run around the building. This idea, which comes from Brenton Adrian, is reminiscent of Johannes Itten's classes in the Bauhaus, where students would begin with calisthenics.[2]

• If you're bilingual, try this experiment: hire a translator, and have the faculty talk to that person. This will produce interesting effects even if your faculty know you can speak English![3]

• Let someone play the role of a famous artist, like Tracey Emin or Yves Klein, and see how those artists' works might get critiqued. (This is from *Art Crits: 20 Questions,* p. 44.)

• There are more ideas in the book *The Critique Handbook,* including the suggestion to have other students write letters about the work, addressed to your instructor; and the idea of conducting the critique like an interview.

Some of these ideas might need a little help from the faculty, especially if you're in a small department and most people know you or your work. I don't think it's a particularly good idea to make fun of the faculty (that would tend to break down conversation, which I am assuming is not a good idea). Each of these suggestions can be arranged so that it is not belligerent. The idea is to learn more about how you and your work are seen, by changing something about yourself or your art. If these strategies work, they will tell you something about how to control viewers' responses—always an important thing to know if you're serious about becoming an artist.

If you're a teacher, you might also use these suggestions as topics for conversation: instead of actually doing them, you can talk about what effect they might have.

Here are some ideas for teachers:

• Try saying the opposite of what you think: anytime you have an opinion, instead of saying it, formulate its opposite.

• Try speaking as if you loved Andrew Wyeth, or Norman Rockwell, or some artist you don't like. Don't name the artist (that might make it too simple to argue against you), but try to make a convincing case for the artist's sensibility.

• Try speaking as if you were Pollock, or Picasso, or some artist you know well. Don't necessarily pretend you are the artist, just try borrowing the artist's language.

• Try erasing yourself from the critique equation, and focusing instead on helping other people (especially faculty) articulate their own ideas. Add to what other people say, but don't contribute new judgments. See how long you can do that before people notice you don't have a position.

These ideas, too, are tools for understanding other people's responses, and they can help illuminate your own habits of thinking. You'll learn something about your own habits and judgments by taking on someone else's. (And of course you can always tell the student afterward.)

A note about performance: I don't intend these proposals as artworks: I'm not suggesting that they're ways of turning the critique into a piece of performance art. That could be interesting, but if you're a student, it won't help you understand your work. On the other hand, any of these ideas could be done as a performative intervention into the usual habits of art classes. If you try one of them as a performance, your work will be your commentary on the art school, not whatever pieces of art you actually present.

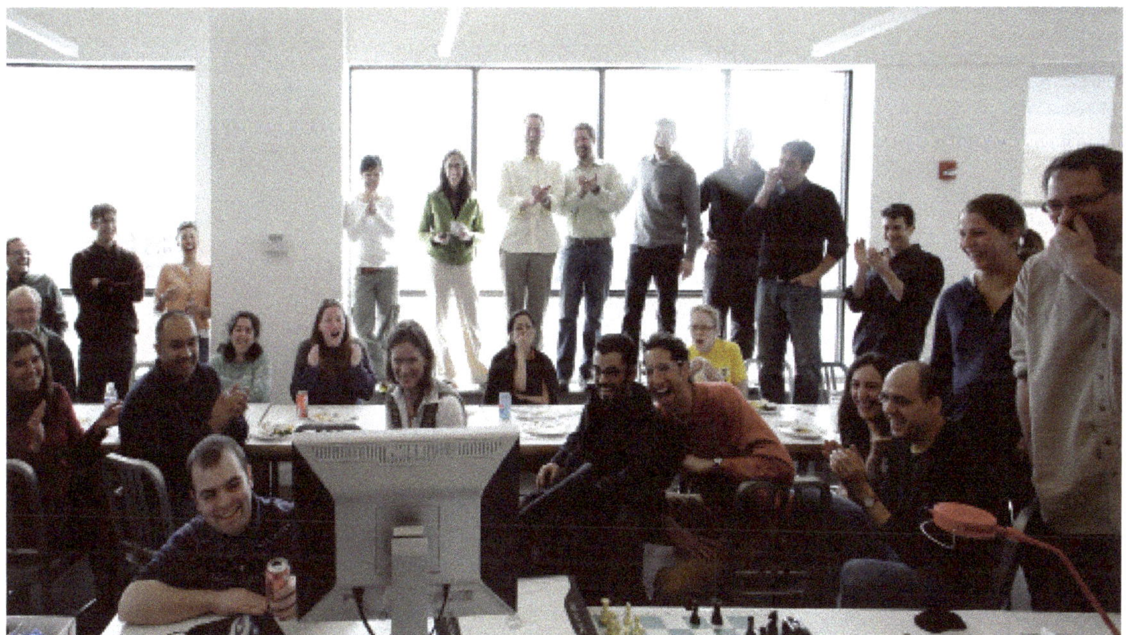

Three Big Projects:

1. Investigate The Chain of Questions

Here are three large-scale proposals. Each takes time, but they are good tools if you want to seriously analyze a critique. This first one is about how to track down the meanings behind what a teacher says. The second is about how to tape critiques and transcribe them, as I have done for this book. And the last is instructions for a six-hour critique centered on a single artwork.

Most conversations about art alternate between dull and creative, repetitious and insightful, superficial and deep. Occasionally a teacher will say something out of the blue that's really interesting, and everyone will fall quiet for a moment thinking about it. Someone might ask the speaker to explain what they said, but much more

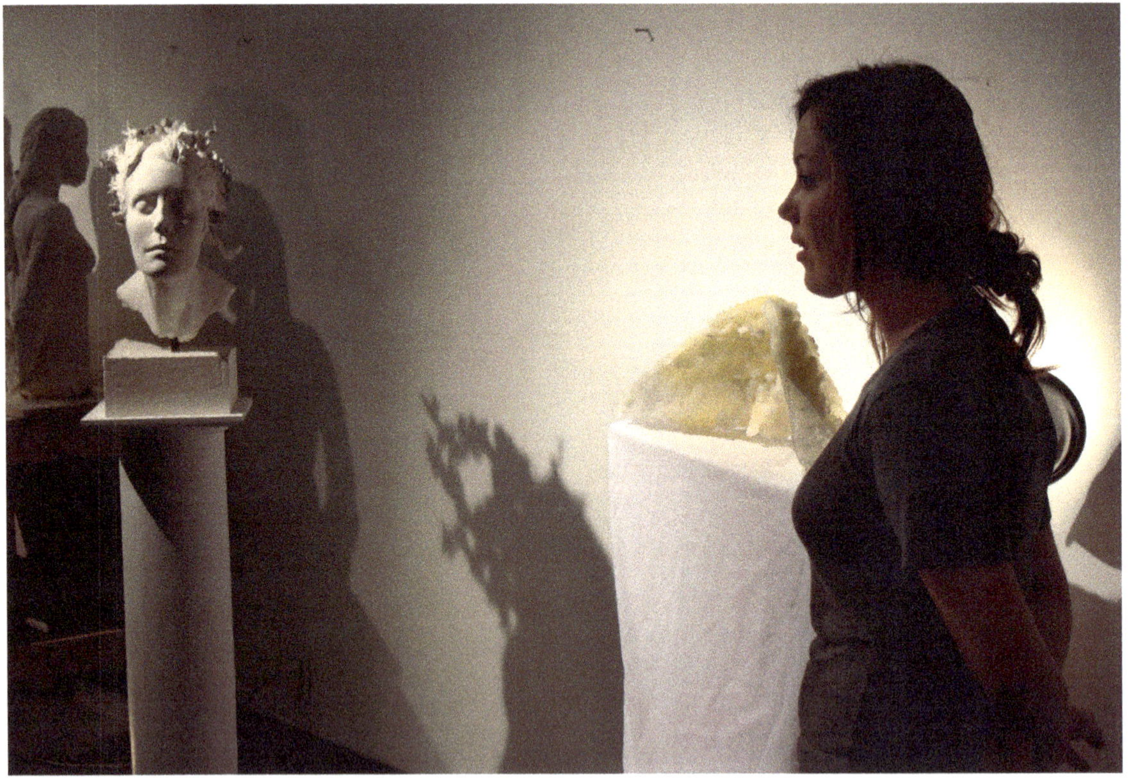

often—really, almost always— teachers say things just once, and then drop the subject before anyone has a chance to follow up on what they've said. The give and take of idea and response, thesis and antithesis, is the ancient art of *dialectic*. In Socratic conversation, which is sometimes called *elenctic argument,* you ask, you think about the reply, you doubt the answer, you ask again, you doubt the answer, you rephrase the question, and so on—you go on, pushing and inquiring, without changing the subject. Essentially, the difference between this kind of questioning and a typical art critique is that elenctic questioning explores a series of questions on one topic, rather than a list of questions on different topics. Though it is artificial and it can be difficult to manage, a dialectic inquiry of this sort is an optimal way to make sense of some talk about art.

There is a serious drawback to statements that are said just once: as a student, you don't always know *why* the statement was made in the first place. "You might want to try more blue," your teacher might say, or "That seems a little odd": those are judgments with no explanations. Many things said in critiques are like this: they're judgments without reasons.

Sometimes a teacher will know her reason for saying something, and will be able to produce it if the student asks. In chapter 31, I used the example of a teacher who says a painting has too much green. If you ask your teacher, "Why did you say I should have less green in the painting?" she might answer, "Because the green is a bit overwhelming." But notice—and this is the crucial point—that this is not a complete explanation. It remains to be said why blue is better, and why any one color, no matter which, should not be overwhelming. (Couldn't overwhelming be good?) There is an important difference here between the *reasons* for statements, which are the explanations that the teacher comes up with when she is asked, and the *unexamined assumptions or dogmas,* which are deeper explanations that the teacher may never have thought about. In this example the *reason* is that green is overwhelming, and the *unexamined assumption* behind the reason might be something like this: "Single colors should not be allowed to dominate."

You can get at your teacher's reasons and unexamined assumptions by asking what I'll call a *chain of questions*. It seems to me that our natural habit of making judgments without giving reasons, and without searching for the underlying assumptions, is the single most important source of confusion in critiques. Teachers tend to have many ideas about what makes art good in general and what makes certain kinds of art good, but many teachers are largely unaware of these ideas: they know a few of them, but the majority go unnoticed. So when a teacher says something about your work, if you don't understand quite why she said what she did, chances are good that she herself is unaware of the assumptions that led her to make the judgment.

(Of course what I'm about to describe doesn't work well when there are lots of confused ideas piles up on each other. A person on Fracebook sent me some notes from a critique that had to do with green. At one point there is a flurry of ideas about green: "Turner said he didn't like trees— [they have] nasty greens. Green doesn't work with the other colors. Constable featured greens.... I don't like to paint the greens... Fairfield Porter is exciting with green.... Feel free not to be a green painter. I'm not saying just because I don't do green painting, doesn't mean other people shouldn't."[1] Each one of those would have to be disentangled separately. In my examples here, I just take a single, simple judgment.)

The *reasons* for statements are usually easy to explain, but the *assumptions* may be hard to get at. It is helpful to look closely at the relation between judgments, reasons, and unexamined assumptions.

Judgments are what normally occur in a critique. A teacher may say,

— I think that this film has too much playfulness about it, it's goofy.

Let's say the student or another instructor questions that judgment, in order to elicit a reason. There are many ways to bring out reasons, but the best is just to behave like a two year old and ask "why":

— Why is that bad?

— Well, because the film starts out seriously, but then it ends up careless.

Things might stop here, either because the critique moves on to another topic, or because the teacher may not be aware of any further explanation. This is the judgment she made:

The film is too playful

1. Judgment

And the reason for her judgment is something like this:

Films like this should not start out
serious and end up playful

2. Reason

Note that the reason is not the end of the line. There is an *unexamined assumption* behind it, something that drove her to think that films like this should not turn

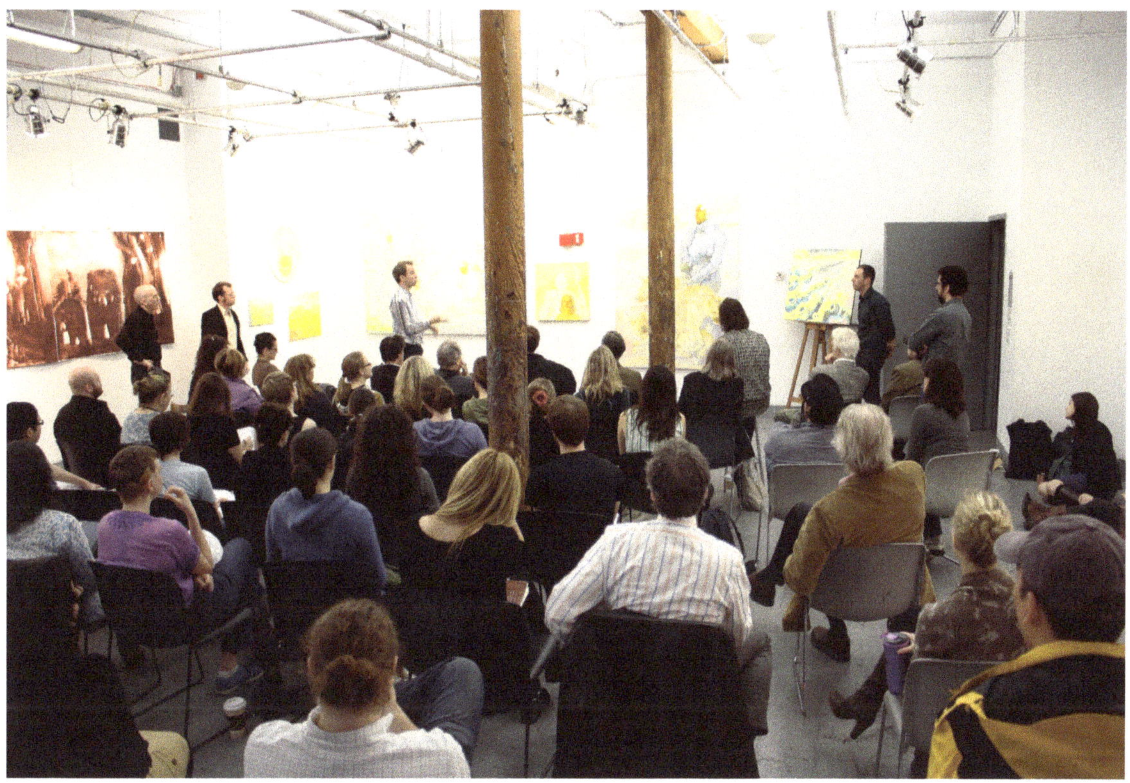

playful. To evoke it, you could ask another two-year-old's "why" question:
   — Why is it bad that the work begins seriously and ends silly?

As a rule, assumptions are usually unexamined—that is, the speaker may never have thought about them—and so this kind of question can be difficult to answer. The response might be a disguised elaboration of the first answer. Your teacher might say:

   — I think the work promises to take itself seriously, and then ends up flippant.
That does not explain *why* it's not desirable to have the work turn silly, and so it is necessary to rephrase the question and ask again. Let's say another teacher helps you out:

   — So does that mean you mistrust the artist?
And let us assume the answer is simply:
   — Yes, I suppose so.

You might guess that an unexamined assumption behind the reason might be:

> *A film like this should not be devious*

3. Unexamined assumption

Like many unexamined assumptions, this one is ambiguous. The assumption might also be:

> *No film should be devious*

or

> *No work of art should be devious*

or

> *This one film should not be devious in this way*

or

> *No work of art should be devious in this way*

Or perhaps openness is real the issue, and the assumption should be something like:

> *A work of art should not hide its intentions*

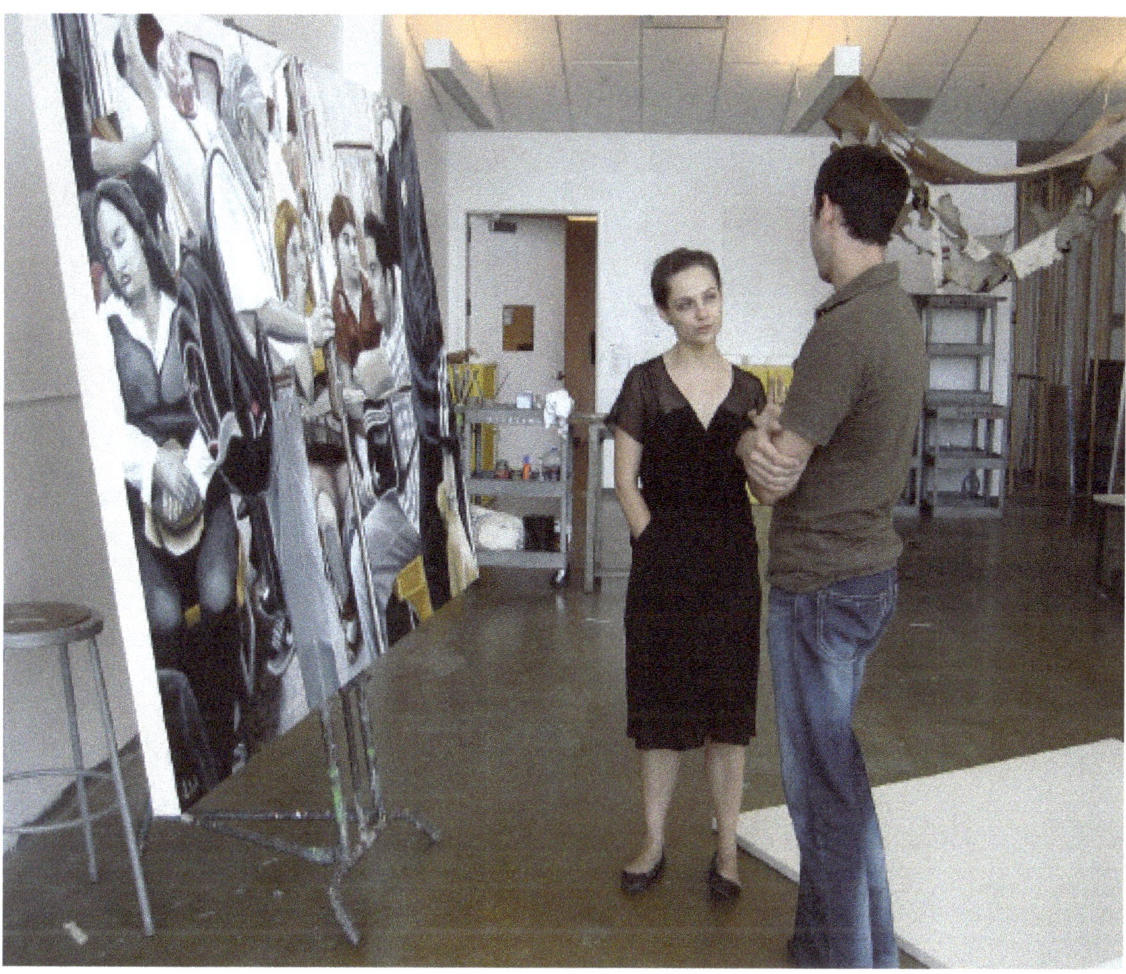

or

A work of art should not lie

Or it may be a more personal issue:

Work should change moods from serious to unserious in a serious or careful manner

These alternatives could be explored after the critique. At this point there is enough information to conclude that your teacher dislikes being tricked, and that *consistency, seriousness, play, trust,* and *intentionality* are all concepts that need further exploration.

The principal difficulty in going further is that evoking deeper unexamined assumptions is like pulling teeth. Even when your teacher doesn't resist the "why" questions—after all, they can seem rather rude—she may not answer in a helpful way. Let's say you, or the other teachers, continue to press the issue, and the teacher finally offers this explanation:

— I like things that are flip, I just don't like the way it's done here.

In that case, the exchange might continue this way:

— What seems wrong about the way it's done here?

— It's done without thinking, too quickly.

— Do you think that work that changes from serious to unserious should do it seriously, or carefully?

Notice that it's getting more difficult to frame the questions. Say the answer is "Yes." Again we have a number of choices:

— Seriousness takes precedence over silliness, and seriousness should control both what is serious and what is not serious.

— Seriousness is fundamental, and playfulness is dependent on it.

— You need to be very careful where silliness is concerned.

The deeper unexamined assumption may be any of these, or several others. Say the assumption was

> *Seriousness is fundamental, and*
> *playfulness is dependent on it*

This is, incidentally, a very common assumption. Does anything lie behind it? Maybe; it could be something like this:

> *Seriousness is part of sanity, and*
> *silliness can be destructive of sanity*

And so the deepest of all the unexamined assumptions would be:

Sanity is an ultimate good

4. Final assumption or axiom

This last assumption could be called an *axiom,* because like the axioms of mathematics it cannot appeal to a higher authority for justification. (You can't argue sanity is good, because you can't argue from the opposing point of view of insanity.) Philosophers and mathematicians also call statements like this dogmas, givens, and postulates. Here I am defining *axiom* as a statement that stands without justification, not because the speaker is unwilling to think further but because she *cannot* think further. Axioms are usually less interesting than reasons or unexamined assumptions because they are things known to everyone. They are sometimes *endoxa,* universal trivial truths, like "Don't go out in public without clothes." Typically they are applicable outside of art—they are principles that apply to art and to life. For these reasons, axioms are not as useful as unexamined assumptions.

Though I find the four-step sequence of judgment-reason-assumption-axiom is widely useful, it goes without saying that it's not always a four-step sequence. In particular, assumptions and axioms can be effectively the same. Any of the terms of praise that I listed in chapter 36, such as "interesting" or "powerful," could also be assumptions or axioms. When people say work is interesting, powerful, moving, authentic, inventive, compelling, gorgeous, or stimulating, the assumption is that interesting work is good, or moving work is good, or something fairly empty along those lines. These might be axioms, because most teachers would be hard pressed to say why a good artwork is compelling, or *why* it's good to be moved.

It also happens that the judgment and the axiom can be one and the same. Many things about the chain of questions can be doubted, but it is often a helpful critical tool. Here are the four links in the chain, with their salient points:

Judgment	A statement made in the course of a critique
Reason	The justification given when someone asks for it
Assumption	The unexamined or unanalyzed principle behind the reason and the judgment
Axiom	The *endoxa*, the general truth that supports the assumption. Often axioms have little to do with art

The four-step chain of questions

Thinking about the chain of questions clarifies a couple of things. First, the chain can be followed to a final link: you can keep questioning your teacher like a two-year-old, and if she doesn't get too pissed off, you may really get somewhere. There is no circularity or infinite regression. Instead, almost everything that is said in art critiques ultimately depends on unexamined assumptions and axioms. I like to think of this like a stream: the individual judgments are like little rivulets, and they converge into streams, which finally converge into rivers, and empty into the very large and common oceans of axioms. The chain of questions also shows that the number of assumptions and axioms in art teaching, like the number of large rivers, is not infinite. People in the art world sometimes assume that visual art has an infinite number of meanings, but in practice it turns out that our thinking runs in a relatively small number of channels. Art discourse is more limited and conventional than we might wish. That will be the moral of my last chapter, on the six-hour critique.

Unexamined assumptions and axioms can be collected the way people collect stamps. There are a large number of them, but I suspect that in any given art department or "interpretive community" there are really not that many. Here are some that were listed by one of my students (Kirsten Lindberg Benson); they dominated the discussion in two painting critiques, without ever being mentioned or directly questioned:

> *Paintings should be primarily concerned with space.*
>
> *A painting should have some sort of unity.*
>
> *It is helpful to use other painters as sources.*
>
> *History is archaeology (and therefore not useful).*
>
> *You can never be sure when a painting is finished.*
>
> *Disruptive qualities are good in a painting.*
>
> *Sensuous paintings are good; materiality is good.*
>
> *Spontaneity is good.*
>
> *Old styles of art need new life to keep them going.*

Unexamined assumptions in painting

These are so common in critiques!

Another interesting thing about the chain of questions is that the teacher's assumptions can turn out to be very surprising. A teacher who thinks of herself as postmodern might make judgments that depend on some old-fashioned assumptions. The list I've just given has some entries that seem dated, like "Sensuous paintings are good." It is the nature of axioms and assumptions to catch us unaware (they are, after all, "unexamined"), and it stands to reason that the general operative principles of our intellectual lives are older, and therefore more dated, than the neologisms we have picked up from the latest art magazine. *Probably a majority of people who teach studio art think of themselves part of the general stream of postmodernism or poststructuralism, but I think most of us are really early modernists, or even late Romantics.* Searching for our unexamined assumptions is a way of finding out just how much many of us owe to modernism, to the late nineteenth century, and even the Romanticism of the early nineteenth century.

I have taught a number of classes on critiques in which students practice finding assumptions and axioms. In one class a student said he thought one of his assumptions was "It is good to put effort into artworks." But that can't be the final term in a chain of questions, because it is not apparent why effort should be good. I suggested that effort might be a moral good, and he said perhaps that was it. (That would make his criticism ethical, as in chapter 35.) But then his axiom would be something like "Good art is moral"—an unsettling thing for a postmodern artist to say.

Another common assumption is that good art can hold our attention for more than a few moments. But if that is pressed, it may turn out that the underlying axiom is that we should be entertained, and then the axiom might be something like "Art relieves boredom." Again, the axiom is unexpected, and it throws light on a common teacher's habit—I do it myself—of asking students to make works that hold the viewer's attention for as long as possible.

In practice, you need to be careful asking teachers to explain themselves more and more deeply. As Nietzsche said, Socrates was one of the most annoying people who ever lived because his ultimate purpose seemed to be demonstrating that everyone, including himself, really knew nothing. Talking about the chain of questions can be annoying because it reveals how little of our reasoning we really understand.

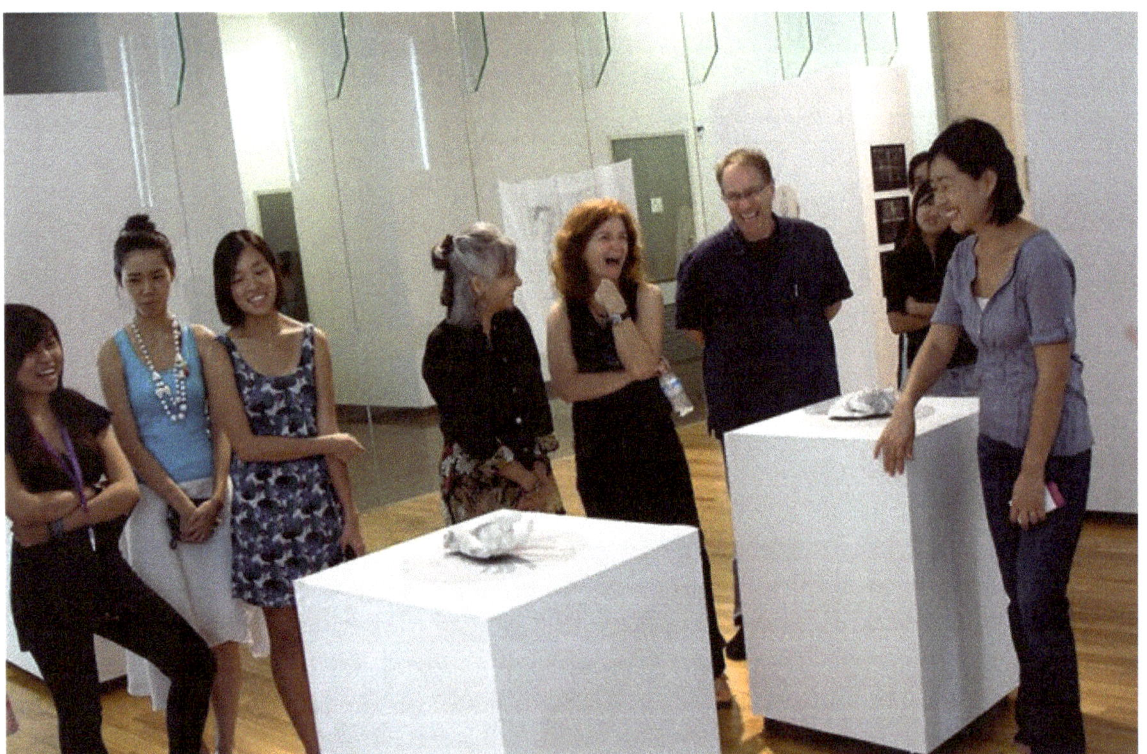

Three Big Projects:

2. Transcribe Your Critique

Several critiques in this book, like the long one in chapter 11, were laboriously transcribed from audiotapes. I did that—and in some cases, the students did it—in order to have the critique as a screenplay or script. That way we could read it out in a seminar class, with the students playing the people in the critique. We could slow it down, and stop to ask about why each person said what they did. A transcription is much better than a videotape, because it makes things very clear, and because the labor involved in producing it ensures that you think about every single word that is spoken.

Taping has to be done carefully. Most important, you have to preserve anonymity: instructors are not likely to talk naturally if they know that everything they say is going to be scrutinized afterward. In my experience the best solution is to have the student tape the critique, and then change everyone's names when the transcripts are made. None of the students in the seminar that reads the transcript should know who the speakers were; they should never hear the tape, and all the names should be expunged from the transcript. (For example, if someone says "he said," that can be replaced in the transcript by "[speaker X] said.") When the artist is present in the seminar, he or she should be cautioned not to give any clues about the identities of the other people in the transcription. The best transcripts, therefore, are those that are several years old, so that the artist and most of the panelists are not known to the students. Anonymity doesn't hinder analysis, and it helps assure everyone in the department or the school that the instructors are not being critiqued behind their backs.

It may seem that the loss of the nuances of speech would impair the usefulness of the transcripts, but it turns out that virtually everything having to do with content can retained without knowing about gestures, body language, mumbles and hrumphs. I think it is best to use italics and scare quotes for emphasis, to transcribe words such as "sort of," "um," and "kind of," and to put in ellipses (…) when speakers hesitate; but in general I have found that the non-verbal parts of speech have less meaning than I had thought. (This is an interesting disproof of the common notion that spoken nuance and body language are all-important.)

Sometimes it is difficult to make sentences out of what the speakers say. Panelists in critiques are usually trying to express the most difficult thoughts that come to their mind, and it can be surprising to find how seldom they speak in complete sentences. I wonder if people only speak in complete sentences when they have very little to say. A paragraph's worth of talk virtually never comes out as a string of grammatically correct sentences. Yet we are oblivious to syntactical transgressions in everyday speech, and we automatically edit what we hear into subjects, verbs, and predicates. In this respect, the project of transcribing can be an illuminating lesson in the difference between the spoken and written word. What should be done, for example, with this speech:

K You could also be printing on Plexiglas […] or any other support that is not, that doesn't have—one of the main connotations that I can think of about glass is fragility or breakability. So I mean, how do you justify its use, maybe given your ideas, given that aspect of that particular material, because it's not a hand-held object and you don't, you know, you don't impose any of these qualities about the material on the viewer, I mean then I would question the use of that as a support.

This is not at all unusual; I chose it almost at random. The question is how much is read into the passage when it is punctuated. If I edit it this way:

K You could also be printing on Plexiglas or any other support that is not, that doesn't have… One of the main connotations that I can think of about glass is fragility or breakability.
So I mean, how do you justify its use? Maybe given your ideas, given that aspect of that particular material… Because it's not a hand-held object and you don't, you know, you don't impose any of these qualities about the material on the viewer. I mean, then I would question the use of that as a support.

Am I imposing a sense that was not intended? The problem here is that if I give this back to the teacher who said it, they will be tempted to remake it into something brilliant. The sense of the critique will be lost.

There are other practical difficulties. When a panelist says, "I like that one there," the transcript needs to have a bracketed interpolation identifying the work, and it needs to be keyed to an image of the work. For that purpose it is essential that the student review the transcript and identify which works the panelists were indicating. All in all, transcribing takes time. The equipment has to be good quality, since a low-quality microphone will miss a great deal of dialogue. It takes me an average of five or six hours to type out a forty-five minute critique: not because I type slowly, but because the transcription requires numerous decisions about punctuation. Photographs have to be taken of the artworks, preferably soon after the critique before they are taken down. Then the transcript has to be given to the artist to be checked. The slides have to be labeled to correspond with the way they're referred to in the critique.

When all that is done, the transcript can then be studied in a classroom setting. It needs to be made clear that the purpose of the class is not to continue the critique by adding more judgments to those the panelists have made. There needs to be a vigilant separation between the juridical statements in the transcript and whatever analysis the students in the seminar propose: their analysis should be descriptive, not judgmental. A good way of putting this is that the function of analyzing transcriptions is to understand the critique, not the artwork.

It can be tempting to make fun of panelists who were, after all, thinking on their feet. Most things that most of us say sound stupid when they are analyzed too carefully. So although it is sometimes useful to say that a given panelist had no particular idea in mind, or that a given statement was particularly obvious, unproductive, or confused, it is essential not to assume that any member of the seminar would do better.

The main advantage of going to all this trouble is that it slows down the critique. If a seminar class reads a critique like a play, it is possible to pause after every speech and analyze it according to any of the topics I have covered. In general, the panelists' unexamined assumptions become much more apparent than they were in real time, and their judgments are easier to understand.

In my classes we read critiques very slowly: we get through a half hour critique, which is about eighteen typed pages, in a three hour class. Usually at that pace it is possible to make a great deal of sense out of the dialogue. But sometimes it doesn't help much, and it seems that *no matter how slowly* we read, the critique remains incomprehensible. Sometimes there is no way to understand a person's train of thought, and no way to see why people respond to each other in certain ways. Why does speaker X say this to speaker Y at this moment? Why doesn't speaker Z listen? There might be no answer to that kind of question.

Studying transcribed critiques is fascinating, but it is not a panacea: it takes a great deal of effort and preparation, and sometimes the only moral that can be drawn is that the critique was somehow doomed from the beginning, or that it will never make sense, no matter how carefully it is studied. At the same time, transcription is the best tool I know for examining how art is taught.

47

Three Big Projects:

3. Do A Six-Hour Critique

In Michael Asher's Silent Teacher critique (chapter 15), students got up to 5 hours each. I have held critiques longer than those, some up to 6 hours long, concentrating on a single work by one student.[1] The idea is to exhaust all the meanings everyone can think of for that one piece. That demonstrates the limits of everyone's imagination; it reveals many of the teachers' and student's guiding assumptions; and it is a great way to think again about more familiar critique formats. It is irritating, exhausting and, in the end, really illuminating.

It isn't just a 3- or 6-hour critique, and it certainly isn't free form like Asher's. In the example I'm giving here, a class of 25 people looked at a single work for 3 hours, trying to name and understand every single meaning that occurred to us. No discussion of anything except meaning was permitted, and to simplify things the artist did not talk. (In other sessions, the artists contributed their own analyses, but it is simpler to begin with a session where the artist doesn't speak.) No one in the class was allowed to suppose that the work was not finished, or that the setting wasn't ideal, or to bring up questions of display or the marketplace. No one was allowed to advise the student: the discussion was purely descriptive. There was no talk about technique unless it bore directly on meaning.

When I've told other teachers about these 6-hour critiques, I've gotten two reactions: either they say it would be impossible to get a class to talk about a single work for 6 hours, or else they think that 6 hours is nowhere near long enough, because meanings are infinite and talk could go on forever. What actually happens is that 3 hours is just about enough to satisfy everyone in a class that they have explored every meaning that they can think of. (Six hours is plenty.)

Most students who have been in these critiques are surprised that they can actually reach the end of a work's meaning—at least for that day, and that class: *the exercise shows that visual art isn't actually endlessly evocative and meaningful.* For the first time, students feel that they really understand a piece of art. Needless to say, that feeling is an illusion, but the discovery that meanings are not infinite is real. As I suggested about the chain of questions, we all usually think along very conventional lines, and it is possible to find most or all of those lines in 6 hours. Students and teachers can then see what appears to be, for that particular class, as the sum total of a work's meanings.

I have found that the best way to organize these explorations of meaning is to divide the critique into three stages.

The first stage (one hour). Students are encouraged to say any meaning that comes to mind. Several volunteers write down everything that is said. I used to start things off with an informal list of things that aren't permitted: no meanings that are personal ("that reminds me of my grandmother"), no judgments, no advice, no talk about the market, no remarks about installation or context (unless the work is site-specific), nothing about the student's life (unless the student's statement is part of the work), no talk about technical questions or technique (unless it is visually apparent in the work). Meanings only.

The second stage (a half hour). At the end of the half hour there is a break. During the break I sit down with the volunteers and try to classify the various things that have been said. We produce a new outline of what's been said, arranging the comments into whatever groupings they suggest. (We don't impose any order: we try to find whatever order the conversation has suggested.)

The third stage (an hour). The provisional outline or list of topics is then read out to everyone, and used to direct another round of comments. I don't impose the ordering of the list, but I try to make sure everyone has a chance to elaborate on everything in the list. Repeating parts of the list helps everyone see what sorts of meanings they have found, and it usually inspires students to find new kinds of meanings.

Then repeat the second and third stages, as many times as possible. In a 6-hour critique, I would usually have 4 sessions with everyone, and 3 or 4 revisions of the list. The critique should not end until everyone has said everything they can think of—and it is especially important not to end when people become exasperated, exhausted or bored.

In this example, the class saw three large, quasi-abstract monoprints that formed a single triptych. The *first stage* is when everyone is encouraged to list whatever meanings come to mind.

A	Okay, let's get started. I think that we should start with some free association. Anyone have any comments on what you see, positive or negative?	
B	Well, I see those two round forms in the one on the right as two suns.	
A	Okay, let's just take this one on the right first, and go through it looking for symbols. Afterward we can do the other two, and then after that I'll ask for other kinds of comments. But as long as we've started, let's keep going on this one, in this way.	*"In this way" means for example that if someone says it's misguided to look for symbolism, their comment will be deferred until the class has exhausted their search for symbols.*
E	Well, I think that purple form is a pair of calipers.	
A	Does anyone agree with that, or with the observation about the suns?	*It is always important to see what consensus the reading has, to distinguish idiosyncratic comments from those closer to the "interpretive community's" position.*

The next twenty minutes were spent adding symbolic meanings. At the end I opened the floor to any kind of reaction other than symbolic meanings.

C	I don't know, I just think these pictures are a little boring.	*The idea of boredom is tricky: it is partly suggested by the 6-hour critique format, and partly inherent in the work.*
A	Uh-huh. Let me just say parenthetically that that's an entirely different kind of reaction, and maybe we might want to think whether or not it belongs—how it belongs—with that list we have just been making. So anyway, I'd like to know if you just thought that recently, or from the very beginning.	*The question is intended to distinguish the student's idea from the boredom that was beginning to settle on the class.*
C	Yes, at the beginning, but much less. This is maybe just too much time to spend on one print.	
F	Yes, I see some of the symbols, but I really don't… I really wouldn't see them unless we had been looking for them.	*This comment also has to do with how long the prints can hold a viewer's attention.*
A	So now I think we have another theme, to go along with our dictionary of symbols, and that is how long the work holds attention. Any comments on that?	

We went on another twenty minutes exploring the themes of boredom, the importance of symbols, the existence of forms that were not symbolic, the possibility that the prints were not meant to be interpreted at all. During the *second stage*, the topics have to be arranged as clearly as possible. In this case we began with an unorganized list of topics, including "landscape symbols," "kinds of abstraction," "issues of unity and disunity," "color problems," "boredom," and several others. Some were placed under larger headings. "Boredom," for instance, went under "psychological responses," which also included "fascination," "exasperation," and "mistrust." The outline was about three pages long.

At the beginning of the *third stage*, after a break, I read the list of meanings that had been arranged during the break. We started with the theme of boredom. The purpose of the third stage is no longer the collection of meanings but the analysis of unexamined assumptions.

A	Why did you say this was boring?	
C	At first it seemed like a kind of mysterious landscape or a cityscape, and I liked that. It seemed as if it could have been abstract or figurative.	*This is the reason behind the judgment; actually it is two reasons together. The first might be: "I like mystery, and without it I am bored," and the second "I like ambiguity, and without it I am bored."*
A	So do you think that mystery is good in a work, or a good thing here?	*Making sure that the first reason really was a love of mystery.*
C	Yes, well, it's good here, or it would have been…	*This is the reason behind the initial judgment, but it still requires explanation.*

A	So why is it a negative thing to stop being mysterious? You mean that any work that is not mysterious is less interesting? Can't a work be straightforward and also successful?	*It is not clear why mystery and ambiguity are positive values, or why boredom is not.*
C	No, no, it's that I get the impression that the panels are supposed to be mysterious—	
A	—that they're intended to look mysterious—	
C	Yes, and so, when I see that it is not mysterious, the work quote "fails."	*This may mean that he thinks that the artist's intention has to be carried through in order for a work to be successful.*
D	I think sort of the opposite here. I like the piece very much, and I think what I like is that it is not ambiguous after all, after a while. It is… it says, "I am abstract," and that's good.	*(This student had been speaking in favor of straightforward work earlier in the critique.)*
E	Well, not for me.	

<table>
<tr>
<td>A</td>
<td>That's interesting.
Let me just stop for a second and sum up the assumptions in these statements: boredom is bad; mystery and ambiguity are good (or, as [speaker D] said, bad); boredom is important, or necessary; and the artist should follow through on her intention (and if she means something to be mysterious, it should be). I'm not so sure about that last one. Why can't it just make the work more interesting when it "fails" in that way? —but let's leave that for a second. I want to go back to something [speaker T] said…</td>
<td>These unexamined assumptions should probably remain unexamined for a while, since they are difficult to think about. In a few minutes they can be brought up again.</td>
</tr>
</table>

That part of the critique continued until we had talked about everything on the outline, and about several new topics that had occurred along the way. Twice during the discussion I read the outline aloud so it could be questioned, and the idea of an outline also became a topic. (In particular students wondered if the work's meaning could ever be captured in an outline.)

Here is what might happen in a full 6-hour critique:

— At first you may feel it is so incredibly artificial that nothing good can really come out of it.

— About an hour later it will get really boring.

— About an hour after that you may get really irritated.

— After 2 hours or so, you may feel like you have no more ideas, that no one has any more ideas.

— After 3 or 4 hours, you may become interested in seeing the *shape* of everyone's ideas, taken all together, how they fit, how they are more similar than you had thought.

— After 5 hours, you will be in an unusual frame of mind: *maybe for the first time, you will see that artwork does not have an infinite number of meanings.*

A student, Kyle Riley, pointed out that a six-hour critique might also tilt the power structure of an ordinary critique away from the instructors. If "panelists exhaust their ability to interpret the work in question," their eventual failure to come up with anything new reveals "their failure to represent themselves and their own subjectivity. It is as if failure is inevitable for them, which puts them at least on the same footing as the artist being reviewed, and in fact positions the artist to succeed over the panelists by withstanding the inquiry." I haven't experienced this myself—very long critiques, in my experience, retain the instructors' authority—but it should happen. Perhaps long critiques could continue until the instructors' authority is revealed to be as contingent as the students'.

We think of ourselves as individuals, but we all think along very well-worn paths. And that puts a lot of responsibility on your shoulders, as an artist. The art you produce is no longer something that is entirely subjective, so that it could mean anything to anyone. It has meanings that can—for the duration of one 6-hour class, anyway—be listed. Sometimes visual art is a place for private thoughts and incommunicable feelings: but more often, visual art is something that happens in the public domain, in a world full of thoughts that are widely shared.

The 6-hour critique suggests that there is a limit to what a picture means: a picture is usually worth approximately 20,000 words on any given occasion.

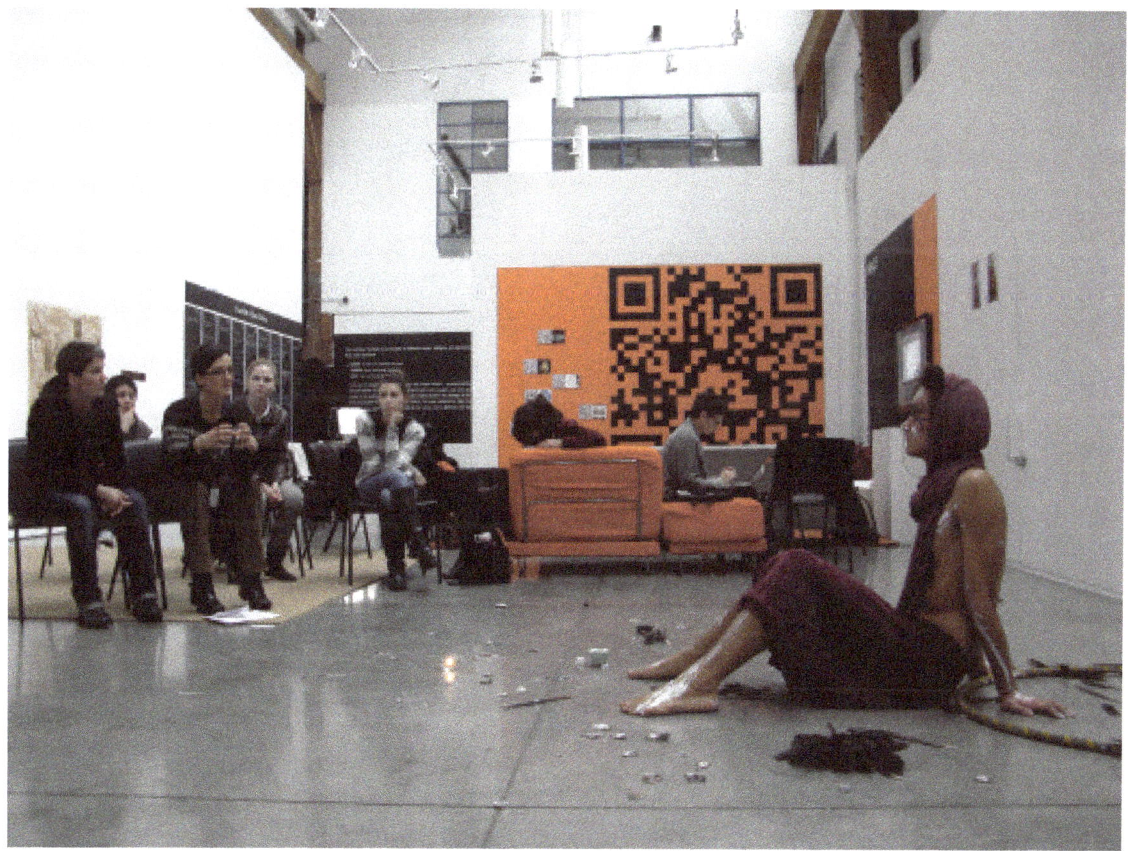

Part Six

PhD Issues

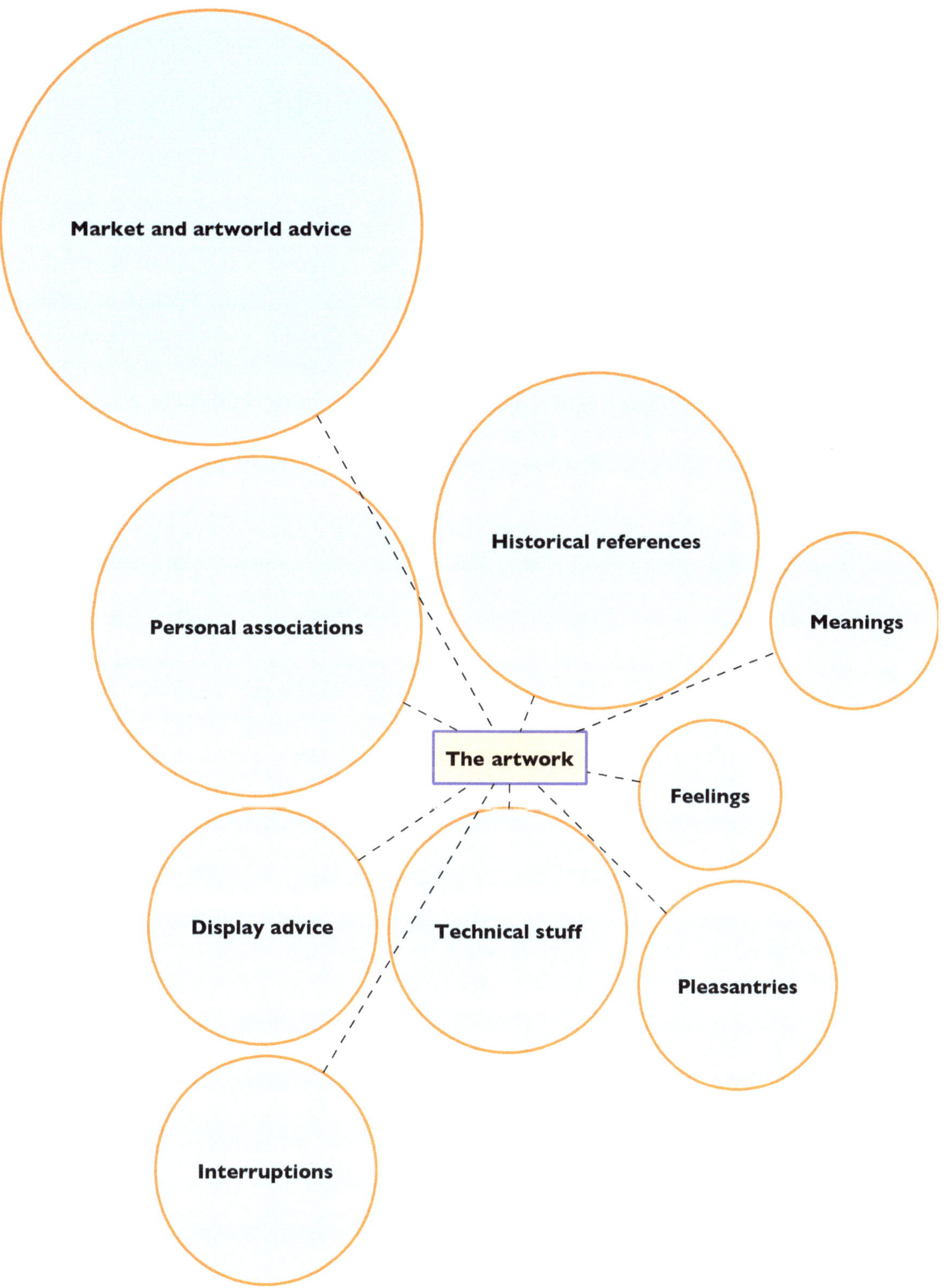

Market and artworld advice
Personal associations
Historical references
Meanings
The artwork
Feelings
Display advice
Technical stuff
Pleasantries
Interruptions

48

The World of the PhD

Most of what I have written has to do with undergraduate critiques and MFA critiques. Almost everything here also happens at the PhD level, but the PhD level can involve very different kinds of interactions between students and teachers. In fact it can be so different that it calls for a different book. And there are many such books: about twenty so far. Those books hardly mention any of the issues I have discussed up to this point: it's as if they are from a different universe, and in many ways they are. The entire subject of art critiques is alien to the literature on the PhD: in all the twenty or so books, I have hardly found a single reference to the sorts of problems I have discussed so far. Those books speak a different language, and they are addressed to educators and professors rather than students.

I suppose it would have been reasonable just to end this book here, and write a separate book on the PhD. That would be in line with the literature: what I've written here seems to have no connection with the problems that concern the authors of books on the PhD.

But I have decided to put in some material here anyway, for a simple reason: the BFA and MFA are continuous with the PhD. Students go from one degree to the next, and there is no break in between for professional courses on art education. I think that the enormous discontinuity between the vast professional literature on the PhD and the scattered, informal literature on BFA and MFA critiques is, all by itself, the single most interesting and challenging problem in visual art education. What could be more challenging than to try to write, or study, or teach, across that gap?

Before I get started, let me just list some of these twenty-odd books. If you are new to this, you might want to look some of these up. But hopefully just their titles will be enough to demonstrate how different things look from the perspective of of the PhD. Compare these titles with the few books and articles I mentioned back in the Preface. The books on the PhD in studio art include:

- *Art Practice as Research: Inquiry in the Visual Arts*
- *Thinking Through Art: Reflections on Art as Research*
- *Artists with PhDs: On the New Doctoral Degree in Studio Art* (this one's mine)

- *Art School (Propositions for the 21st Century)*
- *International Handbook of Research in Arts Education*
- *Art and Artistic Research: Music, Art, Design, Literature, Dance*
- *The Pleasure of Research*
- *The Routledge Companion to Research in the Arts*
- *Practice as Research: Contexts, Method, Knowledge (Approaches to Creative Arts Enquiry)*
- *Handbook of the Arts in Qualitative Research: Perspectives, Methodologies, Examples, and Issues*
- *Practice-led Research, Research-led Practice in the Creative Arts*
- *Design Research Through Practice from the Lab, Field, and Showroom*
- *Intellectual Birdhouse: Artistic Practice as Research*

The titles alone show how different the world of the PhD is: lots of reference to research and practice, nothing at all about judgment or critique.[1]

There are many different kinds of studio-based PhD programs, so it is next to impossible to generalize about them. But they are spreading around the world. As of summer 2012, there are about 40 institutions in the U.K. that grant the PhD, 25 in Australia and New Zealand, 26 in Japan, 8 in China, 6 in the US, about 30 in the European Union, and 6 in Canada. So it's important to ponder how teaching happens at at the PhD level.

(If you're interested in applying for a PhD, try reading one of these books, perhaps starting with the one I edited, which is published by this same publisher. If you still have questions, email me via the website: I try to keep current statistics on the programs.)

Why PhD Programs Leave Critiques Behind

It's important to note that there are no good, pertinent, thorough definitions of the BA, BFA, MA, or MFA. Those degrees have been run in many countries for a century now without any consensus definitions. That is sugnificant because it means there is no clear definition of what the PhD is.

The College Art Association in North America and the Bologna Accords and Tuning Documents in the European Union provide minimal definitions, some less than a page long. NASAD, the National Association of Schools of Art and Design, offers guidelines for accrediting programs in individual media, but the guidelines do not coincide with the things people usually say in studios or classrooms. For example, NASAD says this about painting students: they should "gain functional competence with principles of visual organization, including the ability to work with visual elements in two and three dimensions; color theory and its applications; and drawing."[1] The official definitions of the BFA and MFA are either very brief or not pertinent.

This may come as a surprise if you are in one of these programs! But it is not an exaggeration. Luckily, there is a sort of consensus view, on the street, about what the BFA and MFA are. Roughly speaking, the BFA is thought of as a time for experimentation, as I said in chapter 12. And roughly speaking, the MFA is the time for you to find a voice and consolidate a practice. The PhD, in so far as it can be characterized at all, is an opportunity to develop an existing practice.

That means the PhD level is more like a dialogue between practitioners than a teacher-student situation. The final critique at the end of the MFA is normally an opportunity for the faculty to acknowledge that you are now a peer, an artist in your own right. Final MFA critiques are sometimes just friendly conversations; they are more about understanding and respect than judgment. The same happens, more consistently, in PhD programs. The idea, more or less, is that you already are a mature artist; you have your practice, your language, and your competence. You are in a learning environment, but you are also an adult. For that reason, what happens when you talk to your supervisor or teacher in a PhD program is likely to be more about conversation, dialogue, and analysis than about judgment, quality, or technique. That's why the books on the subject don't mention critique, and it's why it is so difficult for me to switch gears, and talk about conversations instead of critiques.

All that is one reason why "critique" isn't really the right word to describe what happens between teachers and students in PhD programs. Another reason is that PhD programs need to be systematic in order to be accepted in universities, and in systems, like the European Union and the U.K., where new degrees in all subjects need to be comparable. PhDs in studio art involve systematic teaching and learning. Students proceed step by step, and their progress is measured. In that sort of systematic pedagogy there is not much room for the wonderful unpredictability and utter openness of critiques.

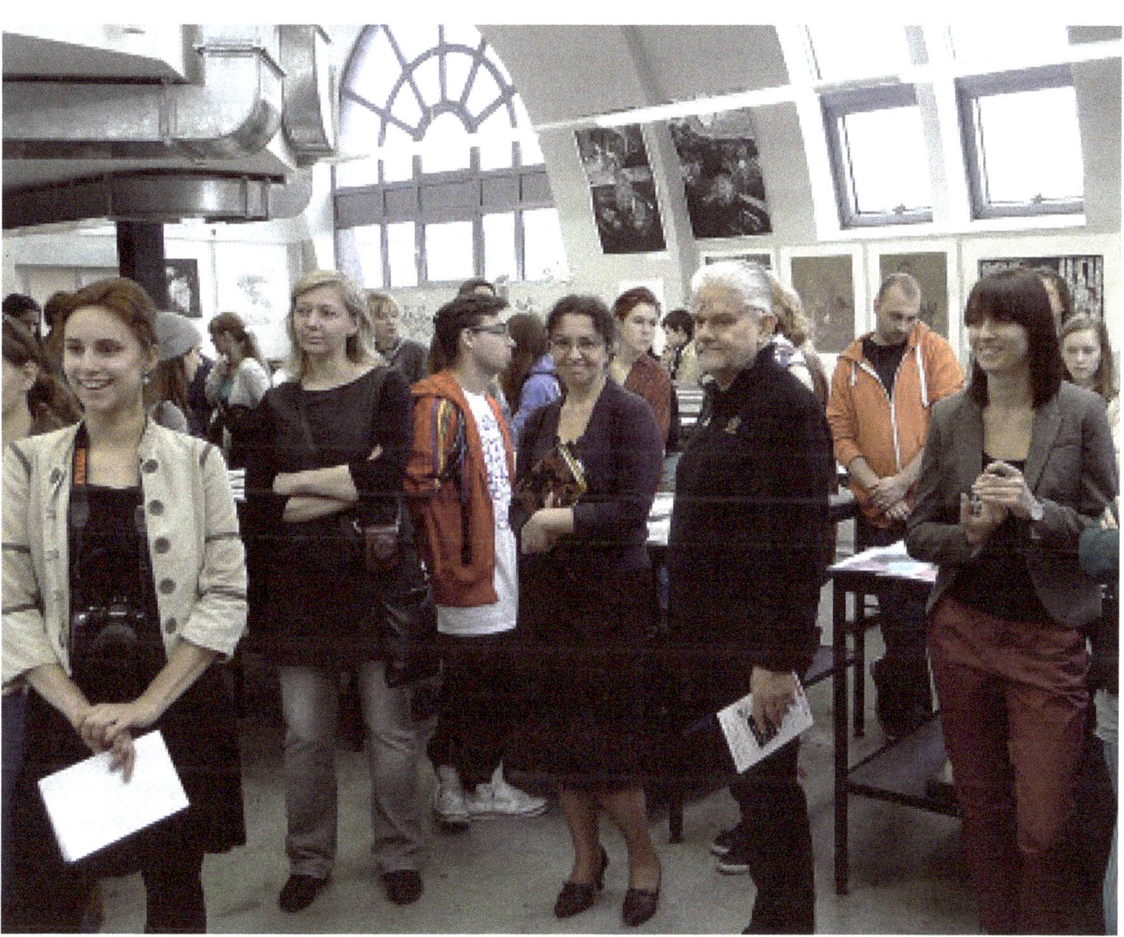

PhD Programs Are Mainly Concerned with Research…

Many PhD programs, especially those based on a model that was begun in the U.K., have a different structure than BFA or MFA programs: they are based on the idea that art, at the professional level, is a matter of *research* that produces *new knowledge*. Teachers (they are usually called "supervisors") ask students (also called "PhD candidates") to analyze their art projects and decide what they hope to accomplish in the next term or year. As a student, you may then be asked to write a proposal, which is sometimes formal and written, and other times verbal, and often includes a research program, along with the methods you will employ, what kind of outcome you hope for, and the means by which that outcome might be assessed by your supervisor. The supervisor then helps develop your research proposal and guide its execution. Conversations between you and the faculty aren't so much critiques as conversations about the viability and interest of your proposal and its possible outcomes.

The problem, from the faculty's point of view, is defining what is meant by "artistic research" and what kind of "knowledge" is produced by art.

There are two large schools of thought forming around these ideas in Europe, where most of the literature is being written. According to one, scientific research is the ultimate model for art research, even if many fundamental terms have to be questioned. In that way of thinking, what matters is how *art research* might be correlated with scientific research pursued elsewhere in the university. According to the other school of thought, *art research* is a polymorphous term, understood in terms of French and other poststructuralist theory, with no fixed relationship to the sciences. Because no one has named these, I'll call them the *university art model* and the *poststructural academy.*[1]

The former is oriented by an interest in quantifiable outcomes, research programs, hypotheses, repeatable research methodologies, and the creation of new knowledge. The latter is oriented by an interest in experimental knowledge, theories of understanding, performativity, identity, and the construction of pedagogy. In general the *poststructural academy* is an initiative of art schools and academies, and the *university art model* takes place more in university and college art departments.

But these are early days, and in another ten years things may have settled.

I will give some examples of each.

A. *The university art model,* the one that stresses quantifiable, empirical, assessable strategies of art making, is the one closest to scientific research. An extreme example is Ilpo Koskinen's guidelines for prospective students to the Aalto University School of Art, Design and Architecture, in Finland. Koskinen uploaded a detailed set of criteria in 2008. He asks prospective students to determine if their art research is "hypothetico-deductive," "interpetive," or "constructive." If you opt for the first one, "you must describe your research design. How many experiments you plan; what are your independent, dependent, control and intervening variables; how many people you study; how you randomize them; what is your null hypothesis and also alternative hypotheses; what kinds of laboratory procedures you follow; which methods of analysis you use (typically ANOVA, ANCOVA, but usually even t-tests will do), and so forth." If that sounds daunting, you can opt for "interpretive" research. But he warns that if "interpretive research… sounds like an easy alternative, it is not. You need to know exactly what you are doing. You need to read yourself into some interpretive tradition—ike interactionism—and its methodology, write down a claim to justify your research, plan data gathering carefully and in detail, and describe your analytic plan carefully."[2] I could go on (it's a very entertaining website), but you can see the kinds of rigor that are required. Most programs are nowhere near this quantified, but many expect you to describe your art as a form of research, and to describe what and how you hope to research, what you hope to find, and how your findings—your artwork—could be assessed. In general the idea is to provide a structured, hierarchical, quantifiable research environment in which you can develop, explore, and articulate your art practice. Science, in its many forms, is what underwrites the rigor or systematization of these programs.

B. *The poststructural academy* is quite different, although in the young world of the practice-based PhD, the two sometimes overlap. In general, however, the idea of what I am calling poststructural academies is that research in the arts needs to be theorized entirely independently of science. A good example is the Dutch theorist Henk Slager; he describes doctoral art research as "temporary autonomous research" and says it has "no need to be led by the formatted models of the established scientific order." The principal purpose of this is to enable oppositional work in relation to capitalist spectacle: "this will be a form of research," he writes, which is "not swayed by issues dictated by the late-capitalist free market system [or its] knowledge commodification… this will be an authentic research that comes about through an artistic necessity…. Many artistic research projects seem the thwart the well-defined disciplines. They know the hermeneutic questions of the humanities (the alpha-sciences); they are engaged in empirically scientific methods (the beta-sciences); and they are aware of commitment (the gamma-sciences)." These point to a "delta-science," characterized by a "capacity… to continuously engage in novel, unexpected epistemological relations in a methodological process of interconnectivity." Artistic research is therefore "an undefined discipline," a "'nameless science,' directed toward generating flexible constructions, multiplicities, and new reflexive zones."[3]

These two models are both generating a lot of writing, and it is too early to know where they will go, or whether they will entwine. But if you are thinking of applying to a PhD program, you should ask yourself whether you think of your art practice as *research* at all. You'll need to conceive it as research in some way; if you don't, most PhD programs won't be suited to you.[4]

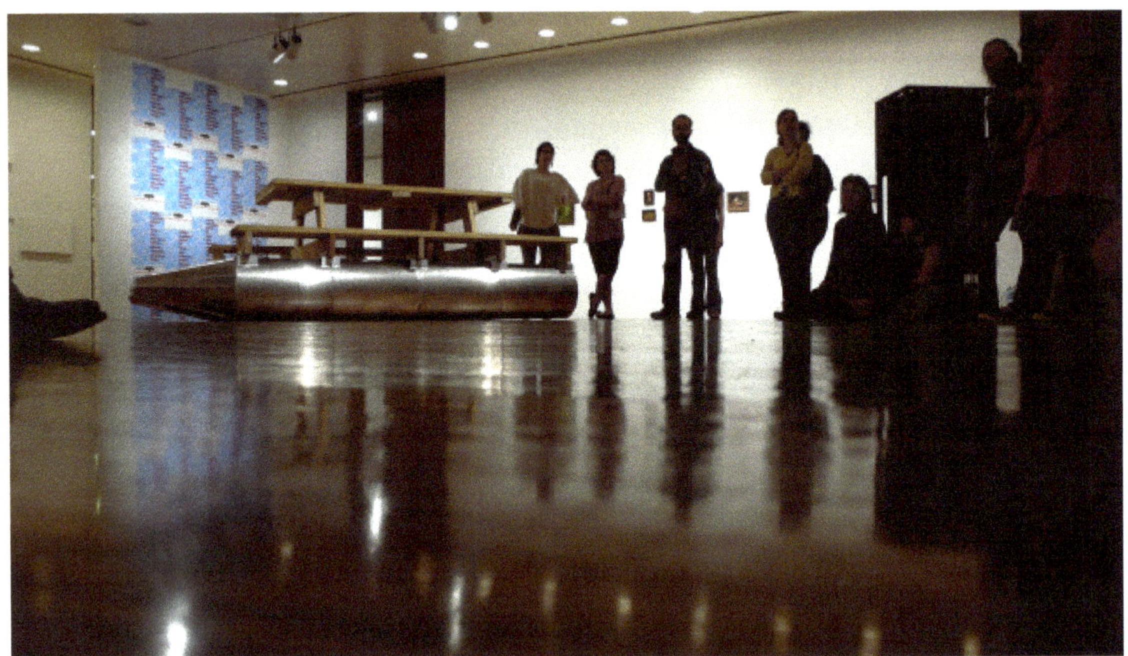

51

… and Knowledge

As a student in a PhD program, you will do a lot of talking about research. The other principal concept you'll be discussing is knowledge. That is because universities require that any subject—art, physics, sociology, whatever—be taught using a consistent research methodology that results in the discovery of new knowledge. So studio-art PhD programs typically talk about art as knowledge.

This, too, can be surprising at first. Only a minority of artists would describe their painting, sculpture, or video as something that produces "knowledge." It is more common to hear artists talking about their work as expressive: it produces moods, feelings, intuitions, and affect, but usually not knowledge. Some people talk about how art produced understanding, or meaning, instead of knowledge. But PhD programs are almost all involved in the idea that art can produce knowledge.

In some institutions, you will be talking about your painting or other artwork as a form of knowledge in itself. You and your supervisor will work out how the painting, or other medium, creates something new in the world, some new form of knowledge. In other institutions, you will be talking about your knowledge of your painting, or the knowledge you've gained by making the painting. Either way, you will also be researching some topic, as a scholar. Typically you'll have a second supervisor who is an art historian or a philosopher, and you'll be writing a research dissertation, anywhere from 10,000 to 100,000 words. Usually students choose topics that help them in their work. If you do performance art, for example, your research dissertation might be on an episode from the history of performance art that can shed some light on your own art practice. The dissertation is supposed to produce new knowledge—that's not a problem—but so is your artwork. No one has clearly theorized how the artwork is related to knowledge: whether it is itself knowledge (in which case what kind of knowledge? Color knowledge? Light knowledge?) or whether your interpretations reveal the knowledge embedded in it (in which case why, exactly, make visual art to begin with, if what matters is the knowledge that you extract from it?).

The majority position on this issue is that knoweldge inheres in visual art, but it has to be extracted. A good example of this position is Henk Borgdorff; he has written that visual art researchers "employ experimental and hermeneutic methods

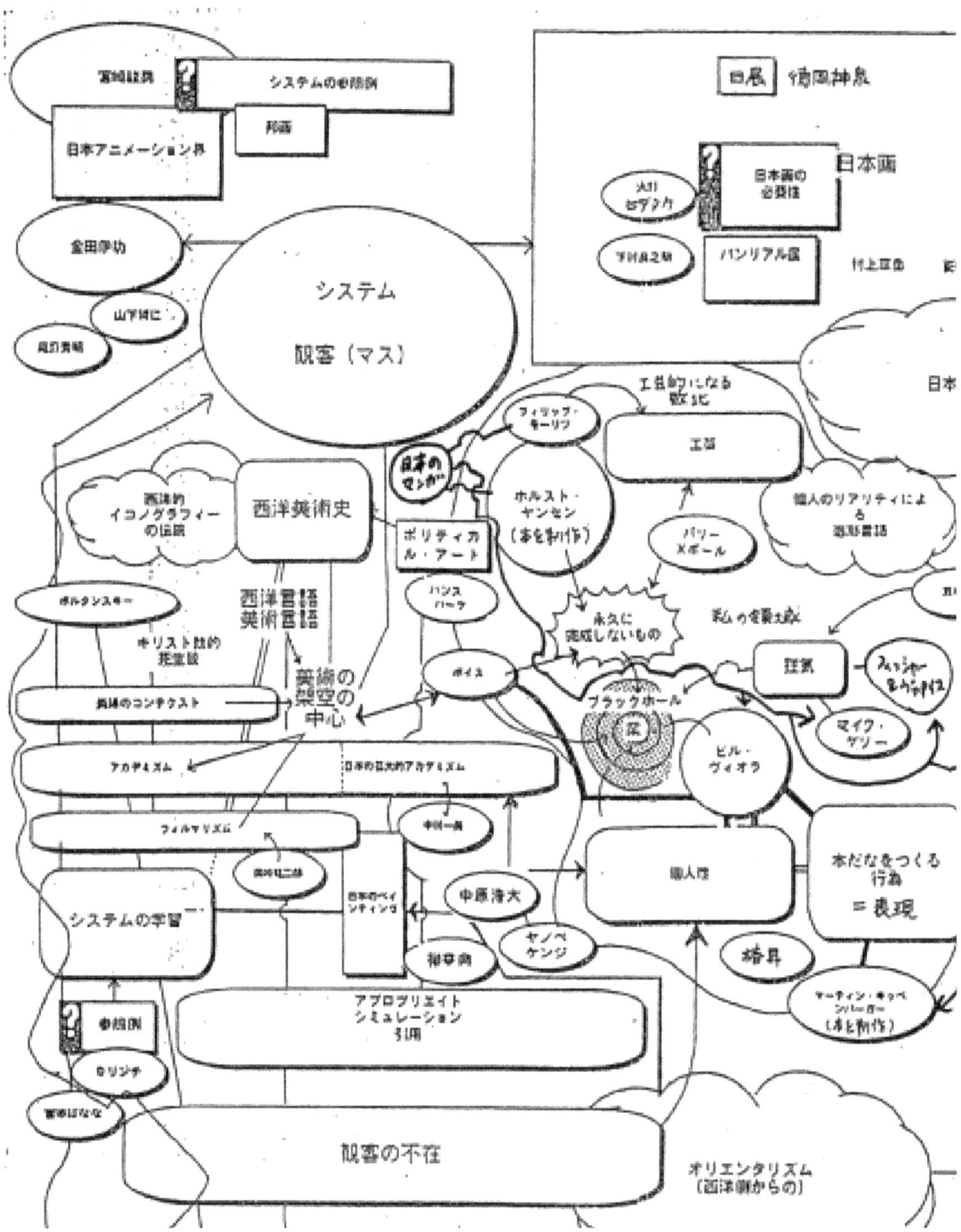

A detail of a diagram of the art world, by Takashi Murakami, from his PhD dissertation, written at the Tokyo University of the Arts.

that reveal and articulate the tacit knowledge that is situated and embodied in specific artworks and artistic processes." That expression, tacit knowledge, is itself a contested one: it names a kind of knowledge that isn't quite knowledge yet—it's not spelled out, it's not yet articulated in words, but it can be made into knowledge if it is properly developed. Lots of philosophic issues swarm around this sort of claim. Luckily they aren't the subject of this book. All that matters here is that in a PhD program, you will be thinking and talking with your supervisor about issues like this.[1]

As in the case of research, if you're thinking of applying to a PhD program, you should ask yourself whether you think of your art practice as something that creates, or produces, knowledge. If you do—and a certain number of artists do think this way—then a PhD program might be right for you.

52

The Future of the PhD

I have tried to sketch the subjects that are discussed in studio-art PhD programs. It is not possible to be much more precise than this, because the programs vary so widely. But I hope this is enough to suggest what sorts of concerns replace critiques at the PhD level.

Although people worry that the PhD will soon be required to teach college-level art, that mostly hasn't happened. There is some evidence from some very different places that faculty are being asked, or required, to get PhDs, but in western Europe and North America that seems very unlikely for the foreseeable future. Most art academies and schools hire people with MFAs as well as PhDs. (Countries where I have heard of the PhD being required or recommended: Malaysia, Poland, Uganda, Kenya.)

So even though the degrees are becoming more common—Australia produces about 50 new PhDs each year—the degree is not something you need in order to pursue a teaching career. It's more a matter of deciding if it could be right for you.

If you use a fairly consistent subject matter, if your work is well formulated and reasonably consistent, if you typically do research to help you with your work, and if you feel you need to continue in a structured learning environment, then the PhD may be right for you. If your work isn't about research, if you don't think of yourself as producing knowledge, if you don't like writing long scholarly papers, if you don't feel you need to understand your work any better than you do now, then you might be better off in a residency, an artist's group, or a shared studio—that is, outside academia once and for all.

But it is strange, isn't it, how the wild and nearly uncontrollable world of critiques suddenly gives way, at the PhD level, to a kind of formal, abstract, sometimes even scientific way of talking. I wonder if in future there will be more flexibility to PhD programs. That is quite possible—some PhD programs are already hybrids of critiques and research discussions—but the opposite is also possible: it could happen that the formal language and protocols of PhDs seeps down into the MFA, creating more research-based MFAs, and even research-based BFAs. I hope not, but I have already seen evidence of that happening.

Envoi

When you first start studying art at the college level, it is best to observe how things are done, and try to participate as much as possible. If you're in a big art school or a university, try to sit in on critiques and classes at all levels. It's also good to keep a notebook of all the interesting things that have been said to you in critiques. I teach a class on art critiques, and I ask students to bring in a list of everything their instructors have ever said to them that is *not* just a matter of technique, medium, or skill. I want to know every judgment and interpretation they can remember, and everything an instructor has ever said their work *means*. Sometimes those lists are frighteningly short. It is all too easy to go through the four years of a BFA, and even the two years of an MFA, and not get a lot of instruction on the *meaning* of your work. So keep notes all the time, and try to observe how things work throughout your department or institution.

I hope this book will help you control and understand some of the things that happen in your critiques. The main thing is: the critique is the time in your life when you'll get the most feedback. It is incredibly precious. After you graduate, you'll get some feedback from your friends, but as I said in the Preface, over the years the feedback you get from your friends will be more and more polite, and less and less valuable. If you're lucky enough to get a show, you'll get some responses at the opening: but that's usually something profound like, "Great work." If you're even luckier, and your show gets reviewed, you may get real criticism: but brief reviews of exhibitions are normally non-judgmental, because critics don't like to mention shows they don't like, unless the artist is famous and has already gotten a lot of press. The newspaper and blog notices for your work are likely to be neutral or positive, and therefore often nearly useless. And, finally, if you get to be famous, and get big shows and books written about you… well, by that time, you'll probably be so stubborn you won't even hear criticism. Think of Jeff Koons or Damien Hirst—is there any evidence they changed anything they did because of critics?[1]

So my moral is: pay attention while you're in school. Listen carefully in critiques. Take notes. Go over the notes. Go back and talk to your instructors about what they said. Try some of the ideas I've set out here. Try anything at all: just keep working at understanding the reactions your work provokes. It is not easy to understand critiques, but that is what makes them so valuable.

Photo Credits

All photos are mine, except the following:

"How This Book is Organized": photo by Laís Pontes (at right in the photo).

Chapter 1: Christine Frerichs's encaustic painting class at the Otis College of Art and Design, 2010. Students, left to right: Catherine Bisson, Rita Coufal Yoshimura, Irene Dolan, Susan Fishbein, Frances Vandal.

Chapter 3: Graduation project critique at the Art University of Tehran. Student: Sepideh Moazzami. Jury, right to left: Saeed Shahlapoor, Helia Darabi, Alireza Isfahanizadeh, Bijan Ghonchepoor. Department of Sculpture, Art University of Tehran, Feb. 2011. Photo Setareh Sepehr.

Chapter 6: An MFA critique at the University of Illinois at Urbana-Champaign, School of Art and Design, fall 2009. Photo by Conrad Bakker.

Chapter 7, photo 1: Steve Daly, February 2011, photo by David McClain.

Chapter 7, photo 2: Critique at the School of the Art Institute, Chicago. Photo courtesy Andre van de Putte.

Chapter 9: A critique at the School of the Art Institute of Chicago, undated. Ray Yoshida is on the right. Photo: Art Institute of Chicago.

Chapter 15: The floor of a critique in the Photography Department, School of the Art Institute of Chicago, photo by David McClain.

Chapter 17: A student at the Art Institute of Chicago. Undated. Photo: Art Institute of Chicago.

Chapter 19: A critique at the School of the Art Institute of Chicago, 1984. Photo: Art Institute of Chicago.

Chapter 20: A Q-Art critique, Jan. 23, 2012, photo by Jeff Ko. Courtesy Sarah Rowles.

Chapter 23: An MFA critique at the University of Illinois at Urbana-Champaign, School of Art and Design, c. 2009. Photo by Conrad Bakker.

Chapter 27: the critique scene is by Buzz Spector; the teacher is Ron Fondaw, Associate Professor of Sculpture at Washington University.

Chapter 28: Courtesy Chris Campe and Sean Lamoureux.

Chapter 29: Andrew Ellis Johnson with freshmen drawing students at Carnegie Mellon School of Art. Photo courtesy Susanne Slavick.

Chapter 30: Critique at the School of the Art Institute of Chicago, April 2013. Molly Zuckerman-Hartung (the teacher, left); Chiara Galimberti (a student, at right); paintings and photo by Magalie Guérin.

Chapter 31, photo 1: Marcel Duchamp, photographed in the Art Institute of Chicago. Photo: Art Institute of Chicago.

Chapter 31, photo 2: A critique at the School of the Art Institute of Chicago, 2013. The student is Youngbin Choi, and her painting is called *Hi, Goodbye*. Lisa Wainwright, Dean of SAIC, is in the red critique dress.

Chapter 32, photo 1: A studio class at the School of the Art Institute of Chicago, c. 1890. Photo: Art Institute of Chicago, from a reproduction in their archives; the location of the original is unknown.

Chapter 32, photo 2: Robert Morris in a critique in the Sculpture Department, School of the Art Institute of Chicago, January 1969. Photo: Art Institute of Chicago.

Chapter 32, photo 3: Sam Tchakalian, still from a YouTube video. (Accessed June 20, 2011)

Chapter 35: New York Academy of Art, MFA critique, 2011. The artist is Christina Barber. Photo Charis Carmichael Braun.

Chapter 36, photo 1: An MFA critique at the University of Illinois at Urbana-Champaign, School of Art and Design, fall 2009. Photo by Conrad Bakker.

Chapter 36, photo 2: School of the Art Institute of Chicago, Contemporary Practices, Research I students in the Crit Room. 2013. Instructor: Edra Soto; guest artists: Chelsea Culp and Ben Foch.

Chapter 38, photo 1: Courtesy Chris Fennell.

Chapter 38, photos 2 and 3: Courtesy elin o'Hara slavick.

Chapter 38, photo 4: School of the Art Institute of Chicago, Contemporary Practices, Research II students in the Crit Room. 2013. Instructor: Edra Soto; foreground student's work, Georgia Notin; background student's work, Juliette Hayt.

Chapter 39: Maria Buszek with Kathryn Van Zante (Minneapolis College of Art and Design, MFA 2014, Drawing and Painting) on 5, 2013, at Whittier Studios. The photographer was Tsu Chi 'Desiree' Niu (MFA 2014, Graphic Design).

Chapter 42, photo 1: A critique at the School of the Art Institute of Chicago, January 1968. Ray Yoshida is on the right. Photo: Art Institute of Chicago.

Chapter 42, photo 2: A critique at the Chautauqua Institute. Photo by Anna Kriger.

Chapter 43: A Q-Art critique, Nov. 27, 2013. Photo by Rachel Wilson; courtesy Sarah Rowles.

Chapter 44: Design critique. Photo by Tim Brown, 2008. From designthinking.ideo.com.

Chapter 45, photo 1: New York Academy of Art, MFA critique, 2011. The artist is Stephanie Lindquist. Photo Charis Carmichael Braun.

Chapter 45, photo 2: New York Academy of Art, MFA critique, 2011. Photo Charis Carmichael Braun.

Chapter 45, photo 3: The painter Dasha Shishkin, visiting the Tyler School of Art, 2010. Photo by Jenna Weiss.

Chapter 45, photo 4: Reza Hosseini Eshlahghi defending his work at the Department of Sculpture, Art University of Tehran, Iran, 2010. Photo Mitra Samavaki.

Chapter 46: A critique at Nanyang Technological University, Singapore, 2011. Photo by Fareez Ahmad. Left to right: Meridel Rubinstein, Joan Marie Kelly, Paul Khol, Oh Soon Hwa. Photo courtesy Joan Kelly.

Chapter 47: The artists Margit Schild and Elvira Hufschmid (far left) critique a performance by Diego Pacheco in the exhibition space of QR_U, as part of "Questions, Responses & Unofficial Conversations," a project created by Lois Klassen, Heidi May, Adam Stenhouse and Elisa Yon at the Emily Carr University of Art and Design, Vancouver, Canada, Dec. 2011. Photo courtesy Heidi May. For more information on QR_U see qruopenschool.ca.

Chapter 49: Critique at the Wroclaw School of Printmaking, 2013.

Chapter 50, photo 1: Takashi Murakami, diagram of the art world, detail. From his doctoral dissertation,『美術における 「意味の無意味の意味」 をめぐって』, "The Meaning of the Meaninglessness of Art" [in Japanese], March 1993. University of Arts, Tokyo. Courtesy Mina Ando.

Chapter 50, photo 2: An MFA critique at the University of Illinois at Urbana-Champaign, School of Art and Design, c. 2009. Photo by Conrad Bakker.

Notes

Preface, Acknowledgments

1   Thanks to Brenton Adrian for this expression.

2   See the Wikipedia entries "List of art schools" and "List of art schools in Europe'"; and artschools.com.

3   Kendall Buster and Paula Crawford, *The Critique Handbook: The Art Student's Sourcebook and Survival Guide*, second edition (New York: Prentice Hall, 2010). Another book, Terry Barrett's *Why is That Art?* (New York: Oxford University Press, 2008), includes reviews of major philosophic theories such as expressionism, formalism, and cognitivism; it also has brief descriptions of writers such as Lacan and Foucault, and collections of critics' responses to contemporary artists.

4   *Rethinking the Contemporary Art School: The Artist, the PhD, and the Academy*, edited by Brad Buckley and John Conomos (Halifax: The Press of the Nova Scotia College of Art and Design, 2009); Thornton, *Seven Days in the Art World* (London: W.W. Norton, 2009). In addition to other sources I list here, there are two pdf essays on art critiques on Terry Barret's webpage, terrybarrettosu.com/articles.html. One of them, "Studio Critiques of Student Art: As They Are, as They Could Be With Mentoring," has a useful bibliography. (June 23, 2011) There are a few other good references for studio critiques: T. Barrett, "Studio Critiques of Student Art: As They Are, as They Could Be with Mentoring," *Theory into Practice* 39 no. 1 (2000): 29–35; R. Hickman, *Why We Make Art and Why it is Taught* (Chicago: The University of Chicago Press, 2010); and Barbara Martinson, "Alternative Personae: An Irreverent Look at the Role of Instructors in Critique Sessions," *FATE in Review* 21 (1999): 42–45. It might be good to look beyond visual art critiques for literature on critiques; Gage McWeeny, the literary scholar, recommends Mark McGurl, *The Program Era: Postwar Fiction and the Rise of Creative Writing* (Cambridge, MA: Harvard University Press, 2009).

5   *Active Sights: Art as Social Interaction* (Mountain View, CA: Mayfield, 1998). See also Heather Darcy Bhandari and Jonathan Mebler, *Art / Work: Everything You Need to Know (And Do) As You Pursue Your Art Career* (New York: Free Press, 2009). The authors rightly point out that a studio visit isn't a critique (p. 103).

6   *The Art of Teaching Art: A Guide for Teaching and Learning the Foundations of Drawing-Based Art* (Oxford: Oxford Uniuversity Press, 2000), especially chapter 4.

7   *Why Art Cannot be Taught: A Handbook for Art Students* (Urbana, IL: University of Illinois Press, 2001).

8   This book got an early bad review on Amazon because someone said I was repeating myself. "Not His Best Moment," February 23, 2012; the writer says I took passages from several books, giving the impression this book is cobbled together.

9   I thank Kirstin Ilse for suggesting that I "loosen it up" to include critiques in general. (June 24, 2011)

Chapter 4

1   I thank Olga Stefan for bringing this to my attention.

2   www.q-artlondon.com; also "11 Course Leaders: 20 Questions," a collection of interviews with eleven London BA Fine Art course leaders, conducted by Sarah Rowles,with an introduction by Patricia Bickers (London, 2011). I thank Sarah Rowles for bringing this to my attention.

3   Personal correspondence, June 11, 2011; mattk@uakron.edu.

4   Personal correspondence, June 15, 2011.

Chapter 6

1   This is the example of "Kim," from my book *On the Strange Place of Religion in Contemporary Art* (New York: Routledge, 2004). I wrote that book largely because I saw that art students who have religious and spiritual beliefs were not getting full responses in their critiques.

2   It is not hard to find essays and books on talking about race and ethnicity in the classroom, but they are mainly produced by educators based on individual experiences. If you are having difficulty talking to a teacher about any of these subjects, the first recourse should be your institution's Student Affairs Office, Ombudsman, Chair, or Dean—whoever handles student complaints. Another strategy is to get your teacher reading one of the texts on how to talk about these issues in classrooms. My own favorite in this context is Richard Dyer, *White: Essays on Race and Culture* (London: Routledge, 1997). Other helpful essays in this respect include Elizabeth Garber, "Implications of Feminist Art Criticism for Art Education," *Studies in Art Education* 32 (1990):17–26; Judith Butler, *Gender Trouble* (New York, 1990); a forum on feminism in art, in *Artforum International* (2003), with Amelia Jones, Linda Nochlin, Andrea Fraser, and others, online at tinyurl.com/5rom8oj (June 28, 2011); and T. Barrett, "A Comparison of the Goals of Studio Professors Conducting Critiques and Art Education Goals for Teaching Criticism," *Studies in Art Education: A Journal of Issues and Research* 30 no. 1 (1988).

Chapter 7

1   Thanks to Rebekah Modrak.

2   Thanks to Elisa Pritzker.

3   Thanks to Jerry Saltz.

4   Thanks to Dawn Hunter.

5   Thanks to Jenny Eagleton.

6   Thanks to Anthony Cervino.

7   Thanks to Jane Fine.

8   Thanks to Jerry Saltz.

9   Thanks to Elisa Pritzker.

10   Thanks to Jane Fine. She adds: "In this case, very strangely followed by: 'the intended audience is middle-aged women from the Southwest.'"

11   Thanks to Dawn Hunter and Rebekah Modrak, whose version is: "I want the work to be open to whatever viewers want to see in it."

12   Thanks to Jenny Eagleton for the second one and the last two.

13   Thanks to Mutt Silver.

14   This one happened to me in my MFA program, and I still remember it unhappily decades later.

15   Thanks to Elisa Pritzker for this and the next one.

Chapter 11

1   http://www.andreaschumacher.com, May 24, 2011.

2   "The Crit" was first published in The Art Journal in 1999, and is online at www.richardrothstudio.com/writing. I thank Randall Szott for drawing my attention to it. The scene in Art School Confidential, which does capture the usual silences, is at youtu.be/1wz2bAByWyI. There's also a droll animation made by Paul Atkins, called "The Crit," at youtu.be/rJ5t_JTtvGk. Thanks to Cindy Baker for showing me that. (June 7, 2011)

3   There are remarkably few films or videos of entire critiques. So far I have only found fragments and videos with bad sound on YouTube. I haven't had a chance to see Elizabeth Subrin's film Shulie, which depicts a day in Shulamith Firestone's life as a student in 1967. (Thanks to Hilary Robinson for this.)

Chapter 15

1   There are similar categories in Deborah Rockman's *The Art of Teaching Art: A Guide for Teaching and Learning the Foundations of Drawing-Based Art* (Oxford: Oxford Uniuversity Press, 2000), 220–22.

2   *Seven Days in the Art World*, 52.

3   *Seven Days in the Art World*, 52.

4   Thanks to Lucy Parker for this story, which happened to her in the BFA program at Goldsmiths in 2003. She adds that they usually went to a pub afterward, "where opinions were often more frank."

5   Thanks to Jeffrey Dell and Rocio Rodriguez, on Facebook, February 2, 2012. Jeffrey adds: "Interestingly, I also find taking notes, writing literally what the student is saying, helps both me and the student come to realize some central point of what they're trying to do. This realization can often provide a pivotal shift in approach, goal, media, wording or handling, depending on the work at hand. Writing literally what the student says is also a good way to help them with writing about their work; they're better able to capture a good phrase, to get at the essence, when they're not trying to be so formally perfect."

6   Here's a nice expansion of this idea from Amy Ellingson, Facebook, February 2, 2012: "When the Silent Teacher's authority reaches mythic proportions, he or she becomes the only important person or thing in the room, and the beta dogs are left to helplessly, slavishly fall all over themselves to impress the master."

228

Chapter 16

1   *Seven Days in the Art World*, 53.

2   Rosalind Krauss, *"A Voyage on the North Sea": Art in the Age of the Post-Medium Condition* (London: Thames and Hudson, 2000); Alexander Alberro, *Institutional Critique: An Anthology of Artist's Writings* (Cambridge MA: MIT Press, 2009).

3   Among the many possible readings here, I like Thierry de Duve, *Kant after Duchamp* (Cambridge, MA: MIT Press, 1996), chapter 4, "The Monochrome and the Blank Canvas"; Stephen Melville, "As Painting: Problematics," in *As Painting: Division and Displacement* (Cambridge MA: MIT Press, 2001).

4   This is discussed by a number of authors in a book I edited, *Artists with PhDs: On the New Doctoral Degree in Studio Art* (Washington, DC: New Academia Publishing, 2009).

5   *What Do Artists Know?*, co-edited with Frances Whitehead, vol. 3 of The Stone Art Theory Seminars (University Park, PA: Penn State Press, 2012); also "What Do Artists Know? A Preliminary Report," *Mahkuzine* [Utrecht] 8 (winter 2010): 27–30.

Chapter 17

1   This is quoted, slightly modified, in Terry Barret's essay "Studio Critiques of Student Art: As They Are, as They Could Be With Mentoring," on his webpage, www.terrybarrettosu.com/articles.html. (June 23, 2011)

2   Thanks to Gillian Wainwright for this story.

3   Thanks to Brenton Adrian for this.

4   The person who sent me this anecdote, who would like to remain anonymous, says he thinks the teacher's idea was something like this: "Part of my brilliant teaching technique is to help you discover yourself by hating me. And of course then you will come to love me," and my informant adds, "In most cases it didn't work."

5   Thanks to Mark Dutcher for this anecdote (which I have slightly modified so it doesn't name names); he adds: "it was very shocking because it was a drawing by a student who was very impressed by their own work… I instantly got what the teacher was really saying: these aren't masterpieces and we are in here to learn." (June 23, 2011)

6   Thanks to Barbara Takenaga. It's a story from when she was a student. (Emailed November 2011)

7   *Seven Days in the Art World*, 55.

Chapter 18

1   This story is told in *Pictures and Tears: A History of People Who Have Cried in Front of Paintings* (New York: Routledge, 2001).

2   The artist Orly Genger, responding to a thread by Nina Katchadourian, April 25, 2011. Quoted with permission.

3   Thanks to Charis J. Carmichael Braun, too, for other stories.

Chapter 19

1   On Facebook, June 23, 2011, he put it slightly differently: "My main critique with group critiques is that they encourage factions, chatterboxes and suck-ups. Most critically, the worst work gets the most attention. This makes good artists think they have lost in the face-time sweepstakes."

2   *The State of Art Criticism*, co-edited with Michael Newman, vol. 4 of The Art Seminar, with contributions by Stephen Melville, Dave Hickey, Irit Rogoff, Guy Brett, Katy Deepwell, Joseph Masheck, Peter Plagens, Julian Stallabrass, Alex Alberro, Whitney Davis, Abigail Solomon-Godeau, and others (New York: Routledge, 2007).

Chapter 20

1   The philosophic argument here is that without some sense of an intentionality behind a work, the work will not appear as something made by a human at all: it will seem *taphonomic*, made by physical forces. If a wave washes a beach, and leaves a poem in the sand, we won't be able to see the poem as a poem without imagining some intentionality behind it: the Sea, Nature, God. See *Against Theory*, edited by W.J.T. Mitchell (Chicago: University of Chicago Press, 1985).

2   Robert Neffson shared this story with me on Facebook (June 22, 2011): "After I spent a summer painting small, Corot-like landscapes at the Skowhegan School of Painting, we all had a critique with Red Grooms. In a large barn, each elected student/artist would take turns and line their work against a wall in front of a sizable audience. He paced quietly in front of my work and I could feel my heat thumping. After saying very generous and sweet things about their luminosity, space and color, he stopped. Scratching his head, he said 'They are wonderful BUT they need something more… they need, they need…' and with that he preformed a hilarious Charlie Chaplin prat fall and landed flat on the floor. My ears turned bright red and my eyes widened. I could feel the laughter and smile of all the other students. In truth, he was right about the importance of the 'wow' factor and it was an elegantly non-verbal way to teach something important."

3   Buzz Spector makes a point like this in his talk "Crit: Studio Critique and Teaching Art": "If, as Jacques Derrida has argued, perception itself is a kind of writing," then critiques are "multivalent… a social process quite different from how the entirely self-directed activity of reading enters into the consciousness of the reader." College Art Association talk in 2007, unpublished.

Chapter 21

1   More on this in chapter 35, on words for success; for the philosophic issues, see *Beyond the Aesthetic and the Anti-Aesthetic*, vol. 4 of The Stone Art Theory Seminars (University Park, PA: Penn State Press, 2014).

2   Thanks to Hortense Dryburgh for most of these, and also to Marcio Guilarducci, Dorian Nisinson, Christopher Johnson, Lisa Phillips, Joseph Podlesnik, and Paul Litterick.

3   For a meditation on failure at the PhD level, in relation to research, see Bruce Bar-

ber, "The Question (of Failure) in Art Research," *Rethinking the Contemporary Art School: The Artist, the PhD, and the Academy*, edited by Brad Buckley and John Conomos (Halifax: The Press of the Nova Scotia College of Art and Design, 2009), 45–63.

Chapter 24

1   Howard Singerman, in the book *Art Subjects*, has said art critiques are like psychotherapy; earlier I mentioned the idea that some critiques are like psychodramas. I think "therapy" is the optimal word, because psychoanalysis is specific and complex: what I have in mind here is a looser, nontechnical sense in which the artist can suddenly seem to be a patient. Singerman, *Art Subjects: Making Artists in the American University* (Berkeley: University of California Press, 1999).

Chapter 26

1   "Nomadic" thought is Gilles Deleuze's term. It was popular in the 1980s and 1990s as a way of indicating non-hierarchical, anti-disciplinary thought. See Deleuze and Félix Gattari, *Traité de nomadologie*, trans. as *Nomadology: The War Machine*, trans. Brian Massumi (New York, 1986).
2   You can see his recent and current work on http://www.cfennellart.com.

Chapter 28

1   See chapters 12 and 36, and for the fuller history, *What Do Artists Know?*, co-edited with Frances Whitehead, vol. 3 of The Stone Art Theory Seminars (University Park, PA: Penn State Press, c. 2012).
2   See www.seanlamoureux.com.

Chapter 30

1   Even theorists of multiple modernisms and multiple contemporaneities tend to overlook the majority of institutions that teach art in any given country, in favor of the ones that are most international and active. See Terry Smith, *What is Contemporary Art?* (Chicago: University of Chicago Press, 2009); Andreas Huyssen, "Modernism at Large," in *Modernism*, edited by Astradur Eysteinsson and Vivian Liska (Amsterdam and Philadelphia: J. Benjamins Pub., 2007), 53–66.
2   It's another sensitive issue. See "The State of Irish Art History," *Circa* [Dublin] 106 (2003): 56–59, www.recirca.com/backissues/c106/arthistory.shtml, and "The State of Irish Art History Revisited," *Circa* 116 (summer 2006), and "Response" [to eight letters responding to the original essay], Circa 118 (winter 2006): 45-47. The essay is at www.recirca.com/backissues/c116/p48_55.shtml and the responses are at www.recirca.com/backissues/c118/p36-47.shtml. (June 11, 2011)
3   Hermann Broch, *Dichten und Erkennen* (Zurich, 1955), vol. 1, 295, discussed briefly in Karsten Harries, *The Meaning of Modern Art: A Philosophical Interpretation* (Evanston,

1968), 81-83. Commercialism is discussed in J. Morreall and J. Loy, "Kitsch and Aesthetic Education," *The Journal of Aesthetic Education* 23 no. 4 (1989): 63.

Chapter 31

1   In poetics this "judicative" criticism is called "judicial" or "prescriptive" and "descriptive" criticism is called "aesthetic" or "romantic." See *Princeton Encyclopedia of Poetry and Poetics*, edited by A. Preminger (1990), v. "Poetics," 637b.

2   There is a similar schema, called the "Feldman method" of art critiques, which divides critiques into four stages: "describe," "analyze," "interpret," and "evaluate." The first and second would be what I'm calling descriptive, and the third and fourth would be judicative. I am not following this here because I can't see how to clearly distinguish *judicative* from *descriptive*, not to mention description and analysis from interpretation and evaluation. But see "How to Critique and Write About Art," tinyurl.com/lodeml. (June 28, 2011)

3   You can see her recent work on http://www.catherinearnold.com.

Chapter 32

1   *Active Sights: Art as Social Interaction*, 12.

2   There's a good example on YouTube: the artist Stephen Doherty, editor of the realist painting magazine *American Artist*, critiquing a student in 2007, at http://youtu. be/3v0wHY-Balc.

3   Buzz Spector made the same remark about this passage in *Active Sights* in his College Art Association talk in 2007, "Crit: Studio Critique and Teaching Art," unpublished.

4   Stanley Fish, *Is There a Text in this Class? The Authority of Interpretive Communities* (Cambridge, Massachusetts, 1980).

5   This is an amalgam of Stanley Fish's concept and Nelson Goodman's "evanescent ontology." See Goodman, "The Way the World Is," in *Problems and Projects* (Indianapolis, 1972), 24.

6   See samtchakalian.com/Remembering_Sam_Tchakalian; thanks to Gale Antokal for this.

Chapter 33

1   For dance and theater critiques see Liz Lerman's "Critical Response Process," at danceexchange.org/projects/critical-response-process, and a book of the same name she co-authored with John Borstel (2003). I thank Esther Grisham Grimm for bringing this to my attention. (June 11, 2011)

2   For music master classes online or for purchase, see www.masterclassfoundation. org. (June 11, 2011)

3   If you don't play an instrument, try listening to the excerpt "Beethoven - Piano Sonatas No 21 "Waldstein" and No 31, Op 110 (MMF 2-030) - Stephen Kovacevich" on www.masterclassfoundation.org, and see if you can understand what he communicates to the student (he barely whispers the tune and rhythm). (June 11, 2011)

4   See *Music and Gesture*, edited by Anthony Gritten (London: Ashgate, 2006).

Chapter 34

1   See *The State of Art Criticism* co-edited with Michael Newman, vol. 4 of The Art Seminar (New York: Routledge, 2007); *What Happened to Art Criticism?* (Chicago: Prickly Paradigm Press [distributed by University of Chicago Press], 2003); "Art Criticism," article in *The Grove Dictionary of Art* (New York, Grove Dictionaries, 1996), now in Grove Art Online / Oxford Art Online; "Afterword," in *Judgment and Contemporary Art Criticism*, edited by Jeff Khonsary and Melanie O'Brian (Vancouver: Artspeak, Fillip Editions, 2010). The first book in particular has many further references.

2   W. Schneiders, "Venünftiger Zweifel und wahre Eklektik. Zur Entstehung des modernen Kritikbegriffes," *Studia Leibnitiana* 17 no. 2, (1985): 160-61.

3   The academic journal *Critical Inquiry* is an example of critical theory: the journal isn't just called *Inquiry* because the editors have in mind the entire range of social, literary, and philosophic theory. The journal and organization Platypus is an overtly Marxist project, with a special interest in Adorno; see platypus1917.org. (11 June, 2011)

4   Sholette, *Dark Matters: Radical Social Production and the Missing Mass of the Contemporary Art World*; see gregorycholette.com.

5   Rogoff, "What is a Theorist?" in *State of Art Criticism*, 97–110, especially 99–100.

6   *Beyond the Aesthetic and the Anti-Aesthetic*, vol. 4 of The Stone Art Theory Seminars (University Park, PA: Penn State Press, 2014).

Chapter 35

1   John Dewey, *Democracy and Education: An Introduction to the Philosophy of Education* (New York, 1920); William Frankena, "Education," in *Dictionary of the History of Ideas* (New York, 1973), vol. 2, 82-83, and Frankena, *Philosophy of Education* (New York, 1965).

2   Ethical criteria also surface when people argue for or against the idea that postmodern art has no fixed norms, that everything is subject to "an on-going process of reinterpretation." Both sides of that argument rely on *ethical* criteria: they either disparate or praise the current state of affairs. See Charles Jansen, "The Post-Modern Agenda," a flier distributed at the 1991 CAA conference, n.p. [p. 1]. See Jansen, *Studying Art History* (Englewood Cliffs, 1986). For postmodern curricula see also Donald Kuspit, "Postmodernism, Plurality and the Urgency of the Given," in *The Idea of Post-Modernism: Who is Teaching It?* (Seattle, 1981).

3   H. Risatti, "Protesting Professionalism," *New Art Examiner* 18 no. 6 (1991): 23.

4   I thank Shona Macdonald, University of Massachuetts Amherst, for drawing this to my attention.

5   For the division into "traditionalist," "social behaviorist" (skill oriented), and "experientialist," see W. H. Schubert, *Curriculum: Perspective, Paradigm, and Possibility* (New York, 1986). See also J. Baldacchino, "The Practice of Art's Deschooled Practice," *The International Journal of Art and Design Education* 27 no. 3 (2008).

6   I thank Carol Diehl for this; see artvent.blogspot.com/2010/04/art-jury-but-not-really.html. (June 15, 2011)

Chapter 36

1   This was contributed by Bill Rutherford. The others are ones I've heard.

2   That is a point made by Miranda Aschenbrenner, "How to Survive an Art Critique," posted September 24, 2009, learntoart.com/index.php/archives/art-general/how-to-survive-an-art-critique. (June 7, 2011)

3   For the sublime, see *Six Stories from the End of Representation* (Stanford: Stanford University Press, 2008), chapter 1, and "Iconoclasm and the Sublime: Two Implicit Religious Discourses in Art History," in *Idol Anxiety*, edited by Josh Ellenbogen and Aaron Tugendhaft (Stanford, CA: Stanford University Press, 2011), 133–51.

4   For rhetoric see Wayne Booth's still very useful books: *The Rhetoric of Fiction* (Chicago: University of Chicago Press, 1983 [1961]), and *Modern Dogma and the Rhetoric of Assent* (Chicago: University of Chicago Press, 1980).

Chapter 37

1   M. H. Abrams, *The Mirror and the Lamp: Romantic Theory and the Critical Tradition* (New York: Oxford University Press, 1971 [1953]). The account that follows mixes Abrams's somewhat simple "orientations" with the "six types" proposed in an outstanding essay by Richard McKeon, "The Philosophic Bases of Art and Criticism," *Modern Philology* 40 (1943) and 41 (1944): 129–71. McKeon's essay remains one of the very best meditations on criticism; it deserves to be read much more widely.

2   Charles Batteux, *Les Beaux arts réduits à un même principe* (Paris, 1747).

3   *Aristotle's Treatise on Poetry*, edited by Thomas Twining (London, 1789), 4, 21-22, 60-61.

4   For the reference to flute-playing see Aristotle, *Poetics* 6.1449[b], 14.1453[b]. For Socrates on imitation, see the *Republic* 10.596-97.

5   Eva Keuls, *Plato and Greek Painting* (Leiden: Brill, 1978).

6   Richard McKeon, "Literary Criticism and the Concept of Imitation in Antiquity," *Critics and Criticism*, edited by R. S. Crane (Chicago, 1952), 173.

7   There is a discussion of this subject, with further references to Levinas and others, in *What is an Image?*, co-edited with Maja Naef, vol. 2 of The Stone Art Theory Seminars (University Park, PA: Penn State Press, 2011); see section 6 of the Seminars.

8   Abrams, *Mirror and the Lamp*, 35.

9   Here Abrams follows J. S. Mill, "What is Poetry" and "The Two Kinds of Poetry," *Early Essays by John Stuart Mill*, ed. J. W. M. Gibbs (London, 1897), 208, 228, 211–17, 208–9.

10   See Chapter 36.

11   Mentoring also has social and practical dimensions such as sponsorship and career advising, but to the extent that it focuses on a one-to-one relationship, it depends on Ro-

manticism. There is an interesting discussion of mentoring, using contemporary sources that do not cite the Romantic heritage, in Terry Barret's essay "Studio Critiques of Student Art: As They Are, as They Could Be With Mentoring," on his webpage, www.terrybarret-tosu.com/articles.html. (June 23, 2011)

12   The common condition in contemporary art practice is to be a mixture of late Romantic and more recent orientations. Just one example, as a token of the kind of issue that's involved here. In a review of conceptual writing, appropriation, Oulipo, and other rule-bound initiatives in recent poetry and writing, Malcolm Sutton proposes a reconsideration of the postmodern sublime: but Jean-François Lyotard's postmodern sublime is explicitly late Romantic, and doesn't belong with those initiatives. See Sutton, "Between Gut and Intellect: Conceptual Writing and the Postmodern Sublime," *Border Crossings* 30 no. 2 (2011): 68–70; for a more detailed look at conceptual writing see Marjorie Perloff, *Unoriginal Genius: Poetry by Other Means in the New Century* (Chicago: University of Chicago Press, 2010); and for a critique of the sublime in recent writing, my "Against the Sublime," in *Beyond the Finite: The Sublime in Art and Science,* edited by Roald Hoffmann and Iain Boyd Whyte (New York: Oxford University Press, 2011), 20–42; and "Iconoclasm and the Sublime: Two Implicit Religious Discourses in Art History," in *Idol Anxiety,* edited by Josh Ellenbogen and Aaron Tugendhaft (Stanford, CA: Stanford University Press, 2011), 133–51.

13   This sounds like what Mary Kelly does in her critiques in which the student doesn't speak (chapter 19). But she is very much engaged with the problems of audience and the artist; excluding the artist's statement is more a pedagogic strategy.

14   There is a good analysis of formalisms and iconography in Whitney Davis, *A General Theory of Visual Culture* (Princeton NJ: Princeton University Press, 2011).

Chapter 38

1   These comments are inspired by Jean Laplanche's Freudian theory and art criticism that uses seduction as a primary trope. See *New Foundations for Psychoanalysis*, trans. David Macey (Oxford, 1989). An earlier version of this chapter appeared as "Studio Art Critiques as Seductions [Freudian slip! sic]," *Journal of Aesthetic Education* 26 no. 1 (1992): 105-7.

2   The best text here is Roland Barthes, A Lover's Discourse, trans. Richard Howard (New York, 1978). Barthes's entire book could be applied to critiques, as a handbook of affects.

3   See http://www.unc.edu/~eoslavic.

Chapter 39

1   Gerald Graff, "Other Voices, Other Rooms: Organizing and Teaching the Humanities Conflict," *New Literary History* (autumn 1990). See also Graff, *Professing Literature: An Institutional History* (Chicago, 1987); and Goodman, *Languages of Art: An Approach to the Theory of Symbols* (Indianapolis, 1976).

2   For an attempt to develop skin metaphors into a more extended "language" see my *Pictures of the Body: Pain and Metamorphosis* (Stanford, 1999).

3   The Instant Art Critique Phrase Generator, www.pixmaven.com/phrase_generator.html (June 24, 2011)

4   This problem is called *metatheoresis* in my *Our Beautiful, Dry, and Distant Texts*, 9-11.

Chapter 40

1   Paul Ricoeur, *Time and Narrative* (Chicago, 1989), 3 vols.

Chapter 44

1   Thanks to Jane D. Marsching for this idea.

2   There's an interesting contrast between the two. Itten was interested in erasing bad habits, and inculcating a ground-up revision of practice, and his exercises are similar to health initiatives of the time. Running may be the contemporary version. Facebok, June 22, 2011. Itten's practice is noted, for example, in Paul Betts, "Science, Semiotics, and Society," in *The Designed World: Images, Objects, Environments*, edited by Richard Buchanan et al. (Oxford: Berg, 2010), 320. I heard another story, from Bill Catling: in San Francisco State, in the early 1970s, Helene Aylon wan a painting class with belly dancers in it. The students weren't supposed to paint the dancers; they were supposed to put the dancers' energy into their work. Bill adds: "I painted a large canvas with minimal colors and a sort-of mountain formation appeared. Later a critique on the work was 'What a waste of canvas.'"

3   Thanks to Takeshi Moro, who tried this. He "decided to pretend not to speak English," as a "sarcastic comment" on how critiques have "coded messages" that get lost in translation. He says some of his teachers loved it, and spoke directly to him as if the interpreter didn't exist.

Chapter 45

1   Thanks to Anna Kriger for this. My abridged selection includes comments made in succession by several people. (June 2012)

Chapter 47

1   I have heard of other long critiques. Helen Ferguson Crawford teaches a ten hour studio at Georgia Tech, involving twelve to fifteen students (reported 2012).

Chapter 48

1   Graeme Sullivan, *Art Practice as Research: Inquiry in the Visual Arts* (London: Sage, 2004); *The New PhD in Studio Art*, no. 4 in the occasional series called Printed Project (Dublin: Sculptor's Society of Ireland, 2005); *Thinking Through Art: Reflections on Art as Research,* edited by Katy Mcleod and Lynn Holdridge (London: Routledge, 2005); *Artists with PhDs: On the New Doctoral Degree in Studio Art* (Washington, DC: New Academia,

2009). This is my main contribution, with contributions by a dozen scholars, and excerpts from the dissertations of studio-art PhD candidates. *Art School (Propositions for the 21st Century),* edited by Steven Madoff (Cambridge, MA: MIT Press, 2009). This has contributions mainly by prominent artists and critics, so it's outside the usual range of this literature. *International Handbook of Research in Arts Education,* edited by Liora Bresler, 2 vols. (New York: Springer, 2007); *Art and Artistic Research / Kunst und künstlerische Forschung: Music, Art, Design, Literature, Dance,* edited by Corina Caduff, Fiona Siegenthaler, and Tan Walchli (Zürich: Verlag Scheidegger and Spiess, 2010); Henk Slager, *The Pleasure of Research* (Helsinki: Finnish Academy of Fine Arts, 2011); *The Routledge Companion to Research in the Arts,* edited by Michael Biggs and Henrik Karlsson (London: Routledge, 2012); *Texte zur Kunst* (art magazine), special issue on "Artistic Research," 2011; *Practice as Research: Contexts, Method, Knowledge (Approaches to Creative Arts Enquiry),* edited by Estelle Barrett and Barbara Bolt (London: I.B. Tauris, 2007); *Handbook of the Arts in Qualitative Research: Perspectives, Methodologies, Examples, and Issues,* edited by J. Gary Knowles and Ardra Cole (London: sage, 2007); *Practice-led Research, Research-led Practice in the Creative Arts,* edited by Hazel Smith and Roger Dean (Edinburgh: Edinburgh University Press, 2009); *Design Research Through Practice from the Lab, Field, and Showroom,* edited by Ilpo Koskinen et al. (New York: Morgan Kaufmann, 2011); and *Intellectual Birdhouse: Artistic Practice as Research,* edited by Florian Dumbois, Claudia Mareis, Ute Meta Bauer, and Michael Schwab (Cologne: Walther König, 2012).

Chapter 49

1   This is exhaustively documented in *What do Artists Know?*, co-edited with Frances Whitehead, vol. 3 of The Stone Art Theory Seminars (University Park, PA: Penn State Press, 2012). There is lots to read in that book about definitions of the BFA, MFA, and PhD.

Chapter 50

1   I thank Marta Edling, Uppsala University, for the insight that the literature might be productively divided in this fashion. The descriptions and examples are mine.

2   This is available at www2.uiah.fi/~ikoskine/doctoral_studies/tips/index.html, accessed June 2012.

3   Slager, *The Pleasure of Research* (Helsinki: Finnish Academy of Fine Arts, 2011), pp. 14, 68–69.

4   My own thoughts on this are in two essays in the book *Artists with PhDs: On the New Doctoral Degree in Studio Art* (Washington, DC: New Academia, 2009).

Chapter 51

1   Borgdorff is quoted, from an essay published in 2006, by Michael Biggs and Daniel Büchler, in their essay "Communities, Values, Conventions, and Actions," chapter 5 in *The Routledge Companion to Research in the Arts,* edited by Michael Biggs and Henrik Karlsson (London: Routledge, 2012), p. 408. Borgdorff identifies what appears as knowledge with the

non-linguistic aesthetic concept of art, and argues that "artistic research... is the articulation of the unreflective, non-conceptual content enclosed in aesthetic experiences, enacted in creative practices and embodied in artistic products." It remains unclear, I think, exactly what it means to "articulate" "non-conceptual content" without "making explicit... knowledge" in the normative sense of that word: but as I noted, that isn't the subject of this book. (Borgdorff, "The Production of Knowledge in Artistic Research," *The Routledge Companion to Research in the Arts,* p. 44.)

Envoi

1   There are just a few examples of well-known artists whose work was decisively altered by criticism. Mark Kostabi claims that a bad review by Donald Kuspit clipped his "little art wings" and made him decide not to make his own work, but to invent "the Mark Kostabi we all know and hate." This was posted on Facebook June 15, 2011; thanks to Heie Treier for pointing it out to me; she also notes that even though it seems mainly truthful, it was posted on the same day he promoted his new music CD.